Introduction to C++
Programming and Graphics

Introduction to C++
Programming and Graphics

C. Pozrikidis

 Springer

Constantine Pozrikidis
Department of Mechanical and Aerospace Engineering (MAE)
University of California, San Diego
9500 Gilman Drive
La Jolla, CA 92093-0411
dehesa@freeshell.org

Cover illustration: The illustration on the front cover shows a twisted nanoring consisting of a warped hexagonal lattice of carbon atoms.

ISBN-13: 978-1-4419-4337-8   e-ISBN-13: 978-0-387-68993-7

Printed on acid-free paper.

9 8 7 6 5 4 3 2 1

springer.com

Preface

The C++ programming language was introduced by Bjarne Stroustrup of the AT&T laboratories in 1985 as an extension of C, with additional features borrowed from the esoteric language *Simula*. Since then, C++ has grown rapidly in response to the practical need for a programming language that is able to efficiently handle composite and diverse data types. The language implementation is pivoted on the ingenious concept of *object oriented programming* (OOP). Today, C++ dominates the commercial market and is favored among system programmers and application developers.

Object oriented programming

To illustrate the advantages of an object oriented programming language compared to a structured language such as MATLAB, FORTRAN 77, or C, we assume that an international sports competition has been entered by runners from many countries around the globe. The record of each runner consists of several fields including name, country of origin, city of birth, date of birth, and best performance time.

In a structured language, each one of these fields is normally registered in a separate data vector. In an OOP language, each runner becomes an object defined as a member of the class of runners, and each member is described by the collection of these fields. This formalism allows us to record, recall, and manipulate in any desired way the personal data of each runner using simple symbolic operators. Sub-classes consisting, for example, of runners of a particular nationality can be readily defined to facilitate more detailed manipulations.

An OOP language allows us to introduce a data type of our choice viewed as an object in a defined class, and then use the class as a building block for further development. This flexibility essentially allows us to build a language without building a compiler. In this sense, an OOP language is an ultimate language.

C and C++

C++ is a generalization of C, but accomplishes much more than C, to the extent that it should be regarded, studied, and taught as a separate language. It is neither necessary nor recommended to study C as a prerequisite of C++, though knowledge of C can be helpful.

This book

This book is a brief and basic introduction to C++ for everyone and especially for scientists and engineers. The text offers a venue for effectively teaching and rapidly learning the language at the level of an undergraduate course in any discipline of the physical sciences and computer science and engineering. The discussion illustrates step-by-step the grammar, syntax, and main features of the language, and explains the basic premise of OOP with an emphasis on scientific computing.

Chapter 1 reviews basic concepts of computer hardware software and programming.

Chapters 2 and 3 outline the general features of C++ and the basic implementation of the language.

Chapter 4 discusses user-defined functions with an emphasis on scientific computing.

In Chapter 5 introduces pointers to memory addresses and demonstrates their applications.

Chapter 6 explains the basic principles of object oriented programming (OOP) and the implementation of classes.

Chapters 7 and 8 discuss graphics and graphical user interface (GUI) programming based on the fabulous VOGLE library for the X11 server, and on the GLUT, GLUI, and GTK+ utility toolboxes.

Chapter 9 demonstrates the use of MATLAB functions from C++ code for numerics and graphics.

Transition to C++

Many students, scientists, engineers, and other professionals are familiar with the general concepts of computer programming, are proficient in an easy programming language, such as MATLAB or FORTRAN 77, and would like to learn C++. This book is ideally suited for this audience. Translation tables demonstrating the conversion of MATLAB or FORTRAN 77 code into C++ code are given in an appendix. A side-by-side comparison illustrates the syntactic and functional differences between the three languages.

Keeping it simple

The C++ language is pluralistic in two ways. First, it allows different commands (tasks) to be stated (implemented) in alternative ways. Second, it supports several dialects dependent on the chosen compiler. All compilers support the ANSI/ISO standard C++ functions discussed in this text.

In our discussion, structure and forms that make for a transparent and efficient, but not necessarily compact, programming style are adopted. Code obfuscation is avoided at all cost.

Learning from the Internet

This text was written with a new learning model in mind: study a basic text or take a short course to get acquainted with a subject, and then use the Internet to master the subject. A wealth of up-to-date resources and tutorials are available on the Internet on every imaginable subject.

Study this text to get acquainted with C++, and then use the Internet to master the language.

Book Internet site

This book is accompanied by a library of programs that can be freely downloaded from the Internet site:

http://dehesa.freeshell.org/ICPPPG

Further information on C++ and links of interest are also provided.

Unix

A C++ programmer without Unix experience is handicapped in many ways. A number of Unix operating systems are freely available and can be readily installed either by themselves or in a dual boot mode along with Windows on desktops and laptops Examples include *Fedora Core*, *CentOs*, and *BSD*. Appendix A summarizes the basic Unix commands.

cygwin for Windows users

The software package *cygwin* allows Windows users to work in a Unix environment and utilize Unix libraries and applications on top of the windows operating system. Effectively, *cygwin* creates a computer running Unix inside another computer running Windows. To distinguish between the two, we refer to the former as an "environment." MATLAB users are familiar with the concept of a computing environment. *cygwin* derives its name from three components:

1. gnu: standing for "GNU's Not Unix". This is a free, open-source operating system consisting of a kernel, libraries, system utilities, compilers,

and end-user applications. Its development was announced by Richard Stallman in 1983.

2. Cygnus: a genus of beautiful birds.

3. Windows: an operating system produced by the Microsoft corporation.

The *cygwin* package can be freely downloaded and easily installed from the Internet site `http://www.cygwin.com`. The package contains a wealth of applications and tools, including the X11 graphics library and a C++ compiler.

Windows users are strongly advised to download and install the package as a prelude to studying this book.

Acknowledgment

I am grateful to Todd Porteous, Conrad Palmer, and Micheal Waltz for providing hardware, software, and moral support.

I am grateful to anonymous reviewers and to my editor Valerie Schofield who immediately recognized the significance of this book and provided useful comments.

C. Pozrikidis

San Diego, March 2007

Contents

Computers and Computing 1

Computers are intelligent devices that mimic human behavior with respect to remembering data and events, processing information, and making logical decisions. Information is stored, recalled, manipulated, and combined in their circuitry to achieve a desired effect.

To properly understand the design and master the implementation of the C++ programming language, it is necessary to have a general familiarity with the basic computer components and their function, and recognize how instructions are translated into machine language code.

1.1 Hardware and software

Physical components including wires, electronics, circuits, cards, boards, and various peripheral devices are classified as *hardware*. Permanent information is stored in permanent recordable media such as hard disk drives (HDD), commonly called hard drives (HD), compact disks with read-only memory (CD-ROM), and digital versatile discs (DVD). Old-timers fondly recall the era of tapes and floppy disks.

CPU

The centerpiece of computer hardware is the central processor housed in the motherboard. The main component of the processor is a microchip fabricated as a compact integrated circuit, called the central processing unit (CPU) or the microprocessor. A modern CPU contains over fifty million transistors. Its function is to perform numerical computations and make logical decisions, collectively called operations. The control unit (CU) of the CPU interprets and prioritizes instructions, and the arithmetic logic unit (ALU) executes instructions.

A microprocessor can be rated in terms of its clock frequency or clock rate, which is the frequency of an internal vibrating crystal expressed in number of cycles per second (Hertz, abbreviated as Hz). Today's microprocessors vibrate at a few GHz, that is, a few trillion cycles per second. The clock rate is the pulse time of the computer circuitry, representing the highest attainable ideal rate at which the computer can process information or execute an instruction. The clock rate can be compared with the blood pulse of a living organism. However, the clock rate is a meaningful measure of a processor's efficiency only when processors of a certain brand-name are compared side-by-side on the same platform.

The CPU is able to receive data from an external memory bank, manipulate the data as instructed, and send the result back to the data bank. Transient information is stored in high-efficiency local memory units called *registers*. The CPU communicates with other devices through information routes implemented on buses.

Software

Instructions, parameters, settings, and other data are classified as *software*. The instructions allow a computer to recognize the hardware, carry out tasks, learn by experience, and exhibit artificial intelligence. Utility and application software provides further functionality on a multitude of levels for scientific, commercial, and entertainment applications.

The operating system

The most important piece of software is the operating system (OS). An operating system is a program written in a mid-level language such as C or C++, prescribing procedures and parameters that tell the computer how to organize its physical components into logical units, manage the memory, and communicate with the environment.

Examples of operating systems include the Unix system and its many variations, the Windows OS, and the Mac OS. When a computer boots up, it loads the operating system into memory from the recordable medium where it resides, such as a hard drive or a CD-ROM.

The heart of an OS is its kernel. The Unix kernel is a very small portion of the Unix operating system that allows it to run on many types of computers – from personal computers running Linux, to supercomputers running UNICOS. If something goes wrong, the kernel enters a panic mode.

BIOS

The basic input/output system (BIOS) is a small set of instructions executed when the computer is first switched on. The BIOS is unrelated to the installed operating system (OS), and is specific to the electronic hardware. Its purpose is to activate the keyboard and monitor, and then run a small program called the boot loader which, in turn, launches the operating system. The boot loader resides in the first partition of a permanent recordable medium, called the boot sector or master boot record (MBR). If multiple media are present, the BIOS searches through a pre-determined yet programmable list, and launches the first available boot loader.

Dual-boot computers allow the alternative loading of multiple operating systems with the help of an advanced boot loader such as the GRand Unified Bootloader (GRUB). GRUB Stage 1, residing in the master boot record, launches GRUB Stage 2, residing anywhere in the disk. A menu of options is then presented and the OS of choice is loaded.

Problem

1.1.1. Conduct an Internet search to compile a list of six operating systems currently in use.

1.1.2. Conduct an Internet search to learn whether the BIOS also initializes the mouse.

1.2   The binary system

Let us pretend that computers have not yet been invented and consider possible ways by which information can be recorded and communicated by means of an encoded protocol.

In the simplest method, a flag with a black and a white side is introduced, and the black or white side is waved as many times as necessary to convey the information unambiguously in lieu of a Morse code. A record of sequential signals represents a string of binary digits 0 and 1, where 0 stands for white and 1 stands for black.

The binary system thus provides us with a framework for describing numbers with binary strings. Once we know how to manipulate numbers, we can proceed to handle letters of the alphabet by assigning to each one of them a numerical code. Strings of letters form words, and strings of words form sentences, instructions, and conclusions that can be true or false. A comprehensive system may thus be built on the quintessential concept of the binary representation.

Bits

Computers work with the binary or base-two system of numbers that uses the two digits 0 and 1 instead of the ten digits $0-9$ of the more familiar decimal or base-ten system. The number two is the *radix* of the binary system, and the number ten is the radix of the decimal system. Computers are two-fingered devices; humans are ten-fingered creatures. The ancient Mayans used a base-twenty system counting fingers and toes.

In the binary system, a number is denoted as

$$(b_k \, b_{k-1} \, \cdots b_0.b_{-1} \cdots b_{-l} \,)_2 \tag{1}$$

where k and l are two integer indices, the binary digits or *bits*, b_i, take the value of 0 or 1, and the period (.) is the binary point. The implied value is equal to

$$b_k \times 2^k + b_{k-1} \times 2^{k-1} + \cdots + b_0 \times 2^0$$
$$+ b_{-1} \times 2^{-1} + \cdots + b_{-l} \times 2^{-l}. \tag{2}$$

In the decimal system, the same number is expressed as

$$(d_m \, d_{m-1} \, \cdots d_0.d_{-1} \cdots d_{-n} \,)_{10}, \tag{3}$$

where m and n are two integers, the decimal digits d_i take values in the range $0-9$, and . is the decimal point. The subscript 10 is omitted by convention in everyday exchange. The implied value is equal to

$$d_m \times 10^m + d_{m-1} \times 10^{m-1} + \cdots + d_0 \times 10^0$$
$$+ b_{-1} \times 10^{-1} + \cdots + d_{-n} \times 10^{-n}, \tag{4}$$

which is identical to that computed from the base-two expansion.

As an example, the binary representation of the number 6.28125 is

$$
\begin{aligned}
(6.28125)_{10} &= (110.01001)_2 \\
&= 1 \times 2^2 + 1 \times 2^1 + 0 \times 2^0 + 0 \times 2^{-1} + 1 \times 2^{-2} + 0 \times 2^{-3} \\
&\quad + 0 \times 2^{-4} + 1 \times 2^{-5}.
\end{aligned}
\tag{5}
$$

In this case, $k = 2$ and $l = 5$. The conversion from decimal to binary will be discussed later in this section.

Since bits can be represented by the on-off positions of electrical switches that are built in the computer's electrical circuitry, and since bits can be transmitted by positive or negative voltage as a Morse code, the binary system is ideal for developing a computer architecture. However, this convenience comes at the expense of economy, as a binary string is generally much longer than a decimal string.

Largest integer encoded by p bits

The largest integer that can be represented with p bits is

$$(111 \cdots 111)_2 \tag{6}$$

where the ones are repeated p times. The decimal-number equivalent is

$$1 \times 2^{p-1} + 1 \times 2^{p-2} + 1 \times 2^{p-3} + \cdots$$
$$+ 1 \times 2^2 + 1 \times 2^1 + 1 \times 2^0 = 2^p - 1. \tag{7}$$

To demonstrate this equivalence, we recall from our high school years the identity

$$a^p - b^p = (a - b)(a^{p-1} + a^{p-2}b + \ldots a\, b^{p-2} + b^{p-1}), \tag{8}$$

where a and b are two variables, and set $a = 2$ and $b = 1$.

When one bit is available, we can describe only the integers 0 and 1, and the largest integer is 1. With two bits the maximum is 3, with three bits the maximum is 7, with eight bits the maximum is 255, and with thirty-one bits the maximum is 214,748,3647. We see that a very rich person requires a lot of bits to record her fortune. How many bits do you need to record your savings in US dollars?

Signed integers

To encode a signed integer, we allocate the first bit to the sign. If the leading bit is 0, the integer is positive; if the leading bit is 1, the integer is negative. The largest signed integer that can be represented with p bits is then $2^{p-1} - 1$. According to this convention, the integer $-5 = -(101)_2$ is stored as the binary string 1101. To derive this binary string, we may use the method of *two's complement*: we flip the bits of 5 to obtain $(010)_2$, and then add $(1)_2$ to obtain the desired code 1101.

Bytes and nibbles

A set of eight bits is one *byte*. The largest integer that can be represented with one byte is

$$(11111111)_2 \tag{9}$$

whose decimal-number equivalent is

$$1 \times 2^7 + 1 \times 2^6 + 1 \times 2^5 + 1 \times 2^4 + 1 \times 2^3 + 1 \times 2^2 + 1 \times 2^1 + 1 \times 2^0$$
$$= 128 + 64 + 32 + 16 + 8 + 4 + 2 + 1$$
$$= 2^8 - 1 = 255. \tag{10}$$

Large units of bytes are shown in Table 1.2.1. As a point of reference, the deficit of the United States in 2005 was approximately \$400 Billion, that is, \$400,000,000,000, which is on the order of one third of a Gbyte.

Bytes

Byte	8 bits	$2^0 = 1$
Kilobyte (Kbyte)	$2^{10} = 1024$ Bytes	$2^{10} = 1024$
Megabyte (Mbyte)	$2^{10} = 1024$ Kbytes	$2^{20} = 1,048,576$
Gigabyte (Gbyte)	$2^{10} = 1024$ Mbytes	$2^{30} = 1,073,741,824$
Terabyte (Gbyte)	$2^{10} = 1024$ Gbytes	$2^{40} = 1,099,511,627,776$
Petabyte (Pbyte)	$2^{10} = 1024$ Tbytes	$2^{50} = 1,125,899,906,842,624$
Exabyte (Ebyte)	$2^{10} = 1024$ Pbytes	$2^{60} \simeq 1,152,921,504,606,847,000$

Table 1.2.1 Large units of bytes. Each byte consists of eight bits.

One byte is sometimes divided into two groups of four bits called nibbles. Thus, a nibble is half a byte.

Decimal to binary conversion

To express the decimal number 6.28125 in the binary system, we first consider the integral part, 6, and compute the ratios:

$$\frac{6}{2} = 3 + \frac{0}{2}, \qquad \frac{3}{2} = 1 + \frac{1}{2}, \qquad \frac{1}{2} = 0 + \frac{1}{2}. \tag{11}$$

We stop when the integral part has become equal to zero. Collecting the numerators on the right-hand sides expressing the remainder *in reverse order*, we find

$$(6)_{10} = (110)_2 = 1 \times 2^2 + 1 \times 2^1 + 0 \times 2^0. \tag{12}$$

Next, we consider the decimal part and compute the products:

$$\begin{aligned}
0.28125 \times 2 &= 0.5625, \\
0.56250 \times 2 &= 1.1250, \\
0.56250 \times 2 &= 1.1250, \\
0.12500 \times 2 &= 0.2500, \\
0.25000 \times 2 &= 0.5000, \\
0.50000 \times 2 &= 1.0000.
\end{aligned} \tag{13}$$

We stop when the decimal part has become equal to zero. Taking the integer bold-faced figures *in forward order*, we find

$$(0.28125)_{10} = (.01001)_2. \tag{14}$$

Now combining the integral and decimal representations, we find

$$(6.28125)_{10} = (110.01001)_2. \tag{15}$$

Decimal	Binary	Hexadecimal
0	0	0
1	1	1
2	10	2
3	11	3
4	100	4
5	101	5
6	110	6
7	111	7
8	1000	8
9	1001	9
10	1010	A
11	1011	B
12	1100	C
13	1101	D
14	1110	E
15	1111	F
16	10000	10
17	10001	11

Table 1.2.2 Binary and hexadecimal representation of zero and first seventeen integers.

Eight binary units (bits), and one binary point are necessary to represent the number 6.28125.

Table 1.2.2 shows the binary representation of zero and first seventeen integers. Note that the binaries of integers that are powers of two, such as 2, 4, 8, and 16, have only one 1, whereas the binaries of their preceding odd integers have only ones and no zeros. The third column shows the hexadecimal representation discussed in Section 1.7.

Binary to decimal conversion

To compute the decimal number corresponding to a certain binary number, we simply use expression (2). The evaluation of the powers of two requires $k + l$ multiplications; their subsequent multiplication with the binary digits requires an equal number of multiplications; and the final evaluation of the decimal number requires $k + l$ additions: A total of $2(k + l)$ multiplications and $k + l$ additions.

The computational cost can be substantially reduced by expressing the sum in the equivalent form:

$$\Big[... \big[\, (b_k\, 2 + b_{k-1})\, 2 + b_{k-3})\, 2 + ... + b_1 \big]\, 2 + b_0 \tag{16}$$

$$+ \Big[... [(b_{-l}\, 0.5 + b_{-l+1})\, 0.5 + b_{-l+2}\,)\, 0.5 + ... + b_{-1} \Big]\, 0.5,$$

and then carrying out the computations according to Horner's algorithm: First, we set

$$a_k = b_k, \tag{17}$$

and compute the sequence

$$\begin{aligned} a_{k-1} &= 2\, a_k + b_{k-1}, \\ &\cdots, \\ a_i &= 2\, a_{i+1} + b_i, \\ &\cdots, \\ a_0 &= 2\, a_1 + b_0. \end{aligned} \tag{18}$$

Second, we set

$$c_{-l} = b_{-l}, \tag{19}$$

and compute the sequence

$$\begin{aligned} c_{-l+1} &= 0.5\, c_{-l} + b_{-l+1}, \\ &\cdots, \\ c_i &= 0.5\, c_{i-1} + b_i, \\ &\cdots, \\ c_{-1} &= 0.5\, c_{-2} + b_{-1}, \\ c_0 &= 0.5\, c_{-1}. \end{aligned} \tag{20}$$

The required number is equal to $a_0 + c_0$. Computing the decimal number in this manner requires a reduced number of $k + l$ multiplications, and an equal number of additions. When the cost of addition is much less than the cost of multiplications, Horner's algorithm reduces the execution time nearly by a factor of two.

Character representation

Characters include the lower- and upper-case letters of the English alphabet, a–z and A–Z, numbers, special symbols such as % and <, and control characters used to convey messages to printers and storage devices. Computers represent and store characters as encoded binary strings corresponding to integers.

According to the American Standard Code for Information Interchange convention (ASCII), 128 characters are represented by numerical values in the range 0–127, as shown in Appendix D. Thus, seven bits are required to describe the standard set of ASCII characters.

As an example, we consider the familiar equation

$$1 + 1 = 2. \tag{21}$$

Referring to Appendix D, we find the ASCII representation:

$$49 \ 43 \ 49 \ 61 \ 50 \tag{22}$$

which can be readily converted into a binary string and stored in a file or transmitted to a device.

The extended ASCII character set (ECS) includes 128 additional characters encoded by integers in the range 128–254. The extended set includes Greek and other European letters, various mathematical symbols, musical notes and sounds. Eight bits (one byte) are required to describe each member of the standard and extended ASCII character set.

An ASCII file contains bits corresponding to integers encoding ASCII characters. An ASCII file should be contrasted with a binary file which does not necessarily encode ASCII characters. An ASCII file can be viewed on the screen, whereas a binary file can be interpreted by only an intended device.

Problems

1.2.1. Consider a binary string, such as 11010...0011, and its complement arising by flipping the bits, 00101...1100, encoding two integers. What is the sum of these integers?

1.2.2. Compute the decimal equivalent of the binary number 101.101.

1.2.3. Compute the decimal equivalent of the binary number 0.11111..., where the ones continue to infinity.

1.2.4. What is the binary number of Mother Teresa's birth-year?

1.2.5. Compute the binary number of the decimal number 10.1.

1.2.6. The size of an ASCII file containing a document is 328 Kbytes. If each ASCII character is an encoded as an one-byte word, how may characters does the document hold? If the file holds a chapter of a book, how many pages does the chapter have?

1.3 Binary system arithmetic

The English word "arithmetic" derives from the Greek word $\alpha\rho\iota\theta\mu\sigma\varsigma$, which means "number." We can add, subtract, multiply, and divide two numbers in their binary number representation using rules that are similar to those for the decimal representation.

Addition

To compute the sum of two binary numbers, we add the corresponding digits according to four basic rules:

$$
\begin{aligned}
(0)_2 + (0)_2 &= (0)_2 \\
(0)_2 + (1)_2 &= (1)_2 \\
(1)_2 + (0)_2 &= (1)_2 \\
(1)_2 + (1)_2 &= (0)_2, \qquad \text{and carry } (1)_2 \text{ to the left.}
\end{aligned}
\tag{23}
$$

For example, following these rules, we find

$$
(111)_2 + (111)_2 = (1110)_2,
\tag{24}
$$

which is equivalent to $7 + 7 = 14$. The sequence of incremental operations that led us to this result is:

```
        + 111   110    110   100   0100   0000   0000
        + 111   110    100   100   1000   1000   0000
carry:  +         1     1     1
          ----   ---   ---   ---   ----   ----   ----
                  0     0    10    10     110    1110
```

The bits in the third row are the "carry."

To compute the difference between two binary numbers, we subtract the corresponding digits according to four basic rules:

$$
\begin{aligned}
(0)_2 - (0)_2 &= (0)_2 \\
(1)_2 - (1)_2 &= (0)_2 \\
(1)_2 - (0)_2 &= (1)_2 \\
(0)_2 - (1)_2 &= (1)_2, \qquad \text{with } (1)_2 \text{ borrowed from the left.}
\end{aligned}
\tag{25}
$$

For example, following these rules, we find

$$
(1000)_2 - (11)_2 = (101)_2,
\tag{26}
$$

which is equivalent to $8 - 3 = 5$. The sequence of incremental operations that led us to this result is:

```
            + 1000   1000   1000   1000   1000   1000
            -   11     10    100    100   1000   1000
carry:      -           1

              ----   ----   ----   ----   ----   ----
                 1      1     01    101   0101
```

The negative "carry" in the third row are added to those in the second row.

To develop rules for multiplication, we observe that, if we multiply a number by $2 = (10)_2$, the binary digits is shifted to the right by one place. This is analogous to the rule that, if we multiply a number by 10, the decimal digits is shifted to the left by one place. For example,

$$(1101.0)_2 \times (10)_2 = (11010.0)_2, \tag{27}$$

and

$$(10101.001)_2 \times (10)_2 = (101010.010)_2. \tag{28}$$

If we multiply a number by $0.5 = (0.1)_2$, which amounts to dividing by two, the binary point will be shifted to the left by one place.

More generally, if we multiply a number by $2^i = (10\ldots0)_2$, where the binary string contains i zeros, the binary digits will be shifted to the right by i places. For example,

$$(1101.000)_2 \times (1000)_2 = (1101000.0)_2. \tag{29}$$

If the integer i is negative, corresponding to division, the binary digits will be shifted to the right. For example,

$$(1101.0)_2 \times (0.01)_2 = (11.01)_2. \tag{30}$$

The distributive property of multiplication allows us to write for any number α:

$$\alpha \times (b_k\, b_{k-1} \cdots b_0 \cdot b_{-1} \cdots b_{-l})_2$$
$$= b_k \times \alpha \times 2^k + b_{k-1} \times \alpha \times 2^{k-1} \ldots + b_{-l} \times \alpha \times 2^{-l}. \tag{31}$$

This expression serves as a basis for implementing multiplication in terms of binary point shifts and additions. As an example, we compute the product:

$$(111)_2 \times (101)_2$$
$$= 1 \times (111)_2 \times (100)_2 + 0 \times (111)_2 \times (010)_2 + 1 \times (111)_2 \times (001)_2$$
$$= (11100)_2 + (111)_2 = (100011)_2. \tag{32}$$

which confirms the equation $7 \times 5 = 35$. The method is implemented in terms of the intuitive rules of binary digit multiplication:

$$(0)_2 \times (0)_2 = (0)_2$$
$$(0)_2 \times (1)_2 = (0)_2$$
$$(1)_2 \times (0)_2 = (0)_2 \tag{33}$$
$$(1)_2 \times (1)_2 = (1)_2.$$

Using these rules, we confirm the previous calculation,

```
        111
   x    101
        ---
        111   (111 times 1)
        000   (111 times 0 shifted once)
 +      111   (111 times 1 shifted twice)
        ------
        100011
```

The procedure is similar to that learned in elementary school for multiplying two numbers in their decimal representation.

Different processors employ different methods of performing division (see, for example, `http://www.cap-lore.com/Hardware/Divide.html`.) In numerical analysis, we learn that division can be implemented in terms of multiplication. Suppose that we want to compute the ratio $x = a/b$, where a and b are given real numbers. This can be done by writing $x = a \times r$, where we have defined the inverse of b, $r \equiv 1/b$. A simple rearrangement yields $r = r\,(2 - b\,r)$, which suggests the following algorithm:

- Guess the value of r, call it $r^{(0)}$.

- Improve the guess by computing: $r^{(1)} = r^{(0)}\,(2 - b\,r^{(0)})$.

- Further improve the guess by computing: $r^{(2)} = r^{(1)}\,(2 - b\,r^{(1)})$.

- Repeat until convergence.

This algorithm implements Newton's method for solving a nonlinear equation. It can be shown that a necessary and sufficient condition for the iterations to converge is that the initial guess lie inside the interval $(0, 2/b)$.

In computer hardware, addition and subtraction are implemented by straightforward combinations of electrical signals. Multiplication is a more complex operation, involving multiplication by a single binary digit using the rules described above, column shifting, and addition of the various subtotals. For this reason, addition and subtraction are often not counted as floating point operations (flops). Modern CPUs are endowed with a floating point unit (FPU) that performs addition, subtraction, multiplication, division, and sometimes computation of the square root of real numbers at comparable cost.

Problems

1.3.1. Add the binaries of 7 and 10, and confirm that the result is the binary of 17.

1.3.2. Subtract the binary of 7 from the binary of 10, and confirm that the result is the binary of 3.

1.3.3. Multiply the binary of 7 with the binary of 3, and confirm that the result is the binary of 21.

1.3.4. Find the inverse of the number 5.0 by carrying out multiplications alone, using the method discussed in the text.

1.4   Computer memory and addresses

The central processor receives information from, and deposits information to, a memory unit housed in an external memory bank mounted on the motherboard. The individual slots are identified by *memory addresses*. It is important to make a distinction between a memory *address* and a memory *content* at the outset.

In contemporary *byte-addressable architectures*, each address is associated with a memory slot consisting of one byte. Long data are stored in multiple bytes identified by a number of consecutive addresses. The real number 9.34556 absorbs more addresses than the integer 124.

Computer architectures are designed to work with memory addresses whose maximum possible value is expressed by the number of bits allocated to the memory addressing system:

- A 24-bit memory addressing system can accommodate $2^{24} = 1,6777,216$ addresses, and this limits the maximum number of memory slots to sixteen Mbytes.

- A 32-bit memory addressing system can accommodate $2^{32} = 4,294,967,296$ addresses, and this limits the maximum number of memory slots to four Gbytes. At the present time, computers with that much memory are rare.

- A 64-bit memory addressing system can accommodate $2^{64} = 1.8446744\ 07370955 \times 10^{19}$ addresses, and this limits the maximum number of memory slots to sixteen Ebytes.

In a 32-bit memory addressing system, the first memory address is 0 and the last memory address is 4,294,967,296.

RAM

The random access memory (RAM) is the primary memory bank. Its name reflects the ability to access the individual memory addresses at about the same amount of time, independent of the memory location last visited. In contrast, information stored in an external storage device, such as a hard drive or a CD-ROM, is accessed sequentially.

RAM is commonly called "system memory" or "internal memory." Input is sent to the RAM from the CPU through the *address bus* and *control bus*, and information is returned through the *data bus*. RAM memory is non-permanent and volatile; when the computer is switched off, the information disappears. RAM cells are organized in RAM units with different architectures.

RAM should be distinguished from the CPU register memory residing inside the processor. C++ has direct access to both.

SRAM, DRAM, and cache

The fundamental element of the static RAM (SRAM) is the *storage cell unit* consisting of a number of memory cells, each recording one bit in a flip-flop switch. Address lines transmit information regarding the address where information will be recorded or retrieved, read-write control lines dictate whether information will be recorded or retrieved, and data lines transfer the data either way. Other devices incorporated in the storage cell unit include the address register and decoder, the memory buffer register, and drivers in the form of transducers or amplifiers. The SRAM unit preserves its content as long as electricity is supplied, and loses its content when the computer is powered off.

The vast majority of system memory consists of dynamic RAM (DRAM). This inexpensive alternative differs from the SRAM in that each bit is stored as charge in a capacitor. Each DRAM cell incorporates a capacitor used to store the bit, and a transistor used to modify or retrieve the bit. A pulse of electrical current constantly refreshes the memory cells; when the pulse is lost, information is irreversibly erased. Every time information is read, the capacitor holding the data is discharged. DRAM is packaged in 30-pin or 70-pin single in-line memory modules (SIMM) or dual in-line memory modules (DIMM).

Other types of RAM memory include the level 1 (L1) or 2 (L2) cache memory consisting of SRAM cells. Because this memory is closer to the CPU, it has a much shorter access time. L1 cache memory is described as the "internal memory" of the CPU, whereas L2 cache memory is described either as the "secondary cache" or as the "external memory" of the CPU. Newer designs incorporate level 3 (L3) and level 4 (L4) cache memory. Preserved RAM (PRAM) runs on a battery, and its content is preserved even after the main power has been disconnected.

ROM system memory

A small amount of memory is designated as read-only memory (ROM), meaning that the information stored can be read but not modified. Like RAM, ROM addresses can be accessed at about the same amount of time. Many electronic devices such as hand-calculators and clocks use ROM. In a computer,

ROM is used for storing the basic input/output operating system (BIOS). Since information stored in a strict ROM cannot be changed, BIOS recorded cannot be upgraded.

The programmable read-only memory (PROM) allows us to record information after fabrication. In an erasable programmable ROM (EPROM), data is erased and recorded using a special ultraviolet (UV) light burner. In an electronically erasable programmable ROM (EEPROM), data is erased by conventional electronic techniques. Modern hardware uses upgradable flash BIOS recorded in the EEPROM.

Problems

1.4.1. A number is stored in four bytes. How many addresses does this number occupy?

1.4.2. What is the maximum useful memory size of an eight-bit memory addressing system in Mbytes?

1.5 Computer programming

The central processor is designed to respond to only a specific set of instructions written in machine language and encoded as binary strings. An instruction is composed of operation codes and accompanying arguments or parameters. For example, the binary equivalent of instruction 67099098095 may request addition, designated by the digits 98, of the content of the memory positioned at the address 670 and that of the memory positioned at the address 990, placing the sum in the memory positioned at the address 095.

Symbolic languages

Symbolic languages employ words instead of operation codes, and refer to operations by symbolic terms such as **add**. An instruction in the lowestlevel symbolic language, called the *assembly language*, is translated into the machine language code (object code) using a translation program called the *assembler*. The instructions of an assembly language make reference to the loading of variables to memory locations and fetching variables from memory locations. The mapping of assembly language commands to machine language instructions is one-to-one: each command is implemented by one instruction. The assembly language implements the lowest level of communication that is meaningful to humans.

A typical assembly command is: `mov b2, 3Ah`, meaning "move the hexadecimal value 3A to the processor register b1"; the hexadecimal representation is explained in Section 1.7. An assembly code implementing the bubble-sort algorithm for sorting a list of numbers or names reads:

```
bs proc array:DWORD,len:DWORD
  mov ecx,len
  mov edx,array
  bs_o:
  xor ebp,ebp
  bs_i:
  mov eax,DWORD PTR [edx+ebp*4+4]
  cmp DWORD PTR [edx+ebp*4],eax
  jb @F
  xchg eax,DWORD PTR [edx+ebp*4]
  mov DWORD PTR [edx+ebp*4+4],eax
  @@:
  add ebp,1
  cmp ebp,ecx
  jb bs_i
  loop bs_o
  pop ebp
  retn 8
bs endp
```

(See: http://www.codecodex.com/wiki/index.php?title=Bubble_sort).   Try explaining this code to a relative! The assembly language is esoteric, to say the least, let alone notoriously difficult to debug. Today, assembly programming is used for writing BIOS, real-time applications such as programs initializing television sets, and device drivers.

It is much more convenient to work with high-level symbolic languages that employ English words and standard mathematical notation. Examples are:

- The BASIC language (Beginner's All-purpose Symbolic Instruction Code) developed in the mid 1960s and still surviving.

- The fabulous FORTRAN (FORmula TRANslator) developed in the mid 1950s and still thriving.

- The UCSD Pascal introduced in the early 1970s.

- The C language developed in the mid 1970s.

- The C++ language developed in the mid 1980s.

A plethora of other languages have been developed for general and special-purpose applications. Because C and C++ allow the manipulation of bits, bytes, and memory addresses, they are considered mid-level languages, half a step above the assembler. The ranking of these computer languages in terms of efficiency and convenience can be the subject of great debate.

In a typical symbolic language, we issue statements such as A=A+B, which means "add the number B to the number A." The CPU executes this task through a sequence of steps:

- (FETCH A,R1): copy the binary of A from RAM to the CPU register R1.

- (FETCH B,R2): copy the binary of B from RAM to the CPU register R2.

- (ADD, R1,R2,R3): copy the contents of R1 and R2 to the adder, perform the addition, and store the results in register R3.

- (STORE, R3,A): copy the content of R3 to the RAM address of A.

We see that the mapping of an upper-level language command to machine language instructions is one-to-many; each command is implemented by several instructions.

Binary executables

Every computer command or application is implemented in a *binary executable file* encoding machine-language instructions. This file is loaded into the RAM by issuing the name of the command or typing the name of the application, and then hitting the ENTER key; on a graphical interface, we click on an icon. To locate a specified binary executable file, the operating system searches through a user-defined ordered execution *directory path.*

The instruction cycle, also called the fetch-decode-execute cycle (FDX), describes the time required for a single instruction written in machine language to be fetched from the RAM, decoded, and executed by the CPU.

Compiling and creating an executable

To write a set of instructions in a mid- or high-level language, we first generate one file or a number of files containing the main program, subroutines, and necessary data. The files are created using a text editor, such as the legendary *vi* editor that comes with any Unix distribution, and is also available in Windows. These files constitute the *source code.*

Secondly, we compile the program and subroutines using the language compiler to create each file's *object code.* The object code is the translation of the source code into machine language that can be communicated to the CPU. The compiler basically assigns memory addresses to variables and translates arithmetic and logical operations into the machine-language instructions. The compiler itself is a binary executable installed in a directory that must be included in the user's executable directory path. The main difference between a compiler and an assembler is that the former understands logical structures, whereas the latter performs a blind translation.

Thirdly, we link the object codes with other installed or system binary libraries called by the program, thereby producing the *executable*. Library files may contain mathematical functions, graphical tools, and graphical user interfaces that allow a program to run in its own exclusive space on the computer desktop. Some compilers have their own linkers, other compilers use linkers that are provided by the operating system.

Finally, we load the executable code into the memory and thereby launch the executable; the presence of the compiler is not necessary. Since different CPUs have different machine languages, an executable produced on one CPU will not necessarily run on another. Moreover, the object files are not necessarily portable across different versions of an operating system on the same hardware platform.

Some language compilers produce *bytecode*, which is portable across a variety of platforms. The bytecode is further compiled to produce machine code, or else executed directly through an interpreter.

While these are the general rules, there are exceptions. A program written in the standard version of the BASIC language or in MATLAB is compiled, or, more accurately, interpreted line-by-line as it runs. The presence of the compiler or interpreter is thus necessary for the program to run. A buggy interpreted code may run until failure, whereas a buggy compiled code will not compile. Executable codes run much faster than interpreted programs.

Data files

Numerical and other parameters are either contained in separate files, called data or configuration files, or are entered from the keyboard as the program runs. Data files are usually denoted with the suffix `.dat`, and configuration files are usually denoted with the suffix `.conf`.

Problems

1.5.1. Conduct an Internet search to prepare a list of ten computer languages.

1.5.2. An executable was generated using an operating systems with a particular CPU. Is it possible that this executable may also run under a different operating system on the same CPU?

1.6   Floating-point representation

The floating-point representation allows us to store real numbers (non-integers) with a broad range of magnitudes, and carry out mathematical operations between numbers with disparate magnitudes.

Consider the binary number:

$$1001100101.01100011101$$

To develop the floating-point representation, we recast this number into the product:

$$1.00110010101100011101 \times 1000000000 \qquad (34)$$

Note that the binary point has been shifted to the left by nine places, and the resulting number has been multiplied by the binary equivalent of 2^9. The binary string 1.00110010101100011101 is the *mantissa* or *significand*, and 9 is the *exponent*.

To develop the floating-point representation of an arbitrary number, we express it in the form:

$$\pm s\, 2^e$$

where s is a real number called the *mantissa* or *significand*, and e is the integer *exponent*. This representation requires one bit for the sign, a set of bytes for the exponent, and another set of bytes for the mantissa. In memory, the bits are arranged sequentially in the following order:

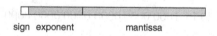

sign exponent   mantissa

The exponent determines the shift of the binary point in the binary representation of the mantissa.

Many combinations of s and e generate the same number. The normalized representation leaves as many zeros as possible at the end of the binary string. This means that the first digit of the mantissa is always non-zero and thus equal to one. We can exploit this convention to avoid storing this bit and thus gain one binary digit of accuracy. We then say that the mantissa has one "hidden bit." The exponent is stored after it has been shifted by an integer bias so as to become positive. This shift saves us from allocating one bit to the exponent sign.

How can we store the number zero? By convention, if all bits of the floating point string after the sign are zero, the hidden bit is also zero, yielding the number zero. Infinity is encoded by a floating point string with all ones for the bits of the exponent, and all zeros for the bits of the mantissa.

When the exponent takes a value that is higher than the maximum value or lower than the minimum value that can be described with the available number of bits, the operating system sends a message (exception) of system overflow or underflow. Improper operations, such as dividing zero by zero or computing the square root of a negative number, activate the *Not-a-Number (NaN)* warning.

Precision

The number of bytes assigned to a real variable (word length) is controlled by the programmer through the option of single, double, and extended precision. A variable can be declared either as integer, in which case the binary point is fixed at the end of the word length, or as real (floating-point) in which case the binary point floats across the word-length.

Single precision

Single precision reserves 32-bit (4-byte) word lengths. A real number in the range 1–2 can be resolved up to only the eighth decimal place, and the machine accuracy is 10^{-8}. The mantissa is usually described by 23 bits, and the biased exponent is described by 8 bits. System overflow or underflow typically occurs when the absolute value of the exponent is higher than 127. The maximum and minimum positive numbers that can be stored are 1.701×10^{38} and 5.877×10^{-39}.

As an example, we consider the floating-point representation:

$$0\ \mathbf{011\ 1111}\ 1000\ 0000\ 0000\ 0000\ 0000\ 0000 \qquad (35)$$

The first bit specifies the sign, the bold-faced digits represent the exponent shifted by 127, and the rest of the bits represent the mantissa. We note that the binary string of 127 is precisely equal to the bold-faced sequence, and find that the exponent is zero. We recall the implicit presence of a hidden bit and the convection that a zero sign bit corresponds to the plus sign, and find that this floating point string represents the number 1.0.

Double precision

Double precision reserves 64-bit (8-byte) word lengths. A real number in the range 1–2 can be resolved up to the fourteenth or sixteenth decimal place. The mantissa is usually described by 52 bits, and the biased exponent is described by 11 bits. System overflow or underflow typically occurs when the absolute value of the exponent is higher that 1023, and the maximum and minimum positive numbers that can be stored are 8.988×10^{307} and 1.123×10^{-308}.

Extended precision

It is sometimes necessary to use extended precision that employs 128-bit (16-byte) word lengths and allows us to describe a number up to the twentieth significant figure. This high level of resolution is necessary for solving a certain class of highly sensitive, nearly ill-posed mathematical problems.

C++ allows us to implement arbitrary precision by dividing a number in piecces and storing them in separate memory slots.

Round-off error

An arbitrary real number that has a finite number of digits in the decimal system generally requires an infinite number of bits in the binary system. In fact, only the numbers $\pm n\, 2^m$ are represented exactly in the single-precision floating point representation, where $0 \leq n < 2^{23}$, and $-127 \leq m \leq 126$, with m and n being two integers. An ideal computing machine would be able to register the number and carry out additions and multiplications with infinite precision, yielding the exact result to all figures. In real life, one must deal with non-ideal machines that work with only a finite number of bits and thus incur round-off error.

Some computers round a real number to the closest number they can describe with an equal probability of positive or negative error. Other computers simply chop off the extra digits in a guillotine-like fashion.

When two real numbers (non-integers) are added in the floating-point representation, the significant digits of the number with the smaller exponent are shifted to align the decimal point, and this causes the loss of significant digits. Floating-point normalization of the resulting number incurs additional losses. Consequently, arithmetic operations between real variables exacerbates the magnitude of the round-off error. Unless integers are only involved, identities that are precise in exact arithmetic become approximate in computer arithmetic.

The accumulation of the round-off error in the course of a computation may range from negligible, to observable, to significant, to disastrous. Depending on the nature of the problem and the sequence of computations, the round-off error may amplify, become comparable to, or even exceed the magnitude of the actual variables.

In certain simple cases, the damaging effect of the round-off error can be predicted and thus minimized or controlled. As a general rule, one should avoid subtracting two nearly equal numbers. In computing the sum of a sequence of numbers, we should start summing the numbers with the smaller magnitudes first, and the largest magnitudes last.

Problems

1.6.1. Derive the floating-point representation in single precision with a hidden bit of (*a*) -2.00, (*b*) -0.50, and (*c*) -2.50.

1.6.2. Find the number whose floating-point representation in single precision with a hidden bit is:

$$1\ \mathbf{100\ 0000\ 0}100\ 1001\ 0000\ 1111\ 1101\ 1011$$

1.7   The hexadecimal system

A number in the hexadecimal system is denoted as

$$(h_k\, h_{k-1}\, \cdots h_0 . h_{-1} \cdots h_{-l}\,)_2 \tag{36}$$

where k and l are two integers, the hexadecimal characters, h_i, take sixteen values, 0–15, and the period (.) is the hexadecimal point. For convenience, the six two-digit numbers, 10–15, are represented by the letters A–F.

The corresponding decimal value is

$$h_k \times 16^k + h_{k-1} \times 16^{k-1} + \cdots + h_0 \times 16^0$$
$$+ h_{-1} \times 16^{-1} + \cdots + h_{-l} \times 16^{-l}. \tag{37}$$

Table 1.1.2 shows the hexadecimal representation of zero and first seventeen integers.

It is easy to find the hexadecimal string of a given binary string. Starting from the left or right or the binary point, we divide the binary string into blocks of four digits, and look up the hexadecimal digit corresponding to each block according to Table 1.1.2. For example,

$$(101111)_2 = (2F)_{16}. \tag{38}$$

The backward translation from hexadecimal to binary can also readily be performed using a similar method.

In C++, hexadecimal numbers are designated by the prefix 0x. Thus, we write

$$(101111)_2 = (2F)_{16}. = \text{0x2F} \tag{39}$$

Storing and retrieving data

Since one byte can hold two hexadecimal digits, the hexadecimal representation is ideal for storing and retrieving data. Consider the floating-point

representation in single precision using four-byte word lengths that accommodate eight hexadecimal digits. Assume that the hexadecimal representation of
a stored number is:

$$0x3F800000 \tag{40}$$

The associated binary string is:

$$0\ \textbf{011 1111}\ 1000\ 0000\ 0000\ 0000\ 0000\ 0000. \tag{41}$$

In Section 1.6, we saw that this is the floating point representation of 1.0.

Problems

1.7.1. Compute the hexadecimal representation of 66.75.

1.7.2. Derive in hexadecimal form the single-precision, hidden-bit floating point
representation of the number (*a*) 0.125, and (*b*) -40.5.

1.7.3. A number in the octal system is denoted as

$$(o_k\ o_{k-1} \cdots o_0.o_{-1} \cdots o_{-l})_8 \tag{42}$$

where k and l are two integers, the octal characters o_i take eight values
0–7, and the period (.) is the octal point. The corresponding decimal
value is

$$o_k \times 8^k + o_{k-1} \times 8^{k-1} + \cdots + o_0 \times 8^0 + o_{-1} \times 8^{-1} + \cdots + o_{-l} \times 8^{-l}. \tag{43}$$

(*a*) Write the octal representation of zero and first seventeen integers.

(*b*) To find the octal representation of a given binary string, we start from
the left or right or the binary point, divide the binary string into blocks
of two digits, and look up the octal digit corresponding to each block.
Apply this procedure to find the octal representation of $(101111)_2$.

General Features of C++ 2

In this chapter, we explain how to write, compile, and execute (run) a basic C++ program.

The program is written in a file using a text editor such as *vi*, *gedit*, or *emacs*. A file containing C++ code is conventionally designated by one of the suffixes:

.c   .cc   .cpp   .cxx

Thus, a C++ source file can be named

kalambaka.c   edessa.cc   kourkoubinia.cpp   mageiras.cxx

The C++ source files are compiled and linked through a C++ compiler to produce the corresponding binary executable, as discussed in Chapter 1.

Free C++ compilers are available for the Linux platform thanks to the *gnu* free-software foundation. Cygwin and Borland offer complimentary compilers for other operating systems. Some compilers are bundled in an integrated development environment (IDE) offering dazzling graphical user interfaces (GUI).

2.1 The main function

Each C++ application (complete code) has a main function that is first loaded into memory and then transferred to the CPU for execution. When execution has been concluded, the main function returns the integer 0. This practice is motivated partly by issues of backward compatibility.

The main function has the general syntax:

```
int main()
{
 ...
 return 0;
}
```

where:

- **int** indicates that an integer will be returned on completion. The penultimate line sets this integer to 0, signaling the success of the execution.

- The parentheses after **main** enclose the arguments of the main function; in this case, there are no arguments.

- The curly brackets mark the beginning and the end of the enclosed main program consisting of various instructions.

- The dots stand for additional lines of code.

- The semicolon is a delimiter, marking the end of the preceding command **return** 0, which concludes the execution.

A simplified version of the main program that returns nothing on execution is:

```
main()
{
...
}
```

However, the previous structure with the return statement included is highly recommended as a standard practice.

In Chapter 5, we will see that the main function can not only return, but also receive information from the operating system. In that case, the parentheses in

```
int main()
```

will enclose command line arguments.

Problem

2.1.1. We saw that C++ uses parentheses and curly brackets. What other bracket delimiters do you anticipate based on the symbols printed on your keyboard?

2.2 Grammar and syntax

Next, we review the most important rules regarding the grammar and syntax of C++. If an error occurs during compilation or execution, this list should serve as a first checkpoint.

C++ is (lower and upper) case sensitive

For example, the variable echidna is different from the variable echiDna, and the C++ command return is not equivalent to the non-existent command Return.

Beginning of a statement

A C++ statement or command may begin at any place in a line and continue onto the next line. In fact, a statement may take several lines of code. We say that C++ is written in *free form*.

End of a statement

The end of a statement is indicated by a semicolon ";" (statement delimiter.) Thus, we write:

```
a=5;
```

If we do not include the semicolon, the compiler will assume that the statement in the next line is a continuation of the statement in the present line.

Multiple commands in a line

Two or more statements can be placed in the same line provided they are separated with semicolons. Thus, we may write:

```
a=5; b=10;
```

White space

An empty (blank) space separates two words. The compiler ignores more than one empty space between two words. A number cannot be broken up into pieces separated by white space; thus, we may not write 92 093 instead of 92093.

Statement and command blocks

Blocks of statements or commands defining procedures are enclosed by curly brackets (block delimiters)

```
{
...
}
```

Note that it is not necessary to put a semicolon after the closing bracket. This practice is consistent with the structure of the main program discussed in Section 2.1.

In-line comments

In-line comments may be inserted following the double slash "//". For example, we may write:

```
a = 10.0; // ignore me
```

The text: `// ignore me` is ignored by the compiler.

To deactivate (comment out) a line, we write:

```
// a = 34.5;
```

A distinction should be made between the slash (/) and the backslash (\). These are two different symbols separated by two rows on the keyboard.

Commentary

All text enclosed between a slash-asterisk pair (/*) and the converse asterisk-slash pair (*/) is commentary and ignored by the compiler. Thus, we may write:

```
/* ---- main program ----- */
```

To provide documentation at the beginning of a code, we may write:

```
/* PROGRAM: late
AUTHOR: Justin Caso
PURPOSE: produce an excuse for being late */
```

Problems

2.2.1. How many commands are executed in the following line?

```
a=3.0; // b=4.0;
```

2.2.2. How does the compiler interpret the following line?

```
/* my other /* car is */ a vartburg */
```

2.3   Data types

In mathematical modeling and computer programming, we introduce variables representing abstract notions and physical objects. Examples are the temperature, the velocity, the balance of a bank account, and the truthfulness of a theorem.

In C++, the name of a variable must start with a letter and contain only letters, numbers, and the underscore (_). Names reserved for C++ grammar and syntax given in Appendix E cannot be employed. Acceptable variables obey the rules discussed in this section.

Numerical variable declaration:

Every numerical variable must be declared either as an integer (whole number) or as a real (floating point) number registered in single or double precision. In the remainder of this text, we adopt a mathematical viewpoint and we refer to a non-integer as a real number.

Suppose that a is an integer, b is a real number registered in single precision, and c is a real number registered in double precision. The statements declaring these variables are:

```
int a;
float b;
double c;
```

Suppose that i is an integer and j is another integer. We can declare either:

```
int i;
int j;
```

or

```
int i, j;
```

Note the obligatory use of a comma.

Why does a variable have to be declared? Appropriate space must be reserved in memory by the compiler.

Numerical variable initialization and evaluation

A numerical variable is not necessarily initialized to zero by default when declared, and may be given a value already recorded previously in the assigned memory address.

Once declared, a numerical variable can be initialized or evaluated. For example, we may write:

```
int a;
a=875;
```

Declaration and initialization can be combined into a single statement:

```
int a = 875;
```

An equivalent but less common statement is:

```
int a (875);
```

In these statements, the numerical value 875 is a *literal*.

To introduce a real number registered in single precision, we may state:

```
float b = -9.30;
```

or

```
float c = 10.45e-3;
```

meaning that $c = 10.3 \times 10^{-3}$. The numerical values on the right-hand sides of these statements are literals.

A literal cannot be broken up into pieces separated by white space. For example, the following declaration is incorrect:

```
double pi=3.141592 653589 793238;
```

The correct declaration is:

```
double pi=3.141592653589793238;
```

Integer evaluation

An integer can be evaluated in the decimal, octal, or hexadecimal system. The statement:

```
int a=72;
```

implies

$$a = 7 \times 10^2 + 2 \times 10^0.$$

The statement:

$$\texttt{int a = 023;}$$

with a leading zero (0), implies

$$a = 2 \times 8^1 + 3 \times 8^0.$$

The statement:

$$\texttt{int a = 0xA4;}$$

with a leading zero (0) followed by x implies

$$a = 10 \times 16^1 + 4 \times 16^0.$$

Boolean variables

A Boolean variables can be either `false` or `true`. When a Boolean variable is printed, it appears as 1 or 0, respectively, for true and false.

The following statements declare and initialize the Boolean variable `hot`:

```
bool hot;
hot = true;
```

An equivalent statement is:

```
bool hot = true;
```

Boolean variables are useful for assessing states and making logical decisions based on deduced outcomes.

Characters

A single character is encoded according to the ASCII protocol described in Appendix D. The following statements declare and initialize a character:

```
char a;
a = 66;
```

In compact form:

```
char a = 66;
```

When the character a is printed, it appears as the letter B. Alternatively, we may define:

```
char a;
a = 'B';
```

or even combine the two statements into one line:

```
char a = 'B';
```

Note the mandatory use of *single* quotes. This example confirms that the ASCII code of the letter B is 66.

To find the ASCII code of a character, we may typecast it as an integer. For example, we may write:

```
char a = 'B';
int c = a;
```

If we print the integer c, it will have the value 66.

Strings

A string is an array of characters. The following statements define and initialize a string:

```
string name;
name = "Kolokotronis";
```

Note the mandatory use of *double* quotes. The two statements can be consolidated into one:

```
string name = "Kolokotronis";
```

Alternatively, we may state:

```
string name ("Kolokotronis");
```

Other data types

C++ supports the data types shown in Table 2.3.1. The number of bytes reserved in memory and the range of the data types depend on the specific system architecture. The values shown in Table 2.3.1 are those found on most 32-bit systems. For other systems, the general convention is that int has the natural size suggested by the system architecture (one word), and each of the four integer types:

Type	Description	Byte size
short int	Short integer	2
short	Ranges from -32768 to 32767	
signed short int	Ranges from 0 to 65535	
unsigned short int		
int	Integer	4
signed int	Ranges from -2147483648 to 2147483647	
unsigned int	Ranges from 0 to 4294967295	
long int	Long integer	4
long	Ranges from-2147483648 to 2147483647	
signed long int	Ranges from 0 to 4294967295	
unsigned long int		
float	Floating point number	4
	Real number inside $3.4\,\mathrm{e}^{\pm38}$	
double	Double precision	8
	Floating point number	
	Real number inside $1.7\,\mathrm{e}^{\pm308}$	
long double	Long double precision	12
	Floating point number	
	Real number inside $1.7\,\mathrm{e}^{\pm308}$	
bool	Boolean value "true" or "false"	1
char	Encoded character	1
signed char	Integer ranging from -128 to 127	
unsigned char	Integer ranging from 0 to 255	
wchar_t	Wide character	4
	Used for non-English letters	
string *stringname*	String of characters	4
char *stringname*[]	Array of characters	

Table 2.3.1 Data types supported by C++ and their common memory allocation. *unsigned* only allows positive integers. *signed* is the default type of integers and characters.

```
char   short   int   long
```

must be at least as large as the one preceding it. The same applies to the
floating point types:

```
float       double     long double
```

Each must provide at least as much precision as the one preceding it.

The size of the different data types listed in Table 2.3.1 can be confirmed
by using the `sizeof` operator discussed in Section 3.1.

Constants

To fix the value of a variable and thus render the variable a constant, we
include the keyword `const`. For example, we may declare

```
const float temperature;
```

Constants are variables that, once evaluated, remain fixed and thus cease to be
variables.

Aliases

We can introduce an alias of a declared variable so that we can refer to
it by a different name. For example, we may declare:

```
float a;
float& a_alias = a;
```

Since `a_alias` and `a` are truly the same variable, any operation on one amounts
to the same operation on the other. In C++, an alias is better known as a
reference.

Defined data types

C++ allows us to duplicate a data type into something that is either more
familiar or more convenient. For example, if *year* is a non-negative integer, we
may declare:

```
unsigned int year;
```

Since the year is positive, we have exercised the `unsigned` option.

We can duplicate the cumbersome "`unsigned int`" into "hronos" meaning year in Greek, by stating:

```
typedef unsigned int hronos;
```

The data types unsigned int and hronos are now synonyms. We may then declare:

```
hronos year;
```

The Unix-savvy reader will notice that the "typedef" command works like the copy command, "cp", the move command, "mv", and the symbolic link command, "ln -l":

```
cp file1 file2
```

copies file1 into file2,

```
mv file1 file2
```

renames file1 into file2, and

```
ln -s file1 file2
```

symbolically links file1 into its alter ego file2.

Problems

2.3.1. Declare and initialize at the value of 77 the integer a using (a) the octal, and (b) the hexadecimal representation.

2.3.2. What are the values of the integers c and d evaluated by the following statements?

```
char a = '='; int c = a;
char b = '1'; int d = b;
```

2.4   Vectors, arrays, and composite data types

The basic data types introduced in Section 2.3 can be extended into composite groups that facilitate notation and book-keeping in a broad range of scientific and other applications.

Vectors

In C++, a one-dimensional array (vector) v_i is declared as v[n], where n is an integer, and $i = 0, \ldots, n - 1$. Thus, the lower limit of an array index is always 0.

For example, a vector **v** with thirty slots occupied by real numbers registered in double precision, beginning at v[0] and ending at v[29], is declared as:

```
double v[30];
```

Note that the elements of the vector are denoted using square brackets, v[i], not parentheses, v(i). Parentheses in C++ enclose function arguments.

Similarly, we can declare:

```
char a[19];
```

and

```
string a[27];
```

Successive elements of a vector are stored in consecutive memory blocks whose length depends on the data type.

In C++ jargon, the term "vector" sometimes implies a one-dimensional array with variable length.

Matrices

A two-dimensional array (matrix) A_{ij} is declared as A[m][n], where n and m are two integers, $i = 0, 1, \ldots, m - 1$ and $j = 0, 1, \ldots, n - 1$. The lower limit of both indices is 0.

For example, the two indices of the 15×30 matrix $A[15][30]$ begin at $i, j = 0$ and end, respectively, at $i = 14$ and $j = 29$. If the elements of this matrix are integers, we declare:

```
int A[15][30];
```

Note that the elements of the matrix are denoted as v[i][j], not v(i,j). The individual indices of a matrix are individually enclosed by square brackets.

Similarly, we can declare the array of characters:

```
char A[13][23];
```

and the array of strings:

$$\texttt{string A[9][38];}$$

Successive *rows* of a matrix are stored in consecutive memory blocks.

Data structures

Consider a group of M objects,

$$o1, o2, \ldots, oM,$$

a group of N properties,

$$p1, p2, \ldots, pN,$$

and denote the jth property of the ith object by:

$$oi.pj$$

The individual properties of the objects can be accommodated in a data structure defined, for example, as:

```
struct somename
{
  int p1;
  float p2;
  double p3;
  double p4;
}
o1, o2, o3;
```

Alternatively, we may define a data structure in terms of the properties alone by declaring:

```
struct somename
{
  int p1;
  float p2;
  double p3;
  double p4;
};
```

and then introduce members by declaring:

```
somename o1;
somename o2, o3;
```

Objects and properties are threaded with a dot (.) into variables that convey expected meanings:

```
int o1.p1;
float o1.p2;
double o2.p3;
char o1.p4;
```

The mathematically inclined reader will recognize that this threading is the tensor product of two vectors, $\mathbf{o} \otimes \mathbf{p}$. In computer memory, the variables

$$o1.p1 \qquad o1.p2 \qquad o1.p3 \ldots$$

are stored in consecutive memory blocks.

As an example, we define the used car lot structure:

```
struct car
{
  string make;
  int year;
  int miles;
  bool lemon;
}
vartburg1, skoda1, skoda2;
```

and then set:

```
skoda1.make = "skoda";
vartburg1.miles= 98932;
skoda1.lemon = true;
skoda2.lemon = false;
```

Data structures and their members are preludes to classes and objects discussed in Chapter 6.

Enumerated groups

One way to represent a property, such as flavor, is to encode it using integers. For example, we may assign:

$$\text{bitter} \to 4, \quad \text{sweet} \to 5, \quad \text{salty} \to 6, \quad \text{hot} \to 7, \quad \text{sour} \to 8.$$

We then know that if `peasoup_flavor=6`, the soup is salty.

C++ allows us to mask this encoding by defining enumerations. In our example, we declare:

```
enum flavor {bitter=4, sweet, salty, hot, sour};
```

where bitter is encoded as 4, sweet is encoded as 5, salty is encoded as 6, hot is encoded as 7, and sour is encoded as 8. The starting integer, 4, is arbitrary and can be omitted, in which case the default value of 0 is used. We may then state:

```
flavor peasoup_flavor;
peasoup_flavor = salty;
```

The broad range of standard features offered by C++, combined with its ability to generate unlimited user-defined structures, explain its popularity and suitability for building large code.

Problems

2.4.1. Define a structure of your choice.

2.4.2. Define an enumerated group of your choice.

2.5   System header files

When a FORTRAN 77 code is compiled to produce an executable (binary) file, the linker automatically attaches the necessary library files that allow, for example, data to be read from the keyboard and data to be written to the monitor. Other library files ensure the availability of intrinsic mathematical and further functions.

In contrast, in C++, supporting functions, mathematical functions, and other ancillary services required during execution must be explicitly requested. This is done by placing at the beginning of each file containing the C++ code an **include** statement or a collection of **include** statements handled by the preprocessor. The C++ preprocessor runs as part of the compilation process, adding to the compiled program necessary code and removing unnecessary code.

An **include** statement asks the preprocessor to attach at the location of the statement a copy of a *header file* containing the definition of a desired class of system or user-defined functions. Both are regarded as *external implementations.*

The system header files reside in a subdirectory of a directory where the C++ compiler was installed, whereas the user-defined header files reside in user-specified directories. For example, in Linux, system header files reside in *include* directories, such as the */usr/include* or the */use/local/include* directory.

Once the header files have been copied, the compiler searches for and attaches the implementations of the required external functions located in system or user-defined library files and directories.

For example, putting at the beginning of the code the statement:

```
#include <iostream>
```

instructs the C++ preprocessor to attach a header file containing the definition, but not the implementation, of functions in the input/output stream library. In the Fedora Core 5 Linux distribution, the `iostream` header file is located in the */usr/include/c++/4.1.1* directory.

Thus, the main function of a code that uses this library has the general structure:

```
#include <iostream>
...
int main()
{
...
return 0;
}
```

where the three dots denote additional lines of code.

Similarly, putting at the beginning of a source code the statement:

```
#include <cmath>
```

ensures the availability of the C++ mathematical library. In this case, *cmath* is a header file containing the definition, but not the implementation, of mathematical functions.

Thus, the main function of a code that uses both the input/output and the mathematical libraries has the general syntax:

```
#include <iostream>
#include <cmath>
...
int main()
{
...
return 0;
}
```

where the three dots denote additional lines of code.

A statement following the # character in a C++ code is a *compiler* or *preprocessor directive*. Other directives are available.

Problems

2.5.1. Locate the directory hosting the `iostream` header file in your computer.

2.5.2. Prepare a list of mathematical functions declared in the `cmath` header file.

2.6 Standard namespace

Immediately after the include statements, we state:

```
using namespace std;
```

which declares that the names of the functions defined in the standard `std` system library will be adopted in the code. This means that the names will be stated plainly and without reference to the `std` library.

In large codes written by many authors, and in codes linked with libraries obtained from different sources or vendors, names may have multiple meanings defined in different namespaces.

If we do not make the "using namespace std" declaration, then instead of stating:

```
string a;
```

we would have to state the more cumbersome:

```
std::string a;
```

What names are defined in the `std` library? We can find this out by trial and error, commenting out the "using namespace std" line and studying the errors issued on compilation.

Thus, the main function of a code that uses the standard input/output library and the mathematical library has the general form:

```
#include <iostream>
#include <cmath>
using namespace std;
...
int main()
{
...
return 0;
}
```

where the three dots denote additional lines of code. This fundamental pattern will be used as a template in all subsequent codes.

Problem

2.6.1. Is the integer declaration `int` in the standard namespace? Deduce this by trial and error.

2.7 Compiling in Unix

Suppose that a self-contained C++ program has been written in a single file named *addition.cc*. To compile the program on a Unix system, we navigate to the directory where this file resides, and issue the command:

```
c++ addition.cc
```

This statement invokes the C++ compiler with a single argument equal to the file name. The compiler will run and produce an executable binary file named *a.out*, which may then be loaded into memory (executed) by issuing the command:

```
a.out
```

It is assumed that the search path for executables includes the current working directory where the *a.out* file resides, designated by a dot (.). To be safe, we issue the command:

```
./a.out
```

which specifies that the executable is in the current directory.

Alternatively, we may compile the file by issuing the command:

```
c++ -o add addition.cc
```

This will produce an executable file named *add*, which may then be loaded (executed) by issuing the command:

```
add
```

or the safer command:

```
./add
```

Other compilation options are available, as explained in the compiler manual invoked by typing:

```
man gcc
```

for the GNU project C and C++ compilers.

Makefiles

C++ programs are routinely compiled by way of Unix makefiles, even if a code consists of a single file. If a complete C++ code is contained in the file *addition.cc*, we create a file named *makefile* or *Makefile* in the host directory of *addition.cc*, containing the following lines:

```
LIBS =
papaya:  addition.o
        c++ -o add addition.o $(LIBS)
addition.o:  addition.cc
        c++ -c addition.cc
```

The empty spaces in the third and fifth lines must be generated by pressing the TAB *key inside the text editor.*

- The first line of the makefile defines the variable LIBS as the union of external binary libraries and header files to be linked with the source code. In this case, no libraries or header files are needed, and the variable LIBS is left empty.

- The second line defines a project named *papaya* that depends on the object file *addition.o*. Subsequent indented lines specify project tasks.

- The third line names the process for creating the executable *add*; in this case, the process is compilation and linking. Note that the name of the executable is not necessarily the same as the name of the the source file. The flag -o requests the production of an executable.

- The fourth line defines the project *addition.o* that depends on the source file *addition.cc*. The flag -c signifies compilation.

- The fifth line states the process for creating the object file *addition.o*; in this case, the process is compilation.

The object file *addition.o* and the executable *add* are generated by issuing the command:

```
make papaya
```

 make is a Unix application that reads information from the file makefile or Makefile in the working directory. In our example, the application performs all operations necessary to complete the project papaya. A condensed version of the papaya project is:

```
papaya:  addition.cc
        c++ -o add addition.cc
```

Other projects can be defined in the same makefile. If we type:

```
make
```

the first project will be tackled. Further information on the make utility can be obtained by referring to the manual pages printed on the screen by issuing the command:

```
man make
```

 In Chapter 4, we will discuss situations in which the C++ code is split into two or more files. Each file is compiled individually, and the object files are linked to generate the executable. In these cases, compiling through a makefile is practically our only option. If the code is written in an integrated development environment (IDE), the compilation process is handled as a project through a graphical user interface (GUI).

Typesetting this book

 This book was written in the typesetting language latex. To compile the source file named book.tex and create a portable-document-format (pdf) file, we have used the makefile:

```
manuscript:
        latex book.tex
        makeindex book
        dvips -o book.ps book.dvi
        ps2pdf book.ps
```

The first line names the task. The second and third lines compile the source code, prepare the subject index, and generate a compiled device-independent (dvi) file named book.dvi. The fourth line generates a postscript (ps) file named book.ps from the dvi file. The fourth line generates a pdf file named book.pdf as a translation of the ps file. To initiate the task, we issue the command:

```
make manuscript
```

Postscript is a computer language like C++. A postscript printer understands this language and translates it into pen calls that draw images and high-quality fonts.

Software distributions

Suppose that a project named *rizogalo* and another project named *trahanas* are defined in the makefile. To execute both, we define in the same makefile the task:

```
all:
        rizogalo
        trahanas
```

and issue the command:

```
make all
```

The tasks `install` and `clean`, defining software installation and distillation procedures, are common in makefiles accompanying software distributions. To install software, we type

```
make install
```

To remove unneeded object files, we type

```
make clean
```

Problems

2.7.1. Define in a makefile a project called *clean* that removes all `.o` object files from the current directory using the Unix *rm* command (see Appendix A.)

2.7.2. Define in a makefile a project that generates the executable of a C++ program and then runs the executable.

2.8   Simple codes

We are in a position to write, compile, and execute a simple C++ code.

The following program declares, evaluates, and prints an integer:

```
#include <iostream>
using namespace std;
```

```
int main()
{
int year;
year = 1821;
cout << year << "\n";
return 0;
}
```

The output of the code is:

1821

The cout statement prints on the screen the value of the variable *year* using the cout function of the internal *iostream* library, and then moves the cursor to a new line instructed by the \n string. The syntax of these output commands will be discussed in detail in Chapter 3.

The fifth and sixth lines could have been consolidated into:

```
int year = 2006;
```

This compact writing is common among experienced programmers, though it is often stretched to the point of obfuscation. Albert Einstein once said: "Things should be made as simple as possible, but not any simpler."

The following C++ code contained in the file *addition.cc* evaluates the real variables a and b in double precision, adds them into the new variable c, and then prints the value of c on the screen along with a comforting message:

```
#include <iostream>
using namespace std;

int main()
{
double a=4;
double b=2;
double c;
c=a+b;
cout << c << "\n";
string message;
message = "peace on earth";
cout << message << "\n";
return 0;
}
```

The output of the code is:

```
6
peace on earth
```

The first cout statement prints the variable *c* on the screen using the *cout* function of the internal iostream library, and then moves the cursor to a new line instructed by the endl directive, as will be discussed in Chapter 3. The second cout statement performs a similar task.

Problems

2.8.1. Write a program that prints on the screen the name of a person that you most admire.

2.8.2. Investigate whether the following statement is permissible:

```
cout << int a=3;
```

2.8.3. Run the following program. Report and discuss the output.

```
#include <iostream>
using namespace std;

int main()
{
bool honest = true;
cout << honest << "\n";
cout << !honest << "\n";
return 0;
}
```

2.8.4. What is the output of the following program?

```
#include <iostream>
using namespace std;

int main()
{
string first_name;
string last_name;
first_name = "Mother";
last_name = "Theresa";
string name = first_name + " " + last_name;
cout << name << endl;
}
```

Programming in C++ 3

Having illustrated the general structure of a C++ program, we now turn to discussing the basic operators, commands, and logical constructs. Most of these are either identical or similar to those encountered in other languages. However, C++ supports some unconventional and occasionally bizarre operations that require familiarization.

In Appendix C, a correspondence is made between MATLAB, FORTRAN 77, and C++ in the form of a dictionary that explains how to translate corresponding code.

3.1 Operators

Operators apply to one variable or a group of variables to carry out arithmetic and logical tasks.

Assignation

The equal sign (=) is the assignation or right-to-left copy operator. Thus, the statement

```
a = b;
```

means "replace the value of a with the value of b", and the statement

```
a = a+5;
```

means "replace the value of a with itself augmented by 5".

The assignation operator is distinguished by lack of reciprocity: the statement a=b is different from the statement b=a.

Arithmetic operators

The basic implementation of C++ supports the following arithmetic operators:

- Addition (+): We may write

  ```
  c=a+b;
  ```

- Subtraction (-): We may write

  ```
  c=a-b;
  ```

- Multiplication (*): We may write

  ```
  c=a*b;
  ```

- Division (/): We may write

  ```
  c=a/b;
  ```

- Modulo (%): We may write

  ```
  c=a%b;
  ```

This operator extracts the remainder of the division a/b. For example

$$5\%3 = 2$$

Unconventional operators

In C++, we can write:

```
a = b = c = 0.1;
```

with the expected result. A perfectly acceptable C++ statement is:

```
a = 1 + (b = 3);
```

meaning:

```
b=3;
a = 1 + b;
```

Compound assignation

Other unconventional statements mediated by compound assignation operators are listed in Table 3.1.1.

Operation	Meaning
a +=b;	a=a+b;
a -=b;	a=a-b;
a *=b;	a=a*b;
a /=b;	a=a/b;
a *= b+c;	a=a*(b+c);
a++;	a=a+1;
++a;	a=a+1;
a--;	a=a-1;
--a;	a=a-1;

Table 3.1.1 Unconventional statements mediated by compound assignation operators in C++. The language name C++ translates into C+1, which subtly indicates that C++ is one level above C. Alternatively, we could have given to C++ the name C and rename C as C--.

To illustrate the difference between the a++ and ++a operators, we issue the commands:

```
a = 5;
b = a++;
```

After execution, a=6 and b=5.

Alternatively, we issue the commands:

```
a = 5;
b = ++a;
```

After execution, a=6 and b=6.

Relational and logical operands

Relational and logical operands are shown in Table 3.1.2. For example, to find the maximum of numbers a and b, we write:

```
max = (a>b) ? a :  b;
```

If $a > b$ is true, the variable max will set equal to a; if $a > b$ is false, the variable max will set equal to b.

Equal to	a == b
Not equal to	a != b
Less than	a<b
Less than or equal to	a<=b
Greater than	a>b
Greater than or equal to	a>=b
And	A && B
Or	A || B
Boolean opposite or true or false	!A
Conditional operator	A ? a : b;

Table 3.1.2 Relational and logical operands in C++; a, b are variables, and A, B are expressions. The conditional operator shown in the last entry returns the value of the variable a if the statement A is true, and the value of the variable b if the statement A is false.

Threading

The statement:

```
c = (a=1, b=2, a+b);
```

is a compact representation of the statements:

```
a=1;
b=2;
c=a+b;
```

In these constructions, the variable c is evaluated from the rightmost expression inside the parentheses.

Byte size operator

To find how many memory bytes are allocated to the variable a, we use the `sizeof` operator:

```
b = sizeof(a);
```

where b has been declared as an integer.

The practical usage of the C++ operators discussed in this section will be demonstrated in following chapters by numerous applications.

Problems

3.1.1. Are the following three statements equivalent?

```
c++;
c+=1;
c=c+1;
```

3.1.2. Implement the conditional operator to compute the absolute value of a
real number.

3.2 Vector and matrix initialization

To declare and initialize a vector v whose three elements are real numbers
registered in double precision, we write

```
double v[3] = {1.0, 2.0, 4.5};
```

or

```
double v[] = {1.0, 2.0, 4.5};
```

which sets: $v[0] = 1.0$, $v[1] = 2.0$, $v[2] = 4.5$.

If we declare and initialize:

```
double v[5] = {1.0, 2.0};
```

then: $v[0] = 1.0$, $v[1] = 2.0$, $v[2] = 0.0$, $v[3] = 0.0$, $v[4] = 0.0$. Thus, the
uninitialized values of a partially initialized vector are set to zero.

If we only declare and not initialize by stating:

```
double v[5];
```

then the vector components are undefined.

Declaration and initialization must be done in a single line. We may not
first declare and then initialize a vector.

Similarly, we can write

```
char u[3]= {78, 34, 78};
```

```
char e[10]= {'a', 'b', 'c'};
```

$$\text{char q[]= 'zei';}$$

$$\text{string n[3]= \{"who", "am", "I?"\};}$$

$$\text{string b[]= \{"who", "are", "they?"\};}$$

The size of q is four, as a final 0 is appended to indicate the end of a character array.

To declare and initialize a 2×2 matrix A whose elements are real numbers registered in double precision, we write

$$\text{double A[2][2] = \{ \{1.0, 2.0\}, \{4.5,-3.5\} \};}$$

or

$$\text{double A[][] = \{ \{1.0, 2.0\}, \{4.5,-3.5\} \};}$$

which sets: $A[0][0] = 1.0$, $A[0][1] = 2.0$, $A[1][0] = 4.5$, $A[1][1] = -3.5$.

Thus, the matrix elements are initialized row-by-row.

Similarly, we can write

```
char D[2][3]= { {60, 61, 65}, {62, 63, 66} };
string C[2][3]= { {"who", "am", "I?"}, {"who", "is", "she?"} };
string C[][]= { {"who", "am", "I?"}, {"who", "is", "she?"} };
```

Problems

3.2.1. A vector is declared and initialized as:

$$\text{double v[128] = \{4.0\};}$$

What are the components of this vector?

3.2.2. A character vector is declared and initialized as:

$$\text{char v[128] = \{67\};}$$

What are the components of this vector?

3.3   Control structures

Control structures are blocks of statements that implement short algorithms
and make logical decisions based on available options. An algorithm is a set of
instructions that achieves a goal through sequential or repetitive steps.

C++ employs control structures with single or multiple statements. The
former are simply stated, while the latter are enclosed by curly bracket delimiters, {}.

- if statement:

    The if statement implements conditional execution of one command or
    a block of commands.

    For example, we may write

    ```
    if(a==10)
      b=10;
    ```

    or

    ```
    if(a==10)
      {
      b=10;
      }
    ```

    If more than one statements is involved, the use of curly brackets is manda-
    tory:

    ```
    if(a!=10)
      {
      b=a+3;
      c=20;
      }
    ```

    We highly recommend using the curly brackets even in the case of one
    statement.

- if/else structure:

    The if/else structure implements conditional execution based on two
    options.

    For example, we may write:

    ```
    if(a!=10)
      {
    ```

```
        b=a+3;
        c=20;
        }
    else
        {
        cout << "angouraki" << endl;
        }
```

The statement

```
        cout << "angouraki" << endl;
```

prints the word "angouraki" on the screen and moves the cursor to the next line.

- if/else if structure:

  The `if/else if` structure implements conditional execution based on several options.

  For example, we may write:

```
        if(a==1)
            {
            b=a+3;
            c=20;
            }
        else if (a==2.3)
            {
            cout << "angouraki" << endl;
            }
        else
            {
            cout << "maintanos" << endl;
            }
```

  We can use multiple `else if` blocks and skip the last `else` block. If two options coincide, the first-encountered option will be executed before exiting the structure.

  Note that `else` and `if` are two separate words separated by white space. In MATLAB, these two words are merged into the ungrammatical `elseif`.

- switch structure:

  Consider an integer or character variable, *diosmos*. If *diosmos* $= n1$

we want to execute a block of commands, if $diosmos = n2$ we want to execute another block of commands, if $diosmos = n3$ we want to execute a third block of commands; otherwise, we want to execute a default block of commands.

These conditional choices are best implemented with the switch structure:

```
switch(diosmos)
case n1:
  {
  ...
  }
  break;
case n2:
  {
  ...
  }
  break;
...
default:
  {
  ...
  }
```

The default block at the end is not mandatory. Note that this block does not contain a break; .

- for loop:

  To compute the sum: $s = \sum_{i=1}^{N} i$, we use the for loop:

```
double s=0;
int i;

for (i=1; i<=N; i+1)
  {
  s = s + i;
  }
```

  The plan is to first initialize the sum to zero, and then add successive values of i. The i+1 expression in the argument of the for statement can be written as i++.

- Break from a for loop:

  To escape a for loop, we use the command break.

For example, to truncate the above sum at $i = 10$, we use:

```
double s=0;

for (int i=1; i<=N; i++)
  {
  if(i==10) break;
  s = s + i;
  }
```

- Skip a cycle in a for loop:

    To skip a value of the running index in a `for` loop, we use the command `continue`.

    For example, to skip the value $i = 8$ and continue with $i = 9$ and 10, we use:

```
double s=0;

for (int i=1; i<=10; i++)
  {
  if(i==8) continue;
  s = s + i;
  }
```

    `for` loops can be nested multiple times. For example, we may write:

```
double a[10][10];

for (int i=0; i<=9; i++)
  {
  for (int j=0; j<=9; j++)
    {
    a[i][j]=i*j;
    }
  }
```

    If we break out from the inner loop, we will find ourselves in the outer loop.

- goto:

    We use this statement to jump to a desired position in the code marked by a label designated by a colon (:).

For example, consider the block of commands:

```
goto mark;
a=5;
mark:
```

The statement a=5 will be skipped.

FORTRAN 77 users are fondly familiar with the Go to statement. MAT-LAB users are unfairly deprived of this statement.

Some programmers consider the goto statement an anathema and a recipe for "spaghetti code." In the opinion of this author, this is only an exaggeration.

- while loop:

  We use the while loop to execute a block of commands only when a distinguishing condition is true.

  For example, the following while loop prints the integers: 1, 2, ..., 9, 10:

```
int i=0;

while(i<10)
{
i=i+1;
cout << i << " ";
}
```

Note that the veracity of the distinguishing condition i<10 is checked *before* executing the loop enclosed by the curly brackets.

The compiler interprets the expression i<10 as a Boolean variable that is true, and thus equal to 1, or false, and thus equal to 0. Accordingly, the loop

```
int i=1;

while(i)
{
i=i-1;
}
```

will be executed only once.

- do-while:

  This is identical to the `while` loop, except that the veracity of the distinguishing condition is examined *after* the first execution of the statements enclosed by the curly brackets. Thus, at least one execution is granted even if the distinguishing condition is never true.

  For example, the do-while loop

  ```
  int i=0;

  do
      {
      i=i+1;
      cout << i << " ";
      }
  while(i<10);
  ```

  prints the integers: 1, 2, 3, ..., 9, 10.

  The `do-while` loop is favored when a variable in the distinguishing condition is evaluated inside the loop itself, as in our example.

- exit:

  To stop the execution at any point, we issue the command:

  ```
  exit(1);
  ```

  The use of these control structures will be exemplified throughout this book.

Problems

3.3.1. Assess whether the following two structures are equivalent:

```
if(i==5) cout << "i=5"; j=i;
```

```
if(i==5) { cout << "i=5"; j=i; }
```

3.3.2. Discuss the function of the following loop:

```
double sum=1.0;
int i=1;
double eps=10.0;

while(eps>0.00001)
{
i=i+1;
eps=1.0/(i*i);
sum=sum+eps;
}
```

What is the value of sum after execution?

3.4 Receiving from the keyboard and displaying on the monitor

The iostream library allows us to enter data from the keyboard and display data on the monitor. In computer science, the keyboard is the standard input and the monitor is the standard output.

It is illuminating to view the keyboard and monitor as abstract objects that can be replaced by files, printers, and other hardware or software devices. The mapping of physical to abstract objects is done by software interfaces called device drivers.

Receiving from the keyboard

To read a numerical variable from the keyboard, we issue the statement:

```
cin >> variable;
```

On execution, the computer will wait for input followed by the ENTER key.

To read two numerical variables, we use either the separate statements:

```
cin >> variable1;
cin >> variable2;
```

or the composite statement:

```
cin >> variable1 >> variable2;
```

On execution, the computer will wait for two inputs separated by a space, comma, or the ENTER keystroke.

Leading white space generated by the space bar, the tab key, and the carriage return is ignored by the `cin` function.

Now consider the following block of commands:

```
double pi;
int a;
cin >> pi;
cin >> a;
```

Suppose that, on execution, we enter the number π in segments separated by white space:

```
3.14159 265358
```

Since the two `cin` statements are equivalent to:

```
cin >> pi >> a;
```

the program will take

```
pi=3.14159        a=265358.
```

Thus, the computer will not pause for the second `cin`, giving the false impression of a coding error.

In professional codes, we circumvent this difficulty by reading all input date as strings, and then making appropriate data type conversions.

Receiving a string

To read a string variable from the keyboard, we use:

```
cin >> astring;
```

The string variable `astring` in this statement is not allowed to have any blank spaces; that is, it cannot be a sentence composed of words. To circumvent this difficulty, we use instead:

```
getline(cin, astring);
```

On execution, the computer will wait for a string to be typed in the keyboard, followed by the ENTER keystroke.

False read

Consider the following *while* loop calculating the square of a typed integer:

```
int a;

while (cin >> a)
{
int a2 = a*a;
}
```

The `while` loop will be executed repeatedly as long as an integer is supplied from the keyboard, and will be exited if a character or a non-integer (real) number is entered, amounting to a *false read*. The reason is that the `cin` function returns to the program a Boolean variable that is true (1) in the case of successful input, and false (0) in the case of unsuccessful input.

The single false read can be generalized to multiple false reads. For example, the following code reads two variables and quits when inappropriate input is entered:

```
int a;
float b;

while(cin>>a && cin>>b)
{
cout << a << " " << b << endl;
}
```

Later in this section, we shall discuss ways of clearing the false read.

Displaying on the monitor

To display the value of a numerical variable on the monitor, we issue the command:

```
cout << variable;
```

To display the value of a numerical variable and move the cursor to the next line, we use:

```
cout << variable << "\n";
```

To print a message on the screen and move the cursor to the next line, we use:

```
cout << "hello\n";
```

```
\'   Print a single quote (')
\"   Print a double quote (")
\?   Print a question mark (?)
\\   Print a backslash (\)
\a   Sound a beep
\t   Press the tab key
\v   Issue a vertical tab
\r   Issue a carriage return
\b   Issue a backspace signal
\f   Issue a page feed
\n   Issue a line break
\\   Continue a string to the next line
```

Table 3.4.1 Printing codes preceded by the backslash.

To display the values of two numerical variables separated by space and move the cursor to the next line, we use:

```
cout << variable << " " << variable1 << " total" << endl;
```

Material enclosed by double quotes is interpreted verbatim as text. The text directive "\n", and its equivalent end-of-line directive "endl", both instruct the cursor to move to the next line.

Other printing codes preceded by the backslash are shown in Table 3.4.1. For example, we can sound a beep by printing: \a.

Printing characters

As an application, we consider a program contained in the file *characters.cc* demonstrating the ASCII code:

```cpp
#include <iostream>
using namespace std;

int main()
{
int i;
char a;

for (i=60; i<=101; i++)
   {
   a=i;
   cout << a;
   }
```

```
cout << endl;
return 0;
}
```

The output of the code is:

<=>?ABCDEFGHIJKLMNOPQRSTUVWXYZ[\]^_'abcde

Note that, although the character variable *a* is evaluated as an integer, it is printed as a character through the output.

Exactly the same output would have been obtained if the for loop were replaced either by:

```
for (i=60; i<=101; i++)
{
cout << (char) i;
}
```

or by:

```
for (i=60; i<=101; i++)
{
cout << char(i);
}
```

The statements (char) i and char(i) invoke integer-to-character conversion functions that perform an operation known as *typecasting*.

To further illustrate that characters are stored as ASCII encoded integers, we consider the instructions:

```
char d = 66;
char e = 'B';
cout << d << e << endl;
```

The screen display is:

BB

Peculiarities of the input buffer

The following code asks for the user's name and age, and then prints the information on the screen:

```
#include <iostream>
using namespace std;

int main()
{
string name;
int age;

cout << "Please enter your name:" << endl;
getline(cin, name);

cout << "Please enter your age:" << endl;
cin >> age;

cout << name << endl;
cout << age << endl;

return 0;
}
```

The code will run without any surprises, as long as the input is reasonable. However, if the order of the input is switched to:

```
cout << "Please enter your age:" << endl;
cin >> age;

cout << "Please enter your name:" << endl;
getline(cin, name);
```

the program will not work properly. In this case, the second `cin` will apparently be skipped, and the user's name will be printed as null. The reason is that the `getline(cin, name)` function accepts the ENTER keystroke character following the age input as legitimate input.

To remedy this problem, we erase this character by inserting immediately after the first `cin` statement the command:

```
cin.ignore()
```

which deletes one character. To delete twenty-six characters, we state:

```
cin.ignore(26)
```

To delete seven characters or discard all characters up to and including a new-line character, whichever comes first, we state:

```
cin.ignore(7, '\n')
```

Ensuring a successful read

If a program expects us to enter a real number and we enter instead a character string, the execution will fail. To ensure a proper read, we use the limits library and engage the program in a do-while loop, as illustrated in the following code:

```
#include <iostream>
#include <limits>
using namespace std;

int main()
{
float a;
int flag;   // for successful read

cout << "Please enter a float number:"<< endl;

do{
  flag=0;
  cin >> a;
  if(!cin)   // execute in case of a false read
    {
    cout << "Inappropriate input; please try again"<< endl;
    flag=1;
    cin.clear();   // reset the false-read flag
    cin.ignore(numeric_limits<streamsize>::max(),'\n');
    }
} while(flag);

cout << a << endl;

return 0;
}
```

The statement:

```
cin.ignore(numeric_limits<streamsize>::max(),'\n');
```

removes from the input stream the bad input.

Greatest common divisor

As an application, we discuss a code that computes the greatest common divisor (GCD) of two integers, defined as the greatest integer that divides both. The GCD is involved in the calculation of the structure of carbon nanotubes parametrized by a pair of integers determining the chirality.

Euclid's algorithm produces the GCD by repeatedly subtracting the smaller from the larger integer, and then abandoning the larger integer in favor of the difference. If at any stage the two integers are the same, the GCD has been identified.

The method is implemented in the following code contained in the file *euclid.cc*:

```cpp
#include <iostream>
using namespace std;

int main()
{
int n=100, m=100, k, save;

cout<<"\n Will compute the Greatest Common Divisor";
cout<<"\n\t of two positive integers\n";
again:
cout<<"\n Please enter the first integer";
cout<<"\n\t 0 quit"<< endl;
cin>>n;

if(n==0) goto quit;

cout<<" Please enter the second integer";
cout<<"\n\t 0 quit\n";
cin>>m;

if(m==0) goto quit;

if(n==m)
  {
  k=n;
  cout<<"\nThe Greatest Common Divisor is:  "<<k<<endl;
  }
else while (n!=m)
  {
  if(n>m) // switch n and m to ensure n<m
    {
    save=m;
    m=n;
    n=save;
    }
  k=m-n; // replace (n,m) with (k,n)
  m=n;
  n=k;
  if(n==m) // done
      {
      k=n;
```

```
                    cout<<"\nThe Greatest Common Divisor is:  "<<k<<endl
                    }
            }

        goto again;
        quit:

        cout<<"\n Thank you for your business\n";
        return 0;
        }
```

The text directive "\t" in the second cout command and elsewhere emulates the TAB key. A typical session follows:

```
Will compute the Greatest Common Divisor
        of two positive integers

Please enter the first integer
        0 quit
34 12

Please enter the second integer
        0 quit

The Greatest Common Divisor is: 2

Please enter the first integer
        0 quit
0

   Thank you for your business
```

Problems

3.4.1. Write a program that receives from the keyboard a vector with three elements consisting of characters, and prints them on the screen.

3.4.2. Write a program that receives your first and last name as a single string from the keyboard, and prints it on the screen.

3.4.3. Write a code that receives from the keyboard an integer and assesses whether it is even or odd based on the modulo operator.

3.4.4. Write a statement that sounds a beep by (*a*) printing an ASCII character, and (*b*) printing a code.

3.4.5. What is the output of the following code?

```
#include <iostream>
using namespace std;

int main()
{
int diosmos=1;

for (diosmos==1;diosmos<=4;diosmos++)
{
  switch(diosmos)
  {
  case 1:{cout << "Two "; }
  break;
  case 2:{cout << "gallons ";}
  break;
  case 3:{cout << "of milk" << endl };
  }
  break;
  default:{cout << "please!!!" << endl;}
  }
}
return 0;
}
```

3.4.6. Compute the greatest common divisor of 1986 and 343.

3.5   Mathematical library

Table 3.5.1 lists functions of the C++ mathematical library. To use these functions, the associated header file must be included at the beginning of the program by stating:

```
#include <cmath>
```

For example, to compute the exponential of a number a, we write:

```
#include <cmath>

float a = 2.3;
float b = exp(a);
```

Equally well, we can write

```
double b = exp(2.3);
```

$m = \text{abs}(n)$	Absolute value of an integer, n
$y = \text{acos}(x)$	Arc cosine, $0 \le y \le \pi$
$y = \text{asin}(x)$	Arc sine, $-\pi/2 \le y \le \pi/2$
$y = \text{atan}(x)$	Arc tangent, $-\pi/2 \le y \le \pi/2$
$y = \text{atan2}(x, z)$	Arc tangent, $y = \text{atan}(y/z)$
$y = \text{ceil}(x)$	Ceiling of x (smallest integer larger than or equal to x)
$y = \cos(x)$	Cosine
$y = \cosh(x)$	Hyperbolic cosine
$y = \exp(x)$	Exponential
$y = \text{fabs}(x)$	Absolute value of a real number, x
$y = \text{floor}(x)$	Floor of x (smallest integer smaller than or equal to x)
$y = \log(x)$	Natural log
$y = \log10(x)$	Base-ten log
$y = \text{pow}(x, a)$	$z = x^a$, where x and a are real
$y = \sin(x)$	Sine
$y = \sinh(x)$	Hyperbolic sine
$y = sqrt(x)$	Square root
$y = \tan(x)$	Tangent
$y = \tanh(x)$	Hyperbolic tangent

Table 3.5.1 Common C++ mathematical functions. The statement #include <cmath> must be included at the preamble of the program.

The argument and return of the mathematical functions are registered in double precision (double). If an argument is in single precision (float), it is automatically converted to double precision, but only for the purpose of function evaluation.

A calculator

An ingenious code due to Fred Swartz implements a simple calculator (see http://www.fredosaurus.com/notes-cpp):

```
// Fred Swartz 10 Aug 2003
// Not robust:  does not check for division by 0

#include <iostream>
#include <iomanip>
using namespace std;

int main()
{
double left, right; // Operands
```

```
double result; // Resulting value
char oper; // Operator

cout << "Please enter:  a (+-*/) b, and hit return" << endl;

while (cin >> left >> oper >> right)
  {
      switch (oper)
      {
      case '+':  result = left + right; break;
      case '-':  result = left - right; break;
      case '*':  result = left * right; break;
      case '/':  result = left / right; break;
      default :  cout << "Bad operator '" << oper << "'" << endl;
      continue; // Start next loop iteration.
      }
      cout << "="<< result << endl << "another (q to quit):   "
                                  << endl;
  }
  return 0;
}
```

The program performs addition, subtraction, multiplication, and division in a text mode.

Problems

3.5.1. Discuss whether the statement

$$y = pow(x, pow(a, b));$$

is equivalent to the statement

$$y = pow(x, a*b);$$

3.5.2. Investigate by numerical experimentation the action of the ceil and floor functions.

3.5.3. Add to the calculator the exponential and the logarithm buttons.

3.6   Read from a file and write to a file

We have learned how to read data from the keyboard and write data to the screen. To read data from a file and write data to a file, we use the intrinsic library fstream.

Read from a file

To read from a file named *stresses.dat*, we simply associate the file with a *device* that replaces `cin` of the `iostream`:

```
#include<fstream>
ifstream dev1;
dev1.open("stresses.dat");
dev1 >> variable1 >> variable2;
dev1.close();
```

The first line declares the device *dev1* as a member of the "input file stream." The second line opens the file through the device, the third line writes to the device, and the fourth line closes the device.

Note that *device* and *filename* are two distinct concepts. A brilliant notion of C++ (and Unix) is that we can change the device but keep the filename.

In compact notation, the lines

```
ifstream dev1;
dev1.open("stresses.dat");
```

can be consolidated into one,

```
ifstream dev1("stresses.dat");
```

which bypasses the explicit use of the `open` statement.

Suppose that we want to read the components of a vector from a file, but the length of the vector is unknown so that we cannot use a `for` loop. Our best option is to use a `while` loop based on a false read.

The implementation of the algorithm is:

```
#include <iostream>
#include <fstream>
using namespace std;

int main()
{
ifstream file9("vector.dat");
int i=1;
double a[10];

while(file9 >> a[i])
{
```

```
        cout << i << " " << a[i] << endl;
        i++;
        }

        file9.close();
        return 0;
        }
```

If the file *vector.dat* reads:

```
                3.4 9.8
                3.0 9.1
                0.45
```

the output of the code will be:

```
                1 3.4
                2 9.8
                3 3
                4 9.1
                5 0.45
```

A false read arises when either the program has reached the end of a file (EOF), or the program attempts to read a certain data type and sees another.

Write to a file

To write to a file named *post_process.dat*, we simply associate the file with a device that replaces cout of the iostream:

```
    #include<fstream>

    ofstream dev2;
    dev2.open("post_process.dat");
    dev2 << variable1 << variable2;
    dev2 << variable << " " << variable1 << " total" << endl;
    dev2.close();
```

The second line declares the device *dev2* as a member of the "output file stream." The third line opens the device, the fourth line writes to the device, and the fifth line closes the device.

The second and third statements can be consolidated into one,

```
        ofstream dev2("post_process.dat");
```

which bypasses the explicit use of the open statement.

Parameter	Meaning
in	Input mode (default for a file of the ifstream class)
out	Output mode (default for a file of the ofstream class)
binary	Binary mode
app	If the file exists, data is written at the end (appended)
ate	For a new file, data is written at the end
	For an existing file, data is written at the current position
	(same as app but we can write anywhere)
trunc	If the file exists, delete the old content (same as out)
noreplace	If the file exists, do not open
nocreate	If the file does not exist, do not open

Table 3.6.1 Open-file parameters for reading data from a file and writing data to a file.

Qualified open

The general syntax of the open statement is:

```
dev.open("filename", ios::xxx | ios::yyy | ... | ios:zzz);
```

where xxx, yyy, ..., zzz are parameter strings defined in Table 3.6.1.

For example, to open a file named *results.dat* for read and write, we state:

```
#include<fstream>

fstream file8;
file8.open("results.dat",ios::in|ios::out);
```

To check whether a file has been successfully opened, we evaluate the Boolean variable:

```
dev.is_open()
```

which is true or false. For example, we can state:

```
if (dev.is_open())
{
dev << variable1 << variable2;
}
```

If the file is not open, the write instructions are bypassed.

Problems

3.6.1. Write a program that reads from a file a vector with three elements consisting of characters, and prints them in another file.

3.6.2. Write the a code that reads from a file your name and prints it in another file.

3.6.3. Write a program that opens an existing file and appends the number 0.

3.6.4. Write a program that opens an existing file and inserts the number 0 at the beginning.

3.7 Formatted input and output

The input/output manipulation library `iomanip` allows us to print data in an orderly fashion. As an example, consider the program:

```
#include <iostream>
#include <iomanip>
using namespace std;

int main()
{
double pi;
pi=3.14159265358;
cout << setprecision(5) << setw(10);
cout << pi << endl;
return 0;
}
```

Running the program prints on the screen:

```
3.1416
```

In this case, the set-width manipulator `setw(10)` reserves ten spaces, and the set-precision manipulator `setprecision(5)` allocates five of these spaces to the decimal part, including the decimal point.

The code:

```
for (int i=1;i<3;i++)
{
  for (int j=1;j<5;j++)
  {
  cout <<"+"<< setfill('-')<<setw(4);
  }
  cout<< "+" << endl;
}
```

prints on the screen the pattern:

```
+---+---+---+---+
+---+---+---+---+
+---+---+---+---+
```

The code:

```
cout << setfill('-') << setw(20) << "-" <<endl;
cout << setfill('.')  << setw(20) << " " << endl;
cout << setfill('=') << setw(15) << "Thank you"
                     << setw(5) << ""<< endl;
cout << setfill('.')  << setw(20) <<""<<endl;
cout << setfill('-') << setw(20) <<""<<endl;
```

prints on the screen the pattern:

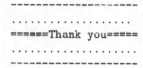

Table 3.7.1 presents I/O manipulators with brief descriptions. Some of these manipulators apply to only one read or write, whereas others apply permanently until reset.

Formatting can also be implemented by the manipulators

```
setiosflags(ios::property1 | ios::property2 | ...);
```

and

```
resetiosflags(ios::property1 | ios::property2 | ...);
```

For example, the property attribute **property1** can be **fixed** or **scientific** (referring to notation), **showpoint**, or other. Thus, the commands:

```
pi=3.14159265358;
cout << setprecision(5) << setw(10);
cout << setiosflags(ios::scientific);
cout << pi << endl;
```

produce the output:

```
3.14159e+00
```

Manipulator	Manipulator	Comment
setw(n)	width(n)	Set the minimum field width
setprecision(n)		Set the number of digits printed
		to the right of the decimal point
showpoint	noshowpoint	Decimal point
uppercase	nouppercase	
dec	oct	Decimal or octal form
hex	setbase(8—10—16)	Hexadecimal
left	right	Margin justification
		used after setw(n)
showbase	noshowbase	
setfill(ch)		Fill empty fields with a character
boolalph	anoboolalpha	Boolean format
fixed	scientific	Notation
ends		
showpos	noshowpos	
skipws	noskipws	Skip white space in reading
ws		Ignore white space
		at the current position
internal	flush	
unitbuf	nounitbuf	
setiosflags(f)	resetiosflags(f)	

Table 3.7.1 Input/Output manipulators for formatted reading and printing.

Tabulation

The following code contained in the file *tabulate.cc* prints a table of exponentials:

```
#include <iostream>
#include <iomanip>
#include <cmath>
using namespace std;

int main()
{
  int i;
  double step=0.1;
  cout << setiosflags(ios::fixed | ios::showpoint);

  for (i=1;i<=6;i++)
  {
  double x=(i-1.0)*step;
```

```
        double y=exp(x);
        cout << setprecision(2) << setw(5) << x << " ";
        cout << setprecision(5) << setw(7) << y << endl;
        }

    return 0;
    }
```

The output of the code is:

```
        0.00 1.00000
        0.10 1.10517
        0.20 1.22140
        0.30 1.34986
        0.40 1.49182
        0.50 1.64872
```

What would the output be if the `setiosflags()` manipulator were not included?

Random numbers

As a second application, we discuss a code contained in the file *random.cc* that computes and prints on the screen random numbers with uniform probability distribution in the range [0, 1], also called uniform deviates, using the C++ compiler random-number generator:

```
#include <iostream>
#include <iomanip>
using namespace std;

int main()
{
int N=6, random_integer;

float random_real, random_number, max=RAND_MAX;

cout<< setiosflags(ios::fixed | ios::showpoint);

for(int i=1;i<=N;i++)
{
random_integer = rand();
random_real = random_integer;
random_number = random_real/max;
cout << setw(3) << i << " " << setw(6) << setprecision(5)
            << random_number << endl;
```

```
    }

    return 0;
    }
```

The internal C++ function **rand** generates random integers ranging from 0 up to the maximum value of RAND_MAX. Converting these integers to real numbers and normalizing by the maximum generates the requisite list. The output of the code is:

```
1 0.84019
2 0.39438
3 0.78310
4 0.79844
5 0.91165
6 0.98981
```

Student grades

In the third application, we discuss a code contained in the file *grades.cc* that reads student names and grades from file *grades.dat*, and prints them nicely formatted on the screen:

```
#include <iomanip>
#include <fstream>
using namespace std;

int main()
{
ifstream file2("grades.dat");

string lastname[201], firstname[201]; // 200 students max
float grade[201][11]; // 10 grades max

int i=1; // assume one student

/*------loop over students---------------*/

while(file2 >> lastname[i]) // read the last name
{
cout << setw(3) << right << i << " " ;

file2 >> firstname[i]; // read the first name

cout << setw(15) << left << lastname[i]+" "+firstname[i] << " ";

int j=1;
```

```
/*------loop over student grades---------------*/

    while(file2 >> grade[i][j]) // read the grades
    {
    cout << setw(3) << right << grade[i][j] << " ";
    j++;
    }

cout << endl;
file2.clear(); // allow for more reads
i++;

} // end of loop over students

file2.close();

return 0;
}
```

An interesting feature of the code is the presence of two nested while loops of reads. When a false name-read is encountered, the outer loop is exited. When a false grade-read is encountered, the inner loop is exited, and the cin flag is cleared by issuing the command:

```
file2.clear();
```

to allow for additional name readings.

If the file *grades.dat* contains the data:

```
Johnson Bob 8 10
Kerr Jean 9 10 9
Wang J-Y 8 10 9
```

then the output on the screen is:

```
1 Johnson Bob     8  10
2 Kerr Jean       9  10   9
3 Wang J-Y        8  10   9
```

Problems

3.7.1. Print the value of RAND_MAX set by your compiler.

3.7.2. Pascal's triangle appears as

$$
\begin{matrix}
 & & & & 1 & & & & \\
 & & & 1 & & 1 & & & \\
 & & 1 & & 2 & & 1 & & \\
 & 1 & & 3 & & 3 & & 1 & \\
1 & & 4 & & 6 & & 4 & & 1 \\
\end{matrix}
$$

1   5   10   10   5   1
...   .

Each entry is the sum of the two entries immediately above it, and the outermost entries are equal to unity. The entries of the pth row provide us with the coefficients of the binomial expansion $(a+b)^{p-1}$, where a and b are two variables and p is an integer.

For example, when $p = 3$, the third row provides us with the coefficients of the quadratic expansion,

$$(a + b)^2 = \mathbf{1}\,a^2 + \mathbf{2}\,ab + \mathbf{1}\,b^2.$$

When $p = 4$,
$$(a + b)^3 = \mathbf{1}\,a^3 + \mathbf{3}\,a^2 b + \mathbf{3}\,ab^2 + \mathbf{1}\,b^3.$$

Write a program that computes and prints the Pascal triangle.

3.7.3. Modify the student code so that the number of grades recorded is printed next to the students' names before the grades.

3.7.4. Write a code that reads from a file the names of pets in a pet store, and prints, nicely formatted, their species, age, and usual mood.

3.8   Sample algorithms

We have learned how to enter data from the keyboard, print data to the screen, read data from a file, and write data to a file. In scientific and other applications, the data are manipulated according to carefully designed algorithms to achieve a specific goal.

We have defined an algorithm as a set of instructions that achieves a goal through sequential or repetitive steps. Certain algorithms provide us with systematic ways of eliminating events and narrowing down possibilities. Other algorithms provide us with craftily devised methods of producing a sequence of approximations to a desired solution.

Maximum and minimum of an array

The algorithm implemented in the following code identifies the maximum number in an array, $a[i]$, where $i = 1, 2, \ldots N$. We begin by assuming that the maximum is the first entry, $a[1]$, and update the maximum by successive comparisons:

```
int max_pos = 1;

for(int i=2; i<=N; i++)
{
    if( a[i] > a[max_pos] )
    {
    max_pos = i;
    }
}
```

A slight variation yields the minimum:

```
int min_pos = 1;

for(int i=2; i<=N; i++)
{
    if( a[i] < a[min_pos] )
    {
    min_pos = i;
    }
}
```

Ranking an element of an array

Next, we consider an algorithm that ranks a specified element in a numerical array $a[l]$, where $l = 1, 2, \ldots N$. If the specified element is the largest number in the array, its rank is 1; if the specified element is the smallest number in the array, its rank is N.

The ranking algorithm is based on the observation that, if $a[i]$ is the element to be ranked, then its rank is equal to one plus the number of times that a[i]<a[j] for $j = 1, 2, \ldots, N$ and $j \neq i$. The last exception is included to safeguard against round-off error. The implementation of the algorithm is:

```
rank = 1;

for(int j=1; j<=N; j++)
{
if(a[i]<a[j] && i!=j) rank++;
}
```

Indexing an array

Now we want to index the elements of the array a[l], for $l = 1, \ldots, N$, so that the index of the largest number is equal to 1, and the index of the smallest number is equal to N. The following code contained in the file *index.cc* uses the ranking algorithm to index the array:

```
#include <iostream>
#include <iomanip>
using namespace std;

int main()
{
float a[6]={0.0, 8.0, 9.7, -1.4, -8.0, 13.8};
int i,j;
int m[6];   // indexing array
const int N=5;

for(i=1; i<=N; i++)
{
  m[i]=1;
  for(j=1; j<=N; j++)
  {
  if(a[i]<a[j] && i!=j) m[i]++;
  }
}

//--- print the list

cout << fixed << showpoint;
for(i=1; i<=N; i++)
cout << setw(8) << setprecision(2) << a[i] << " " << m[i] << endl;

}
```

The output of the code is:

```
    8.00 3
    9.70 2
   -1.40 4
   -8.00 5
   13.80 1
```

Bubble sort

It is often necessary to sort an array of numbers contained in a vector x[i]. The sorting can be done in ascending order where the largest number is placed at the bottom, or in descending order where the smallest number is placed at the bottom.

In the *bubble-sort* algorithm, we first find the highest number, and put
it at the bottom of the list. This is done by comparing the first number with
the second number and swapping positions if necessary, then comparing the
second with the third number and swapping positions if necessary, and repeating
the comparisons all the way to the bottom. In the second step, we find the
second-largest number and put it in the penultimate position using a similar
method. In this fashion, light numbers "bubble up" to the top. The algorithm
is implemented in the following code contained in the file *bsort.cc*:

```
#include<iostream>
#include<iomanip>
using namespace std;

int main()
{
const int n=5;
float save, x[n+1]={0.0, -0.5, -0.9, 0.3, 1.9, -0.3 };
int Istop, i, k;

//--- bubble sort:

k = n-1; // number of comparisons

do {
   Istop = 1; // will stop if Iflag 1
   for (i=1;i<=k;i++) // compare
   {
   if(x[i]>x[i+1])
     {save = x[i]; // swap
     x[i]=x[i+1];
     x[i+1] = save;
     Istop = 0; // an exchange occurred; do not stop
     }
   }
   k--; // reduce the number of comparisons
}
while(Istop==0);

//--- print the sorted array:

for (i=1;i<=n;i++)
{
cout << setw(5) << right << x[i] << endl;
};

return 0;
}
```

The output of the code is:

```
-0.9
-0.5
-0.3
 0.3
 1.9
```

Selection sort

In the *selection-sort* algorithm, we perform only one swap per pass. In the first pass, we identify the minimum of all elements and put it at the top. In the second pass, we identify the minimum of all elements except for the first, and put it in the second position. In the last pass, we identify the minimum of the last two elements. The implementation of the algorithm is:

```
/*---------selection sort---------*/

int min_pos; float save;

for (int pass=1; pass<n; pass++)
  min_pos = pass;
  for (i=pass+1;i<=n;i++) // compare
  {
  if(x[i]<x[min_pos])
    {
    min_pos = i;
    }
  save = x(pass);
  x(pass) = x(min_pos);
  x(min_pos) =save;
  }
}
```

Alphabetizing a list

The sorting algorithm can be used verbatim to alphabetize a list of names. The only difference is that the float vector x[i] is declared as an array of strings defined, for example, as:

```
x[1]="Johnson";
x[2]="Brown";
x[3]="Smith";
x[4]="Wu";
x[5]="Yang";
```

The C++ compiler interprets the "greater than" or "less than" comparison in the expected alphabetical sense.

Problems

3.8.1. Modify the bubble-sort code to arrange the array in descending order with the smallest number put at the bottom.

3.8.2. Discuss whether it is possible to insert a stopping check in the selection-sort algorithm.

3.8.3. Alphabetize a list of ten cities.

3.9 Bitwise operators

In the binary system, an integer, a, is expressed as the modulated sum of powers of two,

$$a = b_k \times 2^k + b_{k-1} \times 2^{k-1} + \ldots + b_1 \times 2^1 + b_0 \times 2^0, \tag{1}$$

where $b_i = 0, 1$ are the binary digits (bits). The binary representation of this integer is

$$a = (b_k \, b_{k-1} \ldots b_1 \, b_0)_2.$$

For example,

$$50 = 1 \times 2^5 + 1 \times 2^4 + 0 \times 2^3 + 0 \times 2^2 + 1 \times 2^1 + 0 \times 2^0, \tag{2}$$

and thus,

$$50 = (110010)_2. \tag{3}$$

If a is declared as a short integer, the binary digits are stored in a two-byte memory block consisting of sixteen memory cells, as:

$$0 \, 0 \ldots 0 \, b_k \, b_{k-1} \ldots b_1 \, b_0 \tag{4}$$

where an appropriate number of leading bits on the left are set to zero. Thus, the number 50 is stored as:

$$0000000000110010 \tag{5}$$

The bitwise operators of C++ allow us to produce new integers by manipulating the bits of a given integer.

Shift operators

The commands:

```
short a=50;
short b;
b = a << 3;
cout << a << ", " << b << endl;
```

print on the screen:

```
50, 400
```

We note that the binary representation of 400 is:

0000000110010000

and conclude that the statement a << 3 causes the binary string of a to be shifted to the left by three places.

More generally, the statement a << m causes the binary string of a to be shifted to the *left* by m places. The statement a >> m causes the binary string of a to be shifted to the *right* by m places. When the binary string is shifted to the left or to the right by m places, the number a is multiplied or divided by 2^m. Accordingly, << and >> are the left and right SHIFT bitwise operators.

"and" operator

The statements:

```
short a=50;
short b = a << 3;
cout << "a=" << a << " b=" << b << endl;
short c = a & b;
cout << "c=" << c << endl;
```

print on the screen:

```
a=50 b=400
c=16
```

To understand the c=a&b operation in the penultimate line of the code, we consider the binary representation of the three numbers involved,

Bitwise operator	Binary operation
<<	left shift
>>	right shift
&	and
|	or
^	xor (exclusive or)
~	not

Table 3.9.1 Bitwise operators in C++. When operating on a number, these operators produce a new number with altered bits.

a = 50	0000000000110010
b = a << 3 = 400	0000000110010000
c = a & b = 16	0000000000010000

Evidently, the operation a & b produces a number whose ith binary digit is 1 only if the corresponding binary digits of a and b are both 1, and 0 otherwise. Accordingly, & is the **and** bitwise operator.

"or" and "xor" operators

The "or" operation a|b produces a number whose ith binary digit is 1 only if at least one of the corresponding ith binary digits of a and b is 1, and 0 otherwise.

The "exclusive or" operation a^b produces a number whose ith binary digit is 1 if the corresponding binary digits of a and b are different, and 0 otherwise.

"not" operator

The **not** operator ~a produces a number whose ith binary digit is 0 if the corresponding digit of a is 1, and vice versa.

Applications

Table 3.9.1 summarizes the bitwise operators. In practice, these operators are commonly used for packing multiple values into one integer and thus compressing a file. This is done by shifting with **and** to extract values, and using **xor** to add values.

For example, the following code contained in the file *binary.cc* written by Fred Swartz prints the binary number of a specified integer, n, described by 32 bits:

```
for (int i=31; i>=0; i--)
{
    int m = n >> i;
    int bit = m & 1;
    cout << bit;
}
```

The idea is to successively shift to the right the binary digits of n, and then sample the last digit using the bitwise *and* operation with the number 1 whose binary representation is:

$$00...0001$$

In other applications, the or operator is used to ensure that a given bit of a given integer is set to 1, while the xor operator is used to toggle two bits.

Problems

3.9.1. Describe the combined action of the following statements:

```
x = x^y;    y = x^y;    x = x^y;
```

3.9.2. Write a code that uses bitwise operations to assess whether a given integer is a power of two.

Hint: The binary string of the even integer 2^p consists of zeros led by one, whereas the binary string of the odd integer $2^p - 1$ consists of ones.

3.9.3. Write a code that deduces whether the fifth binary digit of an integer is 1 or 0.

3.10   Preprocessor define and undefine

The C++ preprocessor assists the compilation process by making substitutions and by inserting and removing chunks of code. It is important to realize that the preprocessor does not interpret C++ code, and only performs mechanical tasks reminiscent of cut-and-paste.

Consider the following code involving the **define** preprocessor directive:

```
#include <iostream>
using namespace std;
```

```
#define print cout <<

int main()
{
string a = "hello";
print a;
print endl;
return 0;
}
```

Running the code prints on the screen:

```
hello
```

The preprocessor has substituted the C++ command "cout <<" for every in-stance of the "print" statement in the code. Effectively, "print" has become a macro for "cout <<".

A macro can be removed at any time using the undef preprocessor directive. As an example, consider the code:

```
#include <iostream>
using namespace std;
#define print cout <<

int main()
{
#define eol << endl
string a = "hello";
print a eol;
#undef eol
#define eol << " for your business" << endl
string b = "thank you";
print b eol;
return 0;
}
```

Running the code prints on the screen:

```
hello
thank you for your business
```

The define preprocessor directive may also be used to implement simple functions. For example, the block of commands:

```
#define square(x) x*x;
double e = 5.0;
```

```
cout << square(e);
cout << endl;
```

prints on the screen:

```
25
```

Two further uses of the **define** directive are illustrated in the following example:

```
#define andy_kaufman(x) #x;
cout << andy_kaufman(genius) << endl;

#define gatoula(x,y) x ## y;
int iatros = 10;
cout << gatoula(ia,tros) << endl;
```

which prints on the screen:

```
genius
10
```

The first directive places the variable x between double quotes. The second directive glues together the strings represented by x and y. Other preprocessor directives will be discussed in Chapter 5.

Problems

3.10.1. Define a macro so that the following command makes sense:

```
enter a;
```

3.10.2. Define a macro so that the following command makes sense:

```
We will now print the value of x;
```

User-Defined Functions

4

The use of main programs and subprograms that perform modular tasks is an essential concept of computer programming. In MATLAB and C++ we use functions, in FORTRAN 77 we use functions and subroutines. In C++, even the main program is a function loaded in memory on execution. Large application codes and operating systems may contain dozens, hundreds, or even thousands of functions.

In mathematics, a function is a device that receives one number or a group of numbers in the input, and produces a new number or groups of numbers in the output. The input and output may contain vectors and matrices collectively called arrays. Computer programming functions work in similar ways. In addition, the input and output may contain characters, strings of characters, words, sentences, and even more complex objects.

The individual variables comprising the input and output of a C++ function are communicated through the function arguments enclosed by parentheses following the function name. We will see that, for reasons of efficient design, single variables (scalars) are communicated differently than arrays.

4.1   Functions in the main file

The following C++ code contained in the file *ciao.cc* prints on the screen the greeting "Ciao" by invoking the function `ciao`:

```
#include <iostream>
using namespace std;

//--- function ciao:

void ciao()
{
cout << "Ciao\n";
}

//--- main:
```

```
int main()
{
ciao();
return 0;
}
```

The statement `ciao()` in the main program prompts the execution of the function `ciao`, which prints on the screen "Ciao" and returns nothing to the main program; that is, the return is *void*. The mandatory parentheses () enclose the function arguments after the function name; in this case null, the arguments are null.

Note that the function `ciao` has been defined before the main program. If the order is transposed, the compiler will complain that the function is attempted to be used before declaration. To satisfy the compiler, we duplicate the function prototype *before* the main function, as shown in the following code:

```
#include <iostream>
using namespace std;

void ciao();

//--- main:

int main()
{
ciao();
return 0;
}

//--- function main:

void ciao()
{
cout << "Ciao\n";
}
```

A function can call another function. An example is implemented in the following code:

```
#include <iostream>
using namespace std;

void greet1();

//--- main:

int main()
```

```
{
greet1();
return 0;
}

void greet2();

//--- function greet1:

void greet1()
{
cout << "bye now" << " ";
greet2();
}

//--- function greet2:

void greet2()
{
cout << "come again" << endl;
}
```

Running this program prints on the screen:

```
                    bye now come again
```

The second function declaration void greet2() could have been stated before the main program.

Problems

4.1.1. Investigate whether a function can call the main program.

4.1.2. Write a program that calls two functions, one function to print your first name and another function to print your last name. The functions should be declared before the main program and implemented after the main program.

4.2   Static variables

Suppose that a variable is defined inside a function. When the function is exited, the value of the variable evaporates. To preserve the variable, we declare it as static using the qualifier static.

As an example, running the program:

```
#include <iostream>
using namespace std;

void counter();

//--- main:

int main()
{
for(int i=1;i<3;i++)
  {
  counter();
  }
cout << endl;

return 0;
}

//--- function counter:

void counter()
{
static int n=0;
n++;
cout << n << " ";
}
```

prints on the screen:

1 2

Every time the function *counter* is entered, the static variable n increases by one unit. A static variable can be used to count the number of times a function is called from another function.

In another application, we use the `static` declaration to prevent a variable from being reinitialized:

```
for (i=1;i<=5;i++)
{
static int count = 0;
count++;
}
```

At the end of the loop, the value of `count` will be 5, not 1.

Problem

4.2.1. Does it make sense to use a static variable in the main program outside a loop that initializes the variable?

4.3   Function return

A function can return to the main program a scalar, a character, or a string by means of the **return** statement. Thus, running the program:

```
#include <iostream>
using namespace std;

double piev();

//--- main:

int main()
{
double pi = piev();
cout << pi << endl;
return 0;
}

//--- function piev:

double piev()
{
double pidef=3.14157;
return pidef;
}
```

prints on the screen:

```
pi=3.14157
```

A function may contain more than one **return** statement at different places, evaluating the same variable or different variables. When a **return** statement is executed, control is passed to the calling program.

As an example, a function may contain the following structure:

```
...
if(index==1)
{
return value1;
}
```

```
                  else if(index==2)
                    {
                    return value2;
                    }
                    ...
```

where the three dotes indicate additional lines of code.

A scalar, character, or string computed in a function is customarily passed to the calling program through the **return** statement. A less common alternative is to pass it through a function argument enclosed by the parentheses following the function name, as will be discussed later in this chapter. Groups of scalar variables and arrays *must* be communicated as function arguments.

Prime numbers

As an application, we discuss a code that decides whether a given integer is prime. By definition, a prime number is divisible only by itself and unity.

The prime-test is based on the observation that the remainder of the division between two integers is an integer only if the two numbers are divisible.

The following code contained in the file *prime.cc* assesses whether an integer entered through the keyboard is prime:

```
#include<iostream>
using namespace std;

int GetN();

//--- main:

int main()
{
int k,l,m,n=1;

while (n>0)
 {
   n=GetN();

   for(m=2; m<=n-1; m++)
    {
    l=n/m;    //--- Test for the remainder
    k=l*m;

    if(k==n)   //--- Not a prime:
       {
       cout<<"\n"<<n<<" is not a prime number;";
```

```
            cout<<" the highest divisor is:  "<<l<<"\n";
            break;
            }
        }

      if( k!=n && n!=0 || n==2)    //--- Found a prime:
      {
      cout<<"\n"<<n<<" is a prime number";
      }
   }
return 0;
}

//---- Function GetN:

int GetN()
{
int n;
cout<<"\nPlease enter the integer to be tested:  \t";

while (cin>>n)
   {
   if (n<0)
      {
      cout<<"\nThe integer must be positive; try again\n";
      }
   else
      {
      goto dromos;
      }
   }

   dromos:

   return n;
}
```

The user-defined function *GetN* is used to solicit input in a while loop. If an entered number is negative, a request is made for a repeat. The input is then returned to the main program. If the input is not an integer, the while loop in the main program is exited and the execution terminates. A typical session follows:

```
Please enter the integer to be tested:  -10
The integer must be positive; try again
897
897 is not a prime number; the highest divisor is:  299
Please enter the integer to be tested:  q
```

Combinatorial

Imagine that we are given n identical objects and are asked to select from these a group of m objects, where $m = 0, 1, \ldots, n$. The number of possible combinations is given by the combinatorial,

$$p = \binom{n}{m} = \frac{n!}{m!\,(n-m)!}, \tag{1}$$

where the exclamation mark denotes the factorial,

$$n! = 1 \cdot 2 \cdot \ldots \cdot n, \qquad m! = 1 \cdot 2 \cdot \ldots \cdot m,$$
$$(n-m)! = 1 \cdot 2 \cdot \ldots \cdot (n-m), \tag{2}$$

and the centered dot designates multiplication; by convention, $0! = 1$. When $m = 0$, we select no object, and $p = 1$; when $m = n$, we select all objects, and $p = 1$; when $m = 1$, we select one object, and $p = n$; when $m = n - 1$, we select all but one objects, and $p = n$.

The following main program contained in the file *combinatorial.cc* receives the pair (n, m) from the keyboard and calls a function to compute the combinatorial:

```
#include <iostream>
using namespace std;

int combin(int, int);

//--- main:

int main()
{
int n,m;
cout<< endl <<"Please enter n and m (n>=m);";
cout<<"'q' for either one to quit" << endl;

while(cin>>n && cin>>m)
{
if(m>n|n<0|m<0)
  {
  cout<<"Invalid input; please try again\n";
  }
else
  {
  int p = combin(n,m);
  cout<<"Combinatorial:" << p << endl;
  cout<< endl << "Please enter a new pair" << endl;
  }
}
}
```

```
        return 0;
    }
```

If a non-integer is entered for either n or m, the while loop is exited due to the false read and the execution terminates.

It would appear that the combinatorial requires the computation of three factorials. Even when f n and m are moderate, the factorial can be huge leading to memory overflow. To prevent this, we use the expression

$$p = n \cdot \frac{n-1}{2} \cdots \cdot \frac{n-k+1}{k} \cdots \frac{n-l+1}{l}, \tag{3}$$

where l is the minimum of m and $n - m$. This formula is implemented in the following function:

```
int combin(int n, int m)
{
int l,p;

//--- Find the minimum of m and n-m:

l = m;
if(n-m<l)
    {
    l=n-m;
    }

//--- Apply the formula:

p=1;
for(int k=1; k<=l;k++)
    {
    p=p*(n-k+1)/k;
    }
return p;
}
```

Problems

4.3.1. Prepare and print a list of the first twenty prime numbers.

4.3.2. Using a home computer, twenty-nine-year-old programmer Joel Armengaud discovered that $2^{1398269} - 1$ is a prime number. Confirm his finding.

4.3.3. Write a function that computes the combinatorial in terms of the three factorials, and discuss its performance.

#include <file>	*file* is a system header file provided with the compiler
#include "file"	*file* is either a user-defined header file or a system header file

Table 4.4.1 Syntax of the include directive system and user-defined header files. The current directory is searched first for a user-defined header file.

4.4   Functions in individual files and header files

Medium-size and large codes are split into a number of source files hosting the main program and various functions. Each file is compiled independently to produce the corresponding object file, and the object files are linked to build the executable. In C++, each file containing user-defined functions must be accompanied by a *header file* that declares these functions.

As an example, consider a code that has been split into two files. The first file named *greetings_dr.cc* contains the following main program:

```
#include "greetings.h"
using namespace std;

int main()
{
greetings();
return 0;
}
```

The second file named *greetings.cc* contains the following user-defined function:

```
#include <iostream>
using namespace std;

void greetings()
{
cout << "Greetings\n";
}
```

The first line of the main program is a compiler preprocessor directive requesting the attachment of the header file *greetings.h*. The significance of the double quotes in the syntax #include "greetings.h" is illustrated in Table 4.4.1.

The content of the header file *greetings.h* is:

```
#ifndef GREETINGS_H

#define GREETINGS_H

#include<iostream>
using namespace std;
void greetings();

#endif
```

The "if not defined" loop checks whether the variable GREETINGS_H has been defined. If not, the enclosed block of commands is executed:

- The first of these commands defines the variable GREETINGS_H, so that the loop will not be executed if the header file is linked for a second time. By convention, the name GREETINGS_H arises by capitalizing the name of the header file and then appending _H.

- The rest of the statements in the "if not defined" loop duplicate the function preamble and declaration.

The overall procedure ensures that a function is not defined multiple times.

A makefile that compiles the individual files and links the object files to form an executable named *greetings* reads:

```
OBJ1 = greetings_dr.o greetings.o

greetings:  $(OBJ1)
      c++ -o greetings $(OBJ1)
greetings_dr.o:  greetings_dr.cc
      c++ -c greetings_dr.cc
greetings.o:  greetings.cc
      c++ -c greetings.cc
```

- The first line defines the variable OBJ1 as the union of two object files. This variable is subsequently cited as $(OBJ1).

- The second line states that the executable depends on $(OBJ1).

- The third line performs the linking.

- The last four lines compile the individual source files and generate the object files.

The white space in the third, fifth, and seventh lines must be generated by pressing the TAB key in the text editor.

Problems

4.4.1. Split the prime-number code discussed in Section 4.3 into two files, one containing the main program and the second containing the getN function, and write the necessary header file.

4.4.2. Split the combinatorial code discussed in Section 4.3 into two files, one containing the main program and the second containing the combin function, and write the necessary header file.

4.5   Functions with scalar arguments

An important concept in C++ is the distinction between global and local variables. The former are pervasive, whereas the latter are private to the individual functions.

Global variables

Global variables are defined outside the main function and user-defined functions. Because their memory addresses are communicated implicitly, their values do not need to be passed explicitly through the function argument list enclosed by parentheses.

The following code employs three global variables:

```
#include <iostream>
using namespace std;

void banana(); // function declaration

double a = 2.0;
double b = 3.0;
double c;

//---- main ---

int main()
{
banana ();
cout << a << " " << b << " " << c << endl;
return 0;
}

//---- banana ---

void banana ()
{
```

```
         a = 2.0*a;
         b = -b;
         c = a+b;
         }
```

Running the executable prints on the screen:

4 -3 1.

Numerical global variables do not have to be initialized, and are set to zero by
the compiler.

Local variables

Local variables are defined inside the main function or user-defined functions, and are private to the individual functions.

The following code employs only local variables:

```
#include <iostream>
using namespace std;

double pear (double, double); // function declaration

//---- main

int main()
{
double a = 2.5;
double b = 1.5;
double c = pear (a, b);
cout << a << " " << b << " " << c << endl;
return 0;
}

//--- pear ----

double pear (double a, double b)
{
a = 2.0*a;
b = 3.0*b;
double c = a+b;
return c;
}
```

Running the executable prints on the screen:

2.5 1.5 9.5

Note that the function **pear** is unable to permanently change the values of the variables a and b defined in the main program. When these variables are communicated to the function **pear**, they are assigned new memory addresses, all calculations are done locally, and the temporary variables disappear when control is passed to the main program.

Thus, *scalar variables passed to a function are not automatically updated.* This feature of C++ represents an important difference from MATLAB and FORTRAN 77.

Referral by address

To allow a function to change the value of a communicated scalar, we specify that the scalar is *not* stored in a new memory address, but is referred instead to the original address pertinent to the calling program. This is done by employing the *reference declarator* "&", which causes the argument of the scalar to be the *memory address* instead of the actual *memory content*.

The implementation of the reference declarator is illustrated in the following code:

```
#include <iostream>
using namespace std;

void melon (double, double, double&);

//--- main ---

int main()
{
double a = 2.0;
double b = 3.0;
double c;
melon (a, b, c);
cout << a << " " << b << " " << c << endl;
return 0;
}

//--- melon ----

void melon (double a, double b, double& c)
{
a = 2.0*a;
c = a+b;
cout << a << " " << b << " " << c << "; ";
}
```

The reference declarator & has been appended to the variable type definition
"double" both in the function `melon` prototype and in the function implementation. Running the executable prints on the screen:

$$4\ 3\ 7;\ 2\ 3\ 7$$

In contrast, if the reference declarators were omitted, the output would have
been:

$$4\ 3\ 7;\ 2\ 3\ 1$$

The reference declarator must be used when a function returns one variable or
a group of scalar variables through the function arguments.

Maximum integer with given bits

For example, we consider a code that computes the maximum integer
that can be described with a specified number of bits, n. According to our
discussion in Section 1.2, this is equal to

$$2^0 + 2^1 + \ldots 2^n = 2^{n+1} - 1$$

It is convenient to split the code into two files, one file containing the
main program and the second file containing a function `ipow` that computes
the integral power of an integer. The content of the main file named *bits.cc* is:

```
/* -----------------------------------------------------------------
Greatest integer that can be described a specified number of bits
-------------------------------------------------------------*/

#include <iostream>
#include <iomanip>
#include "ipow.h"
using namespace std;

int main()
{
int n, i;
const int two = 2;
cout << " Will compute the greatest integer" << endl;
cout << " that can be described with n bits" << endl;

while(n!=0)
    {
    cout << endl;
    cout << " Please enter the maximum number of bits" << endl;
```

```
    cout << " (should be less than 32)" << endl;
    cout << " q to quit" << endl;
    cout << " ---------------------------" << endl;
    if(!(cin >> n)) break;
    cout << setw(13) << " bits " << " "
    << setw(10) << " increment" << " "
    << setw(16) << "largest integer" << endl;

    int q = 0;

    for (i=0; i<=n-1; i++)
      {
      int p = ipow(two, i);
      q = q + p;
      cout << setw(10) << i+1 << " "
      << setw(10) << p << " "
      << setw(10) << q << endl;
      };
    };
  return 0;
  }
```

The while loop is abandoned when a false read is encountered. The content of the second file named *ipow.cc* is:

```
/*-----------------------------------------------
function ipow computes the integer power i^j
----------------------------------------------*/
int ipow(int i, int j)
{
int k, accum=1;
for (k=1; k<=j; k++)
  {
  accum = accum * i;
  };
return accum;
}
```

The content of the header file *ipow.h* is:

```
#ifndef IPOW_H
#define IPOW_H
   using namespace std;
   int ipow (int, int);
#endif
```

Note that the declaration:

```
int ipow (int, int)
```

serves to specify the number and type of arguments. The alternative declaration

```
int ipow (int a, int b)
```

is also acceptable, where a and b are two irrelevant variables serving the role or name-holders.

A makefile that compiles the files and links them into an executable named *bits* reads:

```
bits:  bits.o ipow.o
       g++ -o bits bits.o ipow.o
ipow.o:  ipow.cc
       g++ -c ipow.cc
bits.o:  bits.cc
       g++ -c c bits.cc
```

The executable is built by issuing the Unix command:

```
make bits
```

and is subsequently run by issuing the command

```
./bits
```

A typical session follows:

```
Will compute the greatest integer
that can be described with n bits

Please enter the number of bits
      (should be less than 32)
      q to quit
------------------------------------
31
      bits        increment    largest integer
       1             1              1
       2             2              3
       3             4              7
       4             8             15
       5            16             31
       6            32             63
       7            64            127
       8           128            255
       9           256            511
      10           512           1023
      11          1024           2047
```

```
12         2048          4095
13         4096          8191
14         8192         16383
15        16384         32767
16        32768         65535
17        65536        131071
18       131072        262143
19       262144        524287
20       524288       1048575
21      1048576       2097151
22      2097152       4194303
23      4194304       8388607
24      8388608      16777215
25     16777216      33554431
26     33554432      67108863
27     67108864     134217727
28    134217728     268435455
29    268435456     536870911
30    536870912    1073741823
31   1073741824    2147483647

Please enter the number of bits
      (should be less than 32)
      q to quit
-------------------------------
q
```

Return of an alias

An alias, also called a reference, is a duplicate name of a defined variable. In Chapter 2, we saw that an alias can be declared by stating, for example,

```
double a;
double & b = a;
```

In this case, b is an alias of a.

A function can receive a number of variables, and return an alias to one of these variables. For example, the following function receives two integers and returns a reference to the greater

```
int& max_alias(int& a, int& b)
{
if(b>a)
  {
  return b;
  }
```

```
                    return a;
                    }
```

Now consider the main program:

```
            int main()
            {
            int a=5, b=10;
            int & c = max_alias(a, b);
            c = 20;
            cout << a << " " << b << endl;
            return 0;
            }
```

The output is:

                                    5 20

We can circumvent introducing the alias c by replacing the second and third lines with the single line:

```
            maxal(a, b) = 20;
```

We see that returning an alias allows us to bypass temporary variables and thus save memory space.

Problems

4.5.1. Write a function that returns the product of two real numbers through an argument, and the ratio through the function return.

4.5.2. Write a function that returns the sum and the difference of two real numbers through its arguments.

4.5.3. Explain why the results of the *bits* program discussed in the text are consistent with the data given in Table 2.3.1.

4.6   Functions with array arguments

Unlike scalar variables, array variables communicated to a function are referred to the memory address allocated in the calling program. Thus, array variables are called by *reference* or by *address*. By default, user-defined functions are able to change the values of the elements of a communicated array.

The following main program contained in the file *prj.cc* calls a user-defined function to compute the inner product (projection) of two vector arrays:

```cpp
#include <iostream>
using namespace std;

void prj (double[], double[], int, double&);

//--- main ---

int main()
{
const int n=2;
double a[n] = {0.1, 0.2};
double b[n] = {2.1, 3.1};
double prod;
prj (a,b,n,prod);
cout << "inner product:  " << prod << endl;
return 0;
}

//--- prj ---

void prj (double a[], double b[], int n, double& prod)
{
prod = 0.0;
for (int i=0;i<=n-1;i++)
  prod = prod + a[i]*b[i];
}
```

Running this program prints on the screen:

inner product: 0.83

Constant arguments

To deny a user-defined function the privilege of changing the values of a communicated array, we declare the array as "constant" in the function call. If the function attempts to change the values of this array, an error will be issued during compilation. Consider the following working code:

```cpp
#include <iostream>
#include <cmath>

using namespace std;
```

```
void squirrel (const double[], double[], int);

/*-------main---------*/

int main()
{
const int n=3;
double a[n] = {1, 2, 3};
double b[n] = {1, 4, 9};
squirrel (a, b, n);

for (int i=0; i<=n-1; i++)
   {
   cout << a[i] << " " << b[i] << endl ;
   }
return 0;
}

/*--------squirrel---------*/

void squirrel(const double a[], double b[], int n)
{
for (int i=0; i<=n-1; i++)
   {
//    a[i] = sqrt(a[i]);
   b[i] = sqrt(b[i]);
   }
}
```

If the fourth line from the end is uncommented, the compiler will produce the error message:

```
squirrel.cc:22:   assignment of read-only location
```

Matrix arguments

In the case of vectors, we do not have to specify the length of the arrays in the argument of a function. This is not true in the case of matrices where only the length of the first index can be omitted. The reason is that C++ must know the row width in order to assess the memory addresses of the first-column elements and store the row elements in successive memory blocks.

The following code calculates and prints the sum of the diagonals (trace) of a square matrix:

```
#include <iostream>
using namespace std;

const int n=2;
void trace (double[][n], double&);

//--------------- main -----------------

int main()
{
double a[n][n] = {{0.1, 0.2}, {0.9, 0.5}};
double Trace;
trace (a, Trace);
cout << "Trace:  " << Trace << endl ;
return 0;
}

//--------------- trace -----------------

void trace (double a[][n], double& Trace)
{
Trace= 0.0;
for(int i=0; i<=n-1; i++)
  {
  Trace = Trace + a[i][i];
  }
}
```

Running the core prints on the screen:

Trace: 0.6

An alternative implementation of the **trace** function that passes the trace through the function return is:

```
double trace (double a[][n])
{
Trace=0.0;
for(int i=1; i<=n-1; i++)
  {
  Trace = Trace + a[i][i];
  }
return Trace;
}
```

In this case, the function call is:

```
double Trace = trace (double a[][n]);
```

Vector projections

As an application, we read a matrix and a vector from the file *matrix_v.dat*, and then multiply the vector by the matrix numerous times. The code consists of the main program and a function that performs the multiplication, both contained in the file *mapping.cc*. After each mapping, the vector is optionally normalized so that its length becomes equal to one, and aesthetically printed on the screen.

```cpp
/*------------------------------------------------
Multiply a vector by a square matrix many times
----------------------------------------------*/

#include <iostream>
#include <iomanip>
#include <fstream>
#include <cmath>
using namespace std;

void mat_vec (int, double[][50], double[], double[]);

//--- main ---

int main()
{
int n, i, j, norm;
double b[50],c[50],a[50][50];

cout << endl;
cout << " Normalize the vector after each projection?" << endl;
cout << " Enter 1 for yes, 0 for no" << endl;
cout << " -------------------------" << endl;
cin >> norm;

//--- Read the matrix and the vector:

ifstream input_data;
input_data.open("matrix_v.dat");
input_data >> n;

for (i=1;i<=n;i++)
{
  for (j=1;j<=n;j++)
  {
  input_data >> a[i][j];
  }
}

for (i=1;i<=n;i++)
```

```
{
input_data >> b[i];
}

input_data.close();

//--- Display:

cout << endl ;
cout << " Matrix - initial vector:";
cout << "\n\n";

for (i=1;i<=n;i++)
{
  for (j=1;j<=n;j++)
  {
  cout << setw(8) << a[i][j];
  }
  cout << " " << setw(8) << b[i] << endl;
}
cout << "\n\n";

//--- Mapping:

int icount=0, more=1;

while (more!=0)
{
    mat_vec (n,a,b,c);

    for (i=1;i<=n;i++)
    {
    b[i]=c[i];
    }
//.................
    if(norm == 1)
    {
    double rnorm = 0;
    for (i=1;i<=n;i++)
      {
      rnorm = rnorm + b[i]*b[i];
      }
    rnorm = sqrt(rnorm);
    for (i=1;i<=n;i++)
      {
      b[i]=b[i]/rnorm;
      }
    }
```

```
//..................
```

```
        cout << " Projected vector at stage:  " << icount;
        cout << "\n\n";

        for (i=1;i<=n;i++)
        {
        cout << setprecision(5) << setw(10);
        cout << b[i] << endl;
        }

        icount = icount+1;

        cout << " One more projection?  "<< endl ;
        cin >> more;
     }
     return 0;
     }
```

```
/*----------------------------------------------------
function mat_vec performs matrix-vector
multiplication:   c_i = a_ij b_j
----------------------------------------------------*/

void mat_vec (int n, double a[][50], double b[], double c[])
{
int i, j;
for (i=1;i<=n;i++)
  {
  c[i] = 0;
  for (j=1;j<=n;j++)
    {
    c[i] = c[i] + a[i][j]*b[j];
    }
  }
}
```

The content of the file *matix_v.dat* is:

```
5
 1.0  -2.0   3.0   1.2   2.6
-4.0   2.0  -3.0   8.9  -5.9
 3.0  -3.0   3.0  -2.7   0.1
 1.2   8.9  -2.7   3.2   1.3
 2.6  -5.9   0.1   1.3  -0.2

 0.1   0.4  -0.2  -0.1  -2.9
```

A typical session is:

```
Normalize the vector after each projection?
Enter 1 for yes, 0 for no
------------------------
1
Matrix - initial vector:

      1      -2       3     1.2     2.6     0.1
     -4       2      -3     8.9    -5.9     0.4
      3      -3       3    -2.7     0.1    -0.2
    1.2     8.9    -2.7     3.2     1.3    -0.1
    2.6    -5.9     0.1     1.3    -0.2    -2.9

Projected vector at stage: 0
 -0.45848
  0.88114
-0.077777
 0.006652
-0.085453
One more projection?
1
 Projected vector at stage: 1
 -0.22529
   0.3709
 -0.36126
  0.62582
 -0.53807
One more projection?
1
 Projected vector at stage: 2
 -0.19481
    0.828
 -0.33318
  0.38323
 -0.13635
One more projection?
1
 Projected vector at stage: 3
  -0.1947
  0.54262
  -0.3629
  0.64434
 -0.34753
One more projection?
1
 Projected vector at stage: 4
  -0.1737
  0.74636
```

```
 -0.35276
  0.49945
 -0.19718
 One more projection?
1
 Projected vector at stage: 5
 -0.18376
  0.61676
 -0.36129
    0.608
 -0.29267
 One more projection?
   0
```

Problems

4.6.1. Write a function that returns the Cartesian norm of a vector,

$$L_2 = \sqrt{v[1]^2 + v[2]^2 + \cdots + v[n]^2}.$$

4.6.2. Write a function that returns the p-norm of a vector,

$$L_p = (v[1]^p + v[2]^p + \cdots + v[n]^p)^{1/p},$$

where p is a specified real number.

4.6.3. Write a function that computes and passes to the main function the transpose of a two-dimensional matrix. If A[i][j] is an arbitrary $m \times n$ matrix, its transpose is another $n \times m$ matrix whose elements are defined as: B[i][j]=A[j][i].

4.6.4. Run the *mapping* code to assess the fate of the vector as the iterations continue.

4.7   External variables

Assume that a code has been split into two files, one file containing the main program and the second file containing a function. Moreover, assume that the global integer variable kokoras is defined and possibly evaluated in the first file before the implementation of the main function.

The same global variable cannot be defined in the second file, or the linker may throw an exception on multiple variable definitions. However, if the variable is not defined in the second file, the individual compilation of this file will fail.

To circumvent this difficulty, we declare the variable in the second file as external by issuing the statement:

```
extern int kokoras;
```

which reassures the compiler that the value of this variable will be supplied externally.

As an example, the main program contained in the file *kotoula.cc*, and a function named *kalaboki* are implemented, respectively, as:

```
#include <iostream>
#include "kalaboki.h"
using namespace std;

int kokoras = 10;

int main()
{
kalaboki();
cout << kokoras << endl;
return 0;
}
```

and

```
using namespace std;

extern int kokoras;

void kalaboki()
{
kokoras++;
return kokoras;
}
```

The header file of the function kalaboki.cc is:

```
#ifndef KALABOKI_H
#define KALABOKI_H

using namespace std;
extern int kokoras;
void kalaboki();

#endif
```

If more than two files are involved, a variable may be declared as external in all but one file where it is defined and possibly evaluated. This may be the file hosting the main program or another file hosting a function.

Problems

4.7.1. What is the output of the *kotoula* code?

4.7.2. Write a code contained in three files hosting the main program and two functions. A matrix array should be defined and evaluated in a function file, and should be declared as external in the other two files.

4.8 Function overloading

With the exception of the main function, two entirely different functions are allowed to have the same name, provided they have distinct lists of arguments. The compiler will realize that these are distinct functions, distinguished by the list or type of their arguments.

For example, the following code computes the inverse-distance potential of two charged particles along the x axis. When the particles coincide, the potential is infinite and a warning is issued:

```
#include <iostream>
using namespace std;

/*---------- regular potential ----------*/

double potential(double a, double b)
{
return 1/(a-b);
}

/*---------- singular potential ----------*/

string potential()
{
return "Warning:  singular potential";
}

/*---------- main----------*/

int main()
{
double a=1.1;
double b=2.2;
```

```
if(a!=b)
{
double V = potential(a, b);
cout << "Potential:   " << V << endl;
}
else
{
string message = potential();
cout << message << endl;
}

return 0;
}
```

In this case, we implement the function *potential* twice, the first time with two arguments and the second time with no arguments. The return of these functions is also different, though this is not necessary for the functions to be distinguished by the compiler.

Problems

4.8.1. Write a code that overloads twice a function of your choice.

4.8.2. Consider two functions with the same name and same arguments but different return data types. Are these functions distinguishable?

4.9   Recursive calling

C++ functions are allowed to call themselves in a recursive fashion that is reminiscent of a nested sequence.

For example, recursive function call can be used to compute the factorial of an integer $n! = 1 \cdot 2 \ldots \cdot n$, as implemented in the following algorithm:

```
int factorial (int n)
{
if(n==1)
   int fact = 1;
else
   fact = n * factorial(n-1);
return fact;
}
```

Recursive calling is ideal for computing self-similar objects such as fractals containing an infinite cascade of geometrical patterns. On the down side, recursive calling carries the risk of prolonged execution time.

Problem

4.9.1. What is the output of the following bizarre code?

```
#include <iostream>
using namespace std;

int main()
{
static int i=0;
i++;
cout << i << endl;
i = main();
return 0;
}
```

4.10   Function templates

Assume that a function performs a certain task on numbers, and the same function performs the same task on strings. For example, the function may sort an array of numbers or alphabetize a list.

We can avoid duplicating the function by declaring it as a template and putting it in a header file. This is one instance where the implementation of a function must be included in the header file. The header file then becomes an *implementation-included* or *definition-included* header file.

The reason for including the implementation in the header file is that the template function materializes on demand. If we compile separately the source code of the implementation, we will get an empty object code. Though some compilers allow declaration-only header files for template functions, this is the exception rather than the rule.

The following header file *prsum.h* contains the implementation of a function template that adds and prints two variables:

```
#ifndef PRSUM_H
#define PRSUM_H

#include <iostream>
using namespace std;

template <class T>
void prsum (T x, T y)
{
T z = x+y;
cout << z << endl;
```

```
}
```

```
#endif
```

This function template has two arguments whose data type is left unspecified. The symbol T representing the generic data type of x and y is arbitrary, and can be replaced by any other symbol or variable name. However, it is a standard practice to use T, standing for template.

Replacing T with an actual data type, such as int, we obtain the familiar function definition:

```
void prsum (int x, int y)
```

This example suggests a method of constructing the template of a function: write out the function as usual, and then replace a chosen data type in the input, output, or both with a generic type denoted as T.

The following main program contained in the file *fava.cc* calls this function template to print the sum of two integers, the sum of two real numbers, and the sum of two strings:

```
#include <iostream>
#include "prsum.h"
using namespace std;

int main()
{
int i=5, j=10;
prsum<int>(i,j);

float a=4.5, b=-30.4;
prsum<float>(a,b);

string s="amphi", t="theater";
prsum<string>(s,t);

return 0;
}
```

The executable **fava** is produced by issuing the command:

```
c++ -o fava fava.cc
```

Running the executable produces on the screen:

```
15
-25.9
amphitheater
```

Bubble sort

The header file *bsort.h* containing the implementation of the bubble-sort algorithm discussed in Section 3.8 reads:

```
#ifndef BSORT_H
#define BSORT_H

using namespace std;

template <class T>
T bsort (int n, T x[])
{
int Istop,k,i;
T save;
k = n-1; // number of comparisons
do {
        Istop = 1; // will stop if Iflag 1
        for (i=1;i<=k;i++) // compare
          {
          if(x[i]>x[i+1])
            {save = x[i]; // swap
            x[i]=x[i+1];
            x[i+1] = save;
            Istop = 0; // an exchange occurred; do not stop
            }
          }
        k--; // reduce the number of comparisons
    } while(Istop==0);

return x[n];
}

   #endif
```

This function template returns to the calling program the entry at the bottom of the sorted list. The function has two arguments: the integer n, and the vector variable x[] whose data type is left unspecified.

Replacing T with an actual data type, such as float, we obtain the familiar function definition:

```
float bsort (int n, float x[])
```

The main program *cities.cc* listed below calls this template function to alphabetize a list of cities:

```
#include <iostream>
#include <iomanip>
```

```
#include "bsort.h"
using namespace std;

int main()
{
const int n=6;
string city[n+1];
city[1]="Oslo";
city[2]="Bayreuth";
city[3]="Chevy-Chase";
city[4]="Baltimore";
city[5]="Waco";
city[6]="Kalambaka";

string bottom = bsort<string> (n, city);

for(int i=1;i<=n;i++)
  {
  cout << setw(3) << right << i << " " ;
  cout << setw(15) << left << city[i] << endl;
  }

return 0;
}
```

The executable `cities` is produced by issuing the command:

```
c++ -o cities cities.cc
```

Running the executable produces on the screen the alphabetized list:

```
1 Baltimore
2 Bayreuth
3 Chevy-Chase
4 Kalambaka
5 Oslo
6 Waco
```

The main program *income.cc* listed below calls this template function to sort an array of taxpayer income in dinars:

```
#include <iostream>
#include <iomanip>
#include "bsort.h"
using namespace std;

int main()
{
```

```
const int n=5;
float income[n+1];
income[1]=73020;
income[2]=63250;
income[3]=83890;
income[4]=20340;
income[5]=80234;

float bottom = bsort<float> (n, income);

for(int i=1;i<=n;i++)
  {
  cout << setw(3) << right << i << " " ;
  cout << setw(15) << left << income[i] << endl;
  }

return 0;
}
```

Running the executable produces on the screen the sorted list:

```
1 20340
2 63250
3 73020
4 80234
5 83890
```

Further properties of templates

Templates allow us to transmit values of constant parameters. As an example, consider the code:

```
#include <iostream>
using namespace std;

//------prsum--------

template <class T, int n>
void prsum (T x, T y)
{
T z = x+y;
cout << n << " " << z << endl;
}

//------main--------

int main()
{
```

```
int i=5, j=10;
prsum<int,1>(i,j);

float a=4.5, b=-30.4;
prsum<float, 2>(a,b);

string s="amphi", t="theater";
prsum<string, 3>(s,t);

return 0;
}
```

Running the code produces on the screen:

```
1 15
2 -25.9
3 amphitheater
```

Problems

4.10.1. Write a function template of your choice.

4.10.2. Convert the selection-sort algorithm discussed in Section 3.8 into a template, and then run it for (*a*) a list of real numbers, and (*b*) a list of strings.

Pointers

5

C++ offers an arsenal of tools that allow us to access the inner workings of a code and directly manipulate and allocate memory. Among these tools, pointers play a prominent role. Pointers are both revered and feared for their possible misuse.

A pointer is the identification number of a variable or function, assigned by the CPU on execution. A pointer can be used to identify a variable in the memory bank, reserve space for new data, and erase unwanted data to eliminate memory leaks. The implementation of pointers can be simple or subtle depending on the data types considered.

5.1 Pointers to scalars and characters

As soon as a scalar variable is declared in the main program or in a function, it is given a memory address. The content of the memory address is the value of the variable, which may change during execution. If the variable occupies more than one byte, the memory address of the variable is the memory address of the first byte.

Reference operator

We can extract the memory address of a variable using the *reference operator*, &, which should be read as: "memory address of variable ..."; the name of the appended variable should replace the three dots.

The following code continued in the file *pointer1.cc* evaluates four variables and extracts their memory addresses:

```
#include <iostream>
#include <iomanip>
using namespace std;

int main()
{
int a=4;
```

```
float b=1.2;
double c=3.45;
char d=99;

cout << setw(5) << a << " " << (unsigned int) &a << endl;
cout << setw(5) << b << " " << (unsigned int) &b << endl;
cout << setw(5) << c << " " << (unsigned int) &c << endl;
cout << setw(5) << d << " " << (unsigned int) &d << endl;

return 0;
}
```

The output of the code is:

```
     4 3219066260
   1.2 3219066256
  3.45 3219066248
     c 3219066247
```

The memory addresses printed as unsigned integers appear in the second column.

We can store the memory address of a variable in a new integer variable. In our example, we can state:

```
unsigned int mab = (unsigned int) &b;
```

The parentheses on the right-hand side implement typecasting. When printed, the integer mab will have the value 3219066256.

Pointer variables

Instead of implementing typecasting, we can store the memory address of a variable in another variable of the pointer type called, for example, pname. This practice prevents us from confusing true integer variables with those holding memory addresses.

A pointer corresponding to an integer variable is declared as:

```
int * pname
```

or

```
int *pname
```

A pointer corresponding to a real variable registered in double precision is declared as:

```
double * pname
```

or

`double *pname`

Similar declarations are made for other types.

Once declared, a pointer can be evaluated using the *reference operator*, (&). For example, if `pname` is a pointer to an integer and a is an integer, we may evaluate:

`pname = &a;`

Declaration and initialization can be combined into one statement:

`int * pname = &a;`

The following code contained in the file *pointer2.cc* evaluates four variables and extracts their memory addresses through pointers:

```
#include <iostream>
#include <iomanip>
using namespace std;

int main()
{
int a=4;
float b=1.2;
double c=3.45;
char d=99;

int * memad_a;
float * memad_b;
double * memad_c;
char * memad_d;

memad_a = &a;
memad_b = &b;
memad_c = &c;
memad_d = &c;

cout << setw(5) << a << " " << (unsigned int) memad_a << endl;
cout << setw(5) << b << " " << (unsigned int) memad_b << endl;
cout << setw(5) << c << " " << (unsigned int) memad_c << endl;
cout << setw(5) << d << " " << (unsigned int) memad_d << endl;

return 0;
}
```

The prefix & in the statements evaluating the pointer variables is the reference operator. The output of the code is:

```
4 3219988068
1.2 3219988064
3.45 3219988056
c 3219988055
```

Alternatively, we could have combined pointer declaration and evaluation by stating:

```
int * memad_a = &a;
float * memad_b = &b;
double * memad_c = &c;
char * memad_d = &d;
```

Dereference operator

Conversely, we can extract the memory content of a specified memory address using the *dereference operator*, *, which should be read: "content of the memory address ..."; the name of the appended pointer variable should replace the three dots.

The following statements declare and evaluate an integer, extract its memory address through a pointer, and then deduce the memory content:

```
int a=4;
int * memad_a = & a;
int verify_a = * memad_a;
cout << a << " " << memad_a << " " << verify_a << endl;
```

The prefix * in the statement evaluating the content of the pointer variable is the dereference operator. The output of the code is:

```
4 0xbfa6e2c8 4
```

Note that the memory address is printed in the hexadecimal system.

It is unfortunate that the asterisk is used both in the pointer declaration and as the dereference operator. It would have been much less confusing if a different symbol were chosen for the declaration.

Two ways of changing a variable

We can change the value of variable either directly or indirectly by changing the content of its memory address. The direct route amounts to telling a friend, "I will send you a gift"; the indirect way amounts to saying, "I will send a gift to the occupant of your house."

The indirect way is illustrated in the following code contained in the file *pointer3.cc*:

```
#include <iostream>
using namespace std;

int main()
{
double a = 3.4;
cout << a << " ";

double * memada = &a;
*memada = 3.5;
cout << a << endl;

return 0;
}
```

Running the code prints on the screen:

```
3.4 3.5
```

Null pointer

A declared but non-initialized pointer has an arbitrary and possibly inappropriate value leftover in the memory block where it resides. To ensure a proper value, we initialized the pointer as NULL by stating, for example,

```
int * pnt1 = NULL;
```

Pointer arithmetic

When we increase or decrease the value of a pointer by one unit, we obtain the memory address of a memory cell that is shifted to the right or left by a number of memory cells corresponding to the byte size of the stored data type.

The following code illustrates the memory layout of a two-dimensional array (matrix):

```
#include <iostream>
using namespace std;

int main()
{
float A[2][2]={ {1.1, 1.2}, {1.3, 1.4} };
float * memad1, * memad2; * memad3, * memad4;

memad1 = &A[0][0];
memad2 = memad1+1;
memad3 = memad2+1;
memad4 = memad3+1;

cout << memad1 << " " << *memad1 << endl;
cout << memad2 << " " << *memad2 << endl;
cout << memad3 << " " << *memad3 << endl;
cout << memad4 << " " << *memad4 << endl;

return 0;
}
```

The output of the code is:

```
0xbfafdfe0 1.1
0xbfafdfe4 1.2
0xbfafdfe8 1.3
0xbfafdfec 1.4
```

The memory addresses are printed in the hexadecimal system. We observe that the first and second rows of the matrix are stored in memory addresses that differ by increments of four. The byte size of float is clearly four, in agreement with the data type listing of Table 1.1.1.

Pointer to pointer

A second-order pointer holds the memory address of a pointer associated with a regular (non-pointer) variable.

The following code contained in the file *pointer2p.cc* evaluates a variable, extracts its memory address through a pointer, extracts the memory address of the pointer through a second-order pointer, and then deduces the memory contents:

```
#include <iostream>
using namespace std;

int main()
```

```
{
double a=8.45;
double * memada;
double ** memadb;

memada = &a;
memadb = &memada;

double verifya = *memada;
double verifyb = **memadb;

cout << a << endl;
cout << memada << " " << memadb << endl;
cout << verifya << " " << verifyb << endl;
return 0;

}
```

Running the code prints on the screen:

```
8.45
0xbfd40150 0xbfd4014c
8.45 8.45
```

Third- and high-order pointers are defined in similar ways.

Inverse typecasting

At the beginning of this section, we saw that the memory address of a variable can be stored as a regular integer of a non-pointer type through typecasting.

Double use of the dereference operator allows us to map the integer back into the variable. To demonstrate the method, we consider the statements:

```
float b=1.2;
unsigned int mab = (unsigned int) &b;
cout << b << " " << mab << " " << * (float*) mab << endl;
```

The output on the screen is:

```
                    1.2 3215432204 1.2
```

The expression * (float*) mab typecasts the integer mab as a pointer corresponding to a float, and then extracts the pointer content.

It would seem that this method can be used to extract the content of a given memory address by stating, for example,

```
cout << b << " " << mab << " " << * (char*) 234 << endl;
```

However, since we do not know the data type stored in that address, we will be greeted with the dreaded segmentation fault.

Problems

5.1.1. Assess the data types of the variables p1 and p2 declared in the line:

```
int * p1, p2;
```

5.1.2. Initialize a pointer to a data type of your choice as NULL, and then print and discuss its value.

5.1.3. A collection of pointers to the same data type can be accommodated in a vector array. Write a program that evaluates and prints such an array.

5.1.4. Write a program that defines and prints the fourth-order pointer of a character.

5.2   Pointers to arrays and strings

To locate a vector v in memory, we require the address of the first element, v[0]. Subsequent elements are located in consecutive memory addresses.

The following code contained in the file *pointer_vector.cc* extracts the address of a vector and confirms that it is equal to the address of the first element:

```
#include <iostream>
using namespace std;

int main()
{
double A[4]={1.1, 1.2, 1.3, 1.4};
double * memad1 = A;
double * memad2 = &A[0];
cout << memad1 << " " << memad2 << endl;
return 0;
}
```

The output of the code is:

```
0xbf83b6c8 0xbf83b6c8
```

Note that it is *not* permissible to state:

```
double * memad1 = &A;
```

A vector name is a pointer

The perfectly valid statement:

```
double * memad1 = A;
```

reveals that a *vector name is a pointer*. The statement:

```
cout << *A << endl;
```

will print the first element of the vector (in our case 1.1), and the statement

```
cout << *(A+1) << endl;
```

will print the second element of the vector (in our case 1.2). Thus, the expression A[0] is identical to *A, the expression A[1] is identical to *(A+1), and the expression

```
A[n]
```

is identical to

```
*(A+n)
```

where n is an integer. In fact, the compiler blindly substitutes *(A+n), for every instance of A[n].

Vector layout

The following code contained in the file *pointer_vector1.cc* further illustrates the layout of a vector in a contiguous memory block:

```
#include <iostream>

using namespace std;

int main()
{
double A[3]={1.1, 1.2, 1.3 };
double * memad1 = A;
double * memad2 = memad1+1;
double * memad3 = memad2+1;
```

```
cout << memad1 << " " << memad2 << " "<< memad3 <<endl;
cout << *memad1 << " " << *memad2 << " "<< *memad3 <<endl;
return 0;
}
```

The output of the code is:

```
0xbf9c6e48 0xbf9c6e50 0xbf9c6e58
1.1 1.2 1.3
```

Strings

Pointers of string variables behave in a similar fashion. Consider the following code contained in the file *pointer_string.cc*:

```
#include <iostream>
using namespace std;

int main()
{
string onoma = "iakovos";
string * memad = &onoma;
cout << onoma << endl;
cout << memad << endl;
return 0;
}
```

Running the executable produces the output:

```
iakovos
0xbfa845f4
```

In this example, 0xbfa845f4 is the memory address of the first letter of the string iacovos.

String to character conversion

We can use pointers to convert a string variable to a character array. First, we find the length of the string using the length function and introduce an equal-sized character array. Second, we run through successive pointers of the string characters while evaluating successive elements of the character array, as illustrated in the following block:

```
string onoma= "arkouditsa";
int l = onoma.length();
```

```
char oros[1];
char * memad;

for (int i=0;i<1;i++)
{
memad = &onoma[i];
oros[i] = *memad;
cout << oros[i];
}
```

Running the code produces the output:

arkouditsa

Problems

5.2.1. Describe the action of the following statements:

```
float a[5];
float * pnt = a;
pnt = 3.5;
```

5.2.2. Explore whether it is possible to convert a character array into a string.

5.3   Sorting with the STL

Consider a vector v defined in the main program and passed to a function named *ex_fnc(v)* as a function argument, *ex_fnc(v)*. We have seen that, in fact, the main program passes to the function the memory address of the first element of the vector v. Accordingly, v in ex_fnc(v) should be interpreted as a pointer.

C++ includes the standard template library (STL) offering a variety of utility functions and data structures (see Appendix G). Among them is the function sort that sorts a a subset of a list encapsulated in a vector v[i], where $i = 0, \ldots, N - 1$. This function receives as input the memory address of the first element of the subset, and the memory address of the last element of the subset increased by one unit.

For example, if v is a vector of floats, the following statements will sort the whole list:

```
float * pnt = &v[0];
sort(pnt, pnt+N);
```

These two statements can be replaced by the single statement:

```
sort(v, v+N)
```

which confirms that the vector v is passed to the function as a pointer.

The following code contained in the file *sorting.cc* uses the sort function of the STL to sort and then print a list:

```
#include <iostream>
#include <iomanip>
#include <algorithm>
using namespace std;

int main()
{
const int N=7;
float v[N]={10.0, -9.4, 3.4, -3.4 -10.8, 199.0, -3.56};

sort(v, v+N);

cout<< setiosflags(ios::fixed | ios::showpoint);
for(int i=0;i<=N-1;i++)
  {
  cout << setw(3) << i << " " << setw(6) << setprecision(2)
      << v[i] << endl;
  }

return 0;
}
```

Note that we have included the header file *algorithm* of the STL. Running the code prints on the screen:

```
0   -14.20
1    -9.40
2    -3.56
3     0.00
4     3.40
5    10.00
6   199.00
```

If we only want to sort a subset of the list, we can state, for example,

```
float * pnt = &v[3];
sort(pnt, pnt+2);
```

Order of an algorithm

We can assess the performance of the `sort` function by studying the relation between the elapsed CPU time and the list size, N. The following code contained in file *ransort.cc* generates and sorts a random list of integers:

```
#include <algorithm>

using namespace std;
int main()
{
const int N=1048*1048*2;
int random_integer[N];

for(int i=1;i<=N;i++)
  {
  random_integer[i] = rand();
  }

sort(random_integer, random_integer+N+1);

return 0;
}
```

Now we compile the code into the executable *ransort*, and issue the Unix command:

```
time ransort
```

On execution, we see on the screen:

```
0.664u 0.020s 0:00.70 97.1% 0+0k 0+0io 0pf+0w
```

The first field is the CPU time used by the program (user), the second field is the CPU time used by the operating system in support of the program (system), and the third field is total CPU time (user and system). The significance of the rest of the fields is explained in the `time` manual invoked by issuing the command: `man time`.

Running the program with list size $N = 2^{19}, 2^{20}$, and 2^{21}, requires, respectively, 0.180u, 0.312u, and 0.652u of CPU time. We observe that, as N is doubled, the CPU time also nearly doubles, which means that the algorithm implemented in `sort` is almost linear. In fact, analysis shows that the CPU time scales with $N \log N$. By contrast, if we had used the bubble-sort algorithm discussed in Chapter 3, we would have found that the CPU scales with N^2, which is much inferior.

Problems

5.3.1. Use the `sort` function to alphabetize a list of ten African countries.

5.3.2. Verify by computation that the CPU time of the bubble-sort algorithm scales with N^2. This means that, when N is doubled, the CPU time is multiplied nearly by a factor of four.

5.4   Command line arguments

When execution has been concluded, the main program returns to the operating system (OS) an integer. Conversely, the main program can receive information from the operating system with the help of pointers.

To illustrate the protocol, we consider the following code contained in the file *os.cc* and compiled into an executable named *os*:

```
#include <iostream>
using namespace std;

int main(int argc, char * argv[])
{
   for (int i=0;i<=argc-1;i++)
   {
   cout << i+1 << " " << argv[i] << endl;
   }
return 0;
}
```

Running the executable by typing in the command line:

```
os
```

prints on the screen:

```
1 os
```

The integer `argc` is an argument counter indicating the number of string variables (character arrays) passed from the operating system to the main program. The variables themselves are contained in a string array indicated by the pointer `char * argv` holding the argument values. In this case, the argument counter is one, and the sole component of the string array is the name of the executable.

If we run the executable by typing in the command line:

```
os is running
```

we will see on the screen:

```
1 os
2 is
3 running
```

We can use a double pointer to simplify the arguments of the main function by stating:

```
int main(int argc, char ** argv)
```

Building commands

The ability to receive information from the operating system allows us to build command-line applications. For example, suppose that we want to build a command that generates a file with a specified name, prints a zero in the file, and then closes the file. The command is implemented in the following code contained in the file *nfz.cc* and compiled into an executable named *nfz*:

```
#include <fstream>
using namespace std;

int main(int argc, char **argv)
{
ofstream file1;
file1.open(argv[1]);
file1 << "0";
file1.close();
return 0;
}
```

Running the code by typing in the command line:

```
nfz sage
```

generates a file named *sage* containing a zero.

What if we forget to type the name of the file or accidentally type multiple file names? In the first case argc=1, and in the second case argc>2. To issue a warning, we include the iostream system header file and insert the following block at the top of code:

```
if(argc != 2 )
{
cout<< "Please use:  "<< argv[0] <<" <filename>" << endl;
return 1;
};
```

Print a file

In a more advanced application, we generate a binary executable named *pfile* that displays the content of a file with a specified name *filename* in response to the command:

```
pfile filenme
```

This is accomplished by the following code contained in the file *pfile.cc*:

```
#include <fstream>
#include <iostream>
using namespace std;

int main ( int argc, char *argv[] )
{
ifstream dev1(argv[1])
if(dev1.is_open() )
{
  char x;
  while (dev1.get(x))
  cout<< x;
}
else
{
  cout<<"Unable to open the file" << endl;
}
return 0;
}
```

The Boolean variable `dev1.get(x)` is false if the end of the file *dev1* has been reached, and true otherwise.

Problems

5.4.1. Add to the program *pfile.cc* a check that issues a warning if no file name, or more than one file name, is specified.

5.4.2. Write an application that concatenates two files – that is, it creates a new file consisting of the union of two input files.

5.5   Pointers to functions

Pointers to user-defined functions are employed to concisely represent the functions. Like pointers of regular data types, function pointers can be included in the arguments of functions to give compound functions.

Assume that we need to call a function A which, in turn, calls either function B or function C. We want the call to A to include an argument that allows us to specify which one of the functions B or C will be called. This can be done be introducing pointers to functions B and C, called pA and pB, and calling A with a pointer argument p that is evaluated either as the pointer of B or as the pointer of C – that is, p=pB or p=pC.

If the prototype of a function is:

```
double functionname(double, double);
```

its pointer is declared as:

```
double (*othername)(double, double) = functionname;
```

The function may then be called as

```
c = functionname(a, b);
```

or

```
c = (*othername)(a, b);
```

For example, consider the following code consisting of three functions and the main program, contained in the file *pointer_fun.cc*:

```
#include <iostream>
using namespace std;

double ratio(double, double); // function prototype
double (*point_ratio)(double, double)=ratio; // and its pointer

double product(double, double); // function prototype
double (*point_product)(double, double)=product; // and pointer

/*---------------------------------------------------
The following is a function prototype; the arguments consist of two
"double" scalars and the pointer of a function that receives
two doubles and returns one double
----------------------------------------------------*/

double operate(double, double, double(*)(double, double));

/*--------------- main program --------------------*/

int main()
{
```

```cpp
int menu;
double a = 4.0;
double b = 2.0;
double result;

cout << "Please enter 1 for the ratio and 2 for the product" << endl;
cout << "q to quit" << endl;
cout << "q to quit" << endl;

while(cin >> menu)
{
  if(menu==1)
  {
  result=operate(a, b, prat);
  cout << a << "/" << b <<"=" << result<< endl;
  }
  else if(menu==2)
  {
  result=operate(a, b, pprod);
  cout << a << "x" << b <<"=" << result<< endl;
  }
}
return 0;
}

/*-------------- ratio --------------------*/

double ratio(double a, double b)
{
double c=a/b;
return c;
}

/*-------------- product--------------------*/

double product(double a, double b)
{
double c=a*b;
return c;
}
/*-------------- operate--------------------*/

double operate(double a, double b,
                  double (*funcall)(double, double))
{
double c=(*funcall)(a, b);
return c;
}
```

The syntax of the function-pointer declaration is illustrated near the top of the code. The main program calls the function `operate` with a function-pointer argument that requests division or multiplication. A sample session is:

```
Please enter 1 for the ratio and 2 for the product q to quit
1
4/2=2
2
4x2=8
q
```

Problem

5.5.1. Add to the *pointer_fun* code two more functions to perform addition and subtraction.

5.6   Pointers to free memory

We have discussed pointers associated with declared variables. It is possible to introduce a pointer not associated with a declared variable but corresponding instead to unused or free memory that is available to all programs.

When a new pointer is declared, the corresponding memory address is reserved and the associated memory content is initialized to zero. If the new pointer declaration fails because free memory is not available, the system will throw an exception.

A pointer corresponding to an undeclared integer is introduced by the statements:

```
int * pname;
pname = new int;
```

where `pname` is a chosen pointer name. The two statements can be consolidated into one:

```
int * pname = new int;
```

A pointer corresponding to an undeclared real variable registered in double precision is declared as:

```
double * somename = new double;
```

Similar declarations are made for different data types.

The following code introduces a new pointer and evaluates its content:

```
#include <iostream>
using namespace std;

int main()
{
int * memad = new int;
cout << memad << endl;
cout << *memad << endl;
return 0;
}
```

The output of the code is:

```
0xbff1b08c
0
```

which shows that the memory content is zero. In the same spirit, we can write:

```
double * pnt = new double;
cin >> *pnt;
```

which evaluates the memory content. Note that we do not have to introduce a name for the variable contained in the memory slot addressed by the pointer, and we simply use *pnt.

To free the memory cell, we delete the pointer **pname** using:

```
delete pname;
```

It is highly recommended that the value of a deleted pointer be reset to zero. When the value of zero is assigned to a pointer, the pointer becomes *null*, that is, it points to nothing.

The following code contained in the file *pointer_free.cc* introduces and immediately deletes a new pointer:

```
#include <iostream>

using namespace std;

int main()
{
int * memad = new int;
delete memad;
memad=0;
cout << *memad << endl;
```

```
return 0;
}
```

Running the code produces the system-failure message:

```
Segmentation fault
```

However, running the same code without the `memad=0;` statement yields the irrational answer:

```
0
```

New pointers to arrays have interesting properties. Consider the following declarations:

```
int n=150;
double * pv;
pv = new double[n];

for (int i=0; i<n; i++)
{
pv[i] = 0;
}
```

Here we introduce a pointer, assign it to a vector with n slots, and then evaluate the components of the pointer as though they were the vector. After evaluation, the pointer becomes the vector!

To see this more clearly, consider the code:

```
#include <iostream>
using namespace std;

int main()
{
int n=150;
double * pv;
pv = new double[n];
cout << pv << endl;

for (int i=0; i<n; i++)
  {
  pv[i] = 0;
  }

double * pointer1 = pv;
cout << pointer1 << endl;
```

```
                    return 0;
                    }
```

The output is:

```
                    0x917e008
                    0x917e008
```

To free memory, we can delete the pointer using the commands:

```
                    delete []pv;
                    pv = 0;
```

The pointer-to-array conversion, and vice versa, is as brilliant as it is baffling.

Problem

5.6.1. What would the output of the *pointer_free1.cc* code be without the line
`delete memad; ?`

Classes and Objects

6

The intelligent mind has a natural tendency to classify objects, items, concepts, and abstract notions into groups recognized by given names:

- Races in anthropology

- Species in biology

- Sets and spaces in mathematics

- Elementary particles in physics

- Elementary motions in fluid mechanics

The groups are distinguished by common features and properties, concisely called *attributes*, and the members interact by a well-defined set of rules.

An entity that belongs to a group is formally called a *member*, and an action that can modify a member, make a member disappear, or generate an offspring is called a *member function*.[1] Examples of groups are:

The set of natural numbers: 1, 2, 3, 4, ... :

The member function "addition of unity" operating on the member "2" produces the member "3".

The set of integers: ..., -4, -3, -2, -1, 0, 1, 2, 3, 4, ... :

The member function "subtraction of unity" operating on the member "-3" produces the member "-4".

The set of rational numbers, m/n, where m and n are integers:

The member function "addition" operating on the members m/n and k/l produces the member $(lm + kn)/(nl)$.

---

[1]Groucho Marx once said: "I do not want to belong to any club that would accept me as a member."(http://www.groucho-marx.com).

Generic:	Group	Member	Action
Maths:	Space	Element	Operation
OOP:	Class	Object	Member function
Science:	Discipline	Phenomenon	Dynamics

Table 6.1 Equivalence of groups, spaces, and objects and their relation in object oriented programming (OOP).

The set of real numbers registered as floating-point numbers in computer science:

The member function "multiplication by zero" operating on a member produces the null member "0".

Vector spaces in mathematics:

The member function "inner product" operating on a pair of members produces a number that is a measure of the angle subtended between the two vectors. If the inner product is zero, the two vectors are orthogonal.

The set of all two-index matrices a_{ij}:

Each member is identified by the pair of integers i and j.

In calculus, a "member function" defined on the set of real numbers is a device that receives real numbers (input) and produces new numbers (output). Stated differently, a function maps the input to the output. When the output is the null point "0", the input has been annihilated.

In object oriented programming (OOP), a group is a "class," a member is an "object," and a "member function" implements an operation. By operating on an object with a "function," we can read, record, and change some or all of its attributes. As an example, consider the class of all polygons. A member function can be defined that transforms a rectangle into a triangle in some sensible fashion.

Classes in object oriented programming can be as simple as the set of integers (int) or the set of floating point numbers stored in double precision (double), and as complex as a database whose members (entries) are described by names, numbers, and other fields.

Table 6.1 displays the equivalence of groups, spaces, and objects and their relation in object oriented programming (OOP).

6.1   Class objects and functions

An apple can be declared and initialized as a member of the "fruit" class by stating:

```
fruit apple = fruit(q, w, ..., e);
```

The parentheses enclose names and numbers that define the apple, and can be thought of as a bar code. In English, this line says:

Apple is a fruit uniquely defined by the properties (attributes): q, w, ... e.

The attributes can be words, sentences, or numbers.

A member function can be defined to transform an apple to an orange. Assume that *apple* has been defined as an object of the fruit class, and *change* has been defined as a member function. The C++ command that carries out this operation is stated as:

```
apple.change(x, y, ..., q);
```

The parentheses enclose numbers and strings that ensure the apple-to-orange transformation. In English, this line says:

Mutate the apple in a way that is uniquely determined by the parameters: x, y, ..., q.

The apple may disappear after the operation, or continue to co-exist with the orange. Which will occur depends on how the member function *change* has been defined.

Classes define new data types and corresponding class functions beyond those implemented in the standard C++ library. To see this, we consider the familiar declaration and initialization of a string:

```
string gliko = "koulouraki";
```

We note the similarity with the previously stated apple declaration, and conclude that the string data type is implemented in a corresponding class with a simplified implementation syntax. In this light, C++ endows us with unlimited degrees of freedom for defining new data types and thereby building a language inside another language.

Problem

6.1.1. If the `string` data type were not available, what would be a sensible statement declaring and initializing a string variable?

6.2   Class interfaces

The member functions of a class accomplish a broad range of tasks. First, they construct (initialize) native objects, that is, they evaluate the data fields that uniquely define an object. Second, they allow us to view and visualize an object. Third, they allow us to intrusively operate on an isolated object or groups of objects.

The set of member functions pertinent to a particular class is the *class interface*.

Constructors

These member functions initialize an object. Constructors come in two flavors: *default constructors* and *parametered constructors*.

Suppose that we want to create the beautiful Greek sculpture of the thinking man. To begin, we introduce the class of all sculptures, and use the default constructor to materialize the default sculpture, which can be a square block of clay. Alternatively, we may use the non-default constructor to materialize a rectangular block of clay.

Accessor member functions

These member functions non-intrusively query an object, that is, they do so without altering its properties.

Concerning the class of sculptures, an accessor member function may report the length of the fingernails without actually clipping them.

Mutator member functions

These member functions are able to alter the members on which they operate.

Concerning the class of sculptures, a mutator function can act like a chisel.

Destructors

Destructors are member functions that delete an object for revenge or to free up memory and prevent memory leaks.

Transient objects are generated when we call a function to perform certain operations, and then abandoned when we exit the function. Destructors allow us to abandon the objects before exiting a function.

Problems

6.2.1. A function takes a bite off an apple declared as a member of the fruit class. It this a mutator member function?

6.2.2. Define an accessor and a mutator member function operating on the data type (class) of all integers.

6.3   Class definition

The "fruit" class definition has the general appearance:

```
class fruit
{
    ...
};
```

Here and elsewhere, the dots represent additional lines of code. Note the semi-colon at the end of the class definition.

Member attributes are declared as *public* if they are disclosed to the main program and functions of a different class, and *private* otherwise. Similarly, interface functions are declared as public if they can be called from the main program and from functions of a different class, and private otherwise. This distinction motivates the class-definition structure:

```
class fruit
{
public:
    ...
private:
    ...
};
```

Default constructor

Our first public definition is the default constructor. The fruit class definition reads:

```
class fruit
{
public:
  fruit ();
  ...
private:
  ...
};
```

Note that the default constructor does not have a return type, not even void. The name of the default constructor is identical to the class name.

To define a fruit named "kiwi" using the default constructor, we state in the main program:

```
fruit kiwi;
kiwi = fruit();
```

or

```
fruit kiwi = fruit();
```

or

```
fruit kiwi;
```

It is erroneous to declare:

```
fruit kiwi();
```

as the compiler interprets this statement as the prototype of a function named *kiwi* that receives no arguments and returns a fruit.

Parametered constructor

Including also the parametered constructor, we obtain the class declaration:

```
class fruit
{
public:
  fruit();
```

```
        fruit(q, w, ..., e);
        ...
    private:
        ...
    };
```

Like the default constructor, the parametered constructor does not have a return type, not even void. The name of the parametered constructor is identical to the class name.

To define a fruit named "kiwi" using the parametered constructor, we state in the main program:

```
    fruit kiwi;
    kiwi = fruit(q_value, w_value, ..., q_value);
```

or

```
    fruit kiwi = fruit(q_value, w_value, ..., q_value);
```

or

```
    fruit kiwi(q_value, w_value, ..., q_value);
```

Two constructors

Since the default and parametered constructors have identical names, they are distinguished only by the number and type of arguments enclosed by the parentheses. This duplication is consistent with the notion of function overloading: two functions with the same name are distinguished by the data types of their arguments.

Defining a class constructor is not mandatory. If we do not declare a constructor in the class definition, the compiler will assume that the class has a default constructor with no arguments. However, it is a good idea to always define a constructor.

Default destructor

The declaration of the default destructor is similar to that of the default constructor. The class definition with the default constructor, the parametered constructor, and the default destructor reads:

```
    class fruit
    {
```

```
public:
  fruit();
  fruit(q, w, ..., e);
  ~fruit();
  ...
private:
  ...
};
```

To abandon kiwi, we state

$$kiwi = \text{~}fruit()$$

Accessor function

To query the members of the fruit class on their color, we introduce the accessor member function read_color. The class definition reads:

```
class fruit
{
public:
  fruit();
  fruit(q, w, ..., e);
  ~fruit();
  string read_color(a, b, ..., c) const;
  ...
private:
  ...
};
```

The qualifier string indicates that the function read_color will return a string of characters in the form of a word or sentence describing the color. The qualifier const indicates that the function is non-intrusive, that is, it is an accessor.

To read the color of kiwi, we state in the main program:

```
string chroma;
chroma = kiwi.read_color (a, b, ..., c);
```

Mutator function

To convert one type of fruit into another, we introduce the mutator member function change. The class definition reads:

```
class fruit
{
public:
  fruit();
  fruit(q, w, ..., e);
  string read_color(a, b, ..., c) const;
  void change(g, o, ..., x);
private:
  ...
};
```

The qualifier void indicates that the function change will return neither a number, nor a word, nor a sentence, but will quietly carry out the requested operation.

To change kiwi, we state in the main program:

```
kiwi.change (g, o, ..., x);
```

Public and private functions

If we declare a class function in the private section of the class, then this function could be called from other class functions, but not from the main program or any other external function.

Class implementation

Now we define the precise action taken by the member functions "fruit", "read_color", and "change" of the "fruit" class.

The implementation of the default fruit constructor reads:

```
fruit::fruit()
{
q = dv_q;
w = dv_w;
...
e = dv_e;
}
```

where "dv_q", "dv_w", etc., are specified default values that describe an object of the fruit class.

The implementation of the parametered fruit constructor reads:

```
fruit::fruit(value_q, value_w, ..., value_e)
{
```

```
q = value_q;
w = value_w;
...
e = value_e;
}
```

where "value_q", "values_w", etc., are specified values or names that describe an object of the fruit class.

The implementation of the default fruit destructor reads:

```
fruit::~fruit()
{
delete q;
delete w;
...
delete e;
}
```

In this case, q, w, ..., e are introduced as pointers.

The implementation of the non-intrusive read_color function reads:

```
string fruit::read_color(a, b, ..., c) const
{
...
return color;
}
```

The dots between the angular brackets denote various operations. The prefix string indicates that, after operating on a member, the function read_color will return the string color, which can be evaluated as "red", "green", or any other appropriate shade.

The implementation of the mutator change function is:

```
void fruit::change(g, o, ..., x)
{
...
}
```

The prefix "void" indicates that, when operating on a member, the function "change" acts quietly and returns nothing.

The class implementation may be included in the class declaration either partially or entirely. For example, the fruit class may be defined and implemented as:

```
class fruit
{
public:
  fruit();
    {
    q = dv_q;
    w = dv_w;
    ...
    e = dv_e;
    }
  fruit(q, w, ..., e);
    ...
private:
    ...
};
```

However, this layout obscures the class structure in the absence of a concise class definition. It is thus highly recommended that class definition and class implementation are put in separate sections.

Problems

6.3.1. Explain why it does not make practical sense to define private constructors.

6.3.2. An integer variable is declared as:

$$int\ a;$$

Is this statement consistent with a default constructor?

6.4 Private fields, public fields, and global variables

Next, we discuss the "private" variables of a class. To understand this concept, it is helpful to imagine that a class is a biological cell or capsule whose interior can be accessed, probed, altered or destroyed only by the member (capsule) functions. The capsule encloses data which, if declared "private," can be accessed only by the member functions of the host class, but not by any other functions.

For example, if the string variable *color*, the string variable *shape*, and the real variable *size* are private variables of the "fruit" class, we define:

```
class fruit
{
```

```
public:
  fruit();
  fruit(q, w, ..., e);
  ~fruit();
  string read_color(a, b, ..., c) const;
  void change(g, o, ..., x);
private:
  string color;
  string shape;
  float size;
};
```

If we want to make the color of a fruit available to the main program and any other function that uses objects of the fruit class, we must move the declaration:

```
string color;
```

to the public section of the class definition.

Suppose, for example, that a function *outside* the fruit class declares

```
kiwi = fruit();
```

If `color` is a private field, the statement:

```
cout << kiwi.color;
```

is unacceptable. However, if `color` is a public field, this statement is perfectly acceptable. Class member fields are routinely kept private to prevent inadvertent evaluation in unsuspected parts of a code.

Before proceeding to discuss specific class implementations, we emphasize two important properties regarding variable availability:

- The arguments of the constructor that defines an object, whether public or private, are implicitly available to the member functions. Thus, the calling arguments of a member function operating on an object include by default the arguments of the constructor that defines the object.

For example, suppose that the **vendor** member function has been defined as:

```
void fruit::vendor()
{
  ...
}
```

To operate on an apple with this function, we write:

```
fruit apple = fruit(value_q, value_w, ,...value_e);
apple.vendor();
```

The attributes of the apple do not need to be passed explicitly to the vendor. The first line can be shrunk into:

```
fruit apple(value_q, value_w, ,...value_e);
```

- Global variables are available to all functions of all classes. Though global variables must be declared outside the main program and any classes or functions, they can be initialized and evaluated inside the main program or any function.

6.5   The fruit class

Our definition of the fruit class involves the default constructor, a parameter constructor, and two member functions:

```
#include <iostream>
using namespace std;

//--- CLASS FRUIT DEFINITION

class fruit
{
public:
        fruit();
        fruit(string color, string shape, float size);
        string read_color(bool Iprint) const;
        void change_color(string newcolor);
private:
        string color;
        string shape;
        float size;
};
```

By way of choice, the three fruit attributes – color, shape, and size – have been declared private.

The implementation of the default constructor is:

```
fruit::fruit()
{
color = "green";
shape = "spindle";
```

```
size = 1.2;
}
```

The implementation of the parametered constructor is:

```
fruit::fruit(string clr, string shp, float size)
{
color = clr;
shape = shp;
size = 2.3;
}
```

The implementation of the non-intrusive read_color function is:

```
string fruit::read_color(bool Iprint) const
{
if(Iprint==true)
cout << color << endl;
return color;
}
```

The implementation of the mutator change_color function is:

```
void fruit::change_color(string clr)
{
color = clr;
}
```

The following main program defines and manipulates fruit class members:

```
int main()
{
bool Iprint = true;

fruit fig = fruit();
string fig_color = fig.read_color(Iprint);
cout << fig_color << endl;

fruit apple = fruit("red", "round", 2.0);
string apple_color = apple.read_color(Iprint);

apple.change_color("yellow");
apple_color = apple.read_color(Iprint);

return 0;
}
```

Running this program prints on the screen:

```
green
green
red
yellow
```

Because the attribute `color` has been declared as private, we cannot state in the main program:

```
cout << fig.color << endl;
```

This would be acceptable only if the declaration:

```
string color;
```

were made in the public section of the class.

Problems

6.5.1. Add to the fruit class a member function that prints and returns (*a*) the shape, and (*b*) the size of an object.

6.5.2. Add to the fruit class a member function that changes all three attributes of an object.

6.5.3. Introduce a global variable of your choice and confirm that it can be initialized and evaluated inside the main program or any fruit function.

6.5.4. Define the class of all taxpayers whose attributes include last name, first name, social-security number, and income.

6.6   Friends

Privacy exceptions can be made to friends. If we want to disclose the private fields of the class members to an external function named `package`, we state this in the class definition. In the case of the fruit class, we state:

```
//--- CLASS FRUIT DEFINITION

class fruit
{
friend void package(fruit item);
public:
    fruit();
    fruit(string color, string shape, float size);
```

```
        string read_color(bool Iprint) const;
        void change_color(string newcolor);
private:
        string color, shape;
        float size;
};
```

The function `package` now has access to `color`, `shape`, and `price`. We will implement this function as:

```
//--- FRIEND FUNCTION

void package(fruit item)
{
if(item.size<1.0)
cout << "box" << endl;
else
cout << "crate" << endl;
}
```

We may then state in the main program:

```
fruit watermelon("green", "oval", 12.0);
package(watermelon);
```

The second statement will print on the screen:

```
box
```

We recall that, if we want to disclose a private field of an object to *all* non-member functions, we must declare it as public.

Problems

6.6.1. Implement a friend function that determines whether the color of a fruit is green.

6.6.2. Implement a friend function that determines whether the size of a fruit is less than 3.0 inches.

6.7 Circles and squares

To further illustrate the concept of private variables, we consider a code defining two classes, one containing circles and the second containing horizontal squares.

The circles are defined by their center and radius, and the squares are defined by their center and side length. In both cases, the x and y coordinates of the center are hosted by a two-slot vector named center[2].

The circle class definition is:

```
#include <iostream>
using namespace std;

//--- CIRCLE CLASS DEFINITION

class circle
{
public:
        circle(double, double, double);
        void print() const;
private:
        double center[2], rad;
};
```

The square class definition is:

```
//--- SQUARE CLASS DEFINITION

class square
{
public:
        square(double, double, double);
        void print() const;
private:
        double center[2], side;
};
```

The circle class implementation is:

```
//--- CIRCLE CLASS IMPLEMENTATION

circle::circle(double center_x, double center_y, double radius)
{
center[0] = center_x;
center[1] = center_y;
rad = radius;
}

void circle::print() const
{
cout << center[0] << " " << center[1] << " " << rad << endl;
}
```

The square class implementation is:

```
//--- SQUARE CLASS IMPLEMENTATION

square::square(double center_x, double center_y, double edge)
{
center[0] = center_x;
center[1] = center_y;
side = edge;
}

void square::print() const
{
cout << center[0] << " " << center[1] << " " << side << endl;
}
```

Note that the variable `center` is defined separately in each class. To understand this practice, imagine that a native of Greece and a native of Cyprus have the same name, *Athenoula*. This is permissible, as long as their passports are issued from the respective different countries.

The following main program defines one object in each class and prints its properties:

```
int main()
{
circle A = circle(0.1, 0.2, 0.3);
A.print();

square B = square(0.9, 1.2, 5.3);
B.print();

return 0;
}
```

Running the code produces on the screen:

```
0.1 0.2 0.3
0.9 1.2 5.3
```

Note that the `print` statement behaves in one way when it applies to A, and in another way when it applies to B. This is an example of polymorphism.

The composite Greek word "polymorphism" consists of "poly," which means "many," and "morphi," which means "appearance."

Problems

6.7.1. Add to the circle class a member function that computes and prints the area of a circle, and to the square class a member function that computes and prints the area of a square.

6.7.2. (*a*) Add to the circle class a member function that assesses whether two members overlap. (*b*) Repeat for the square class.

6.8 Algebra on real numbers

As a further example, we introduce the class of points along the x axis described by the x value and their color. If x is positive, the color is black, if x is negative, the color is red, and if x is zero, the color is white.

We will endow the algebra class with several member functions that perform the following tasks:

- Initialize a new point using the default constructor.

- Initialize a new point using the parametered constructor.

- Determine the color from the value of x.

- Get the value of x and the color of a specified point.

- Print the value of x and the color of a specified point.

- Shift a point along the x axis.

The algebra class definition is:

```
/*---------------------------
Algebra on real numbers
-----------------------*/

#include <iostream>

using namespace std;

//--- CLASS DEFINITION

class algebra
{
public:
        algebra();          // default constructor
        algebra(double);        // parametered constructor
        double get(string&) const;
```

```
        void print() const;
        void shift(double string);
   private:
        double x;
        string color;
        string set_color(float);
   };
```

The algebra class implementation is:

```
//--- CLASS IMPLEMENTATION

algebra::algebra() // default constructor
{
x=0.0;
color = "white";
}

//---

algebra::algebra(double value_x) // parametered constructor
{
x=value_x;
color = set_color(x);
}

//---

string algebra::set_color(float x) // set the color:
{
string color;
if(x>eps)
     color="black";
else if(x<-eps)
     color="red";
else
     color="white";
return color;
}

//---

double algebra::get(string& color) const
{
chroma=color;
return x;
}

//---
```

```
void algebra::print() const
{
cout << x << " " << color << endl;
}

//---

void algebra::shift(double y)
{
color = set_color(x+y);
x = x+y;
}
```

Following is a main program that uses the algebra class:

```
int main()
{
string chroma;

algebra A = algebra();
A.print();
cout << A.get(chroma) << " " << chroma << endl;

algebra B = algebra(-0.9);
B.print();

B.shift(2.1);
B.print();

return 0;
}
```

Running this program produces on the screen:

```
0 white
0 white
-0.9 red
1.2 black
```

Two features are worth emphasizing:

- The get function returns the value of x through the function return and passes the color through an argument endowed with the reference declarator (&).

- Because the function set_color has been declared private, it cannot be called from the main program.

Problems

6.8.1. A point in the plane defines a vector starting at the origin, $x = 0, y = 0$, and ending at that point. Add to the algebra class a member function that rotates the vector by a specified angle around the z axis.

6.8.2. Add to the algebra class a member function that implements subtraction, a second function that implements multiplication, and a third member function that implements division.

6.9 Operator overloading

In the main function of the algebra code, we may add a point A to another point B to produce the new point C using the following statements:

```
algebra save = A;          // save A
A.shift(B.get(chroma));    // shift A
algebra C=A;               // C is the shifted A
A=save;                    // reinstate A
```

Alternatively, we can directly add points A and B by overloading the + operator. This is done by defining the algebra class addition function:

```
algebra algebra::operator + (algebra patespani)
{
algebra add;
add.x = x+patespani.x;
add.color = set_color(add.x);
return add;
}
```

and then inserting the following declaration in the public section of the class:

```
algebra operator + (algebra);
```

Once this is done, we can state in the main program:

```
C=A+B;
```

which adds the two points A and B by adding the corresponding x values and calculating the new color to produce a point C.

Table 6.9.1 displays operators that can be overloaded in C++. Because the left-to-right copy assignment operator (=) is overloaded by default, it is declared and implemented only if a special functionality is desired. Tables 6.9.2 and 3 explain the syntax of common overloading declarations. Class overloading

6.9 *Operator overloading*   171

```
+      -      *      /      =      <    >      +=      <<=    >>=    ==
!=     <=     >=     ++     --     ~    &=     ^=      |=     &&     ||
%=     []     -=     *=     /=     <<   >>     delete  %      &      ^
!      |    new[] ()    ,          ->*  ->     new     delete[]
```

Table 6.9.1 Operators that can be overloaded in C++. The right-to-left copy
assignment operator (=) is overloaded by default.

Statement	Operator	Syntax
•a	+ - * & ! ~ ++ --	A::operator •()
a•	++ --	A::operator•(int)
a•b	+ - * / % ^	operator•(A, B)
a•b	&	< > == !=	operator•(A, B)
a•b	<= >= << >> && || ,	A::operator•(B)
a•b	= += -= *= /=	A::operator•(B)
a•b	%= ^= &=	A::operator•(B)
a•b	|= <<= >>= []	A::operator•(B)
a(b, c...)	()	A::operator() (B, C...)
a->x	->	A::operator->()

Table 6.9.2 Syntax of common operators overloaded as class functions. • stands
for an operator, a is a member of class A, b is a member of class B, and c is
a member of class C.

Statement	Operator	Syntax
•a	+ - * & ! ~ ++ --	operator •(A)
a•	++ --	operator•(A,int)
a•b	+ - * / % ^	operator•(A, B)
a•b	&	< > == !=	operator•(A, B)
a•b	<= >= << >> && || ,	operator•(A, B)

Table 6.9.3 Syntax of common operators overloaded as global functions. • stands
for an operator, a is a member of class A, b is a member of class B, and c is
a member of class C.

is implemented by member functions, and global overloading is implemented by
outside functions.

As an example, we overload the ++ operator in the algebra class by
inserting the following declaration in the public section of the class:

```
void operator ++ ();
```

The associated class implementation is:

```
void algebra::operator ++ ()
{
x = x*x;
color= set_color(x);
}
```

Once this is done, we can state in the main program:

```
++A;
```

where A is a declared point.

Even more interesting, we can twice overload the + operator by inserting the following declaration in the public section of the class:

```
algebra operator + ();
```

accompanied by the implementation:

```
void algebra::operator + ()
{
x = 2*x;
color= set_color(x);
}
```

Once this is done, we can write

```
+A;
```

where A is a point.

Consider the classes of circles and squares introduced in Section 6.7. The following global function defined outside these classes overloads the + operator:

```
void operator + (circle A, square B)
{
A.print();
B.print();
}
```

Including in the main program the block of commands:

```
circle A = circle(0.1, 0.2, 0.3);
square B = square(0.9, 1.2, 5.3);
A+B;
```

prints on the screen:

$$0.1 \ 0.2 \ 0.3$$
$$0.9 \ 1.2 \ 5.3$$

Problems

6.9.1. Overload the multiplication operator for the algebra class.

6.9.2. Demonstrate by example the action of the ++ operator and the twice overloaded + operator for the algebra class discussed in the text.

6.9.3. (*a*) Overload the | operator for the circles discussed in Section 6.7, so that the result is a Boolean variable that is true if the areas of two circles are the same, and false otherwise. (*b*) Repeat for the squares.

6.10   Pointers to class members

In Chapter 5, we discussed pointers to scalar variables and various data types including vectors and matrices. A class defines a new data type whose members can also be identified with pointers encapsulating the addresses of memory cells identifying the objects.

As an example, we introduce the algebra class and state in the main program:

```
algebra D = algebra(-9.45);
algebra * pnt = &D;
algebra E = *pnt;
D.print();
E.print();
```

The first line defines object D; the second line defines a pointer to D; the third line identifies point E with point D stated as the content of the memory space identified by the pointer pnt; the last two lines print D and E.

The output of the code is:

```
-9.45 red
-9.45 red
```

Instead of operating on point D with a function, we can operate on its pointer. Thus, in the above example, the statement:

```
D.print();
```

can be replaced by:

```
pnt->print();
```

Note the "ASCII art" pointer designation of the arrow: ->

"this" communicates the memory address of an object

Let us revisit the algebra class discussed in Section 6.8 and introduce the member function print1 defined as:

```
void algebra::print()
{ double * pntx = &x;
string * pntc = &color;
cout << this << " " <<pntx << " " << pntc << " "<< x
                << " " << color << endl;
}
```

Including in the main program the statements:

```
algebra Z(-0.4);
Z.print1();
algebra * pntZ = &Z;
cout << pntZ << endl;
```

prints on the screen:

```
0xbfdb1cc8 0xbfdb1cc8 0xbfdb1cd0 -0.4 red
0xbfdb1cc8
```

We see that this is the memory address of point Z regarded as an object of the algebra class. Furthermore, the memory address of Z is the same as the memory address of its first field, Z.x

When a function operates on an object, its memory address is implicitly passed to the object through the variable this. In practice, this is used to overload the assignation operator and check whether a parameter passed to a member function is the object itself.

Problems

6.10.1. Illustrate the implicit communication of a member's memory address through this for the class of circles discussed in Section 6.7.

6.10.2. What changes are necessary so that the memory address of an algebra point is the same as the memory address of its color?

6.11   The class of points in a plane

As a further example, we consider the class of points in the xy plane. The location of each point is determined by the doublet of real number (x, y) specifying the Cartesian coordinates. The class definition is:

```
class point
{
public:
  point();
  point(double value_x, double value_y);
  double get_x() const;
  double get_y() const;
  void print() const;
  void move(double dx, double dy);
private:
  double x;
  double y;
};
```

The implementation of the default constructor is:

```
point::point()
{
x = 0.0; y = 0.0;
}
```

The implementation of the parametered constructor is:

```
point::point(double a, double b)
{
x = a; y = b;
}
```

The implementation of the non-intrusive *print* function is:

```
void point::print() const
{
cout << x << " " << y << endl;
}
```

The implementation of the non-intrusive *get_x* function is:

```
double point::get_x() const
{
return x;
}
```

The implementation of the non-intrusive *get_y* function is:

```
double point::get_y() const
{
return y;
}
```

The implementation of the mutator *move* function is:

```
void point::move(double dx, double dy)
{
x = x+dx;
y = y+dy;
}
```

The main function is allowed to make any of the following calls:

- Define the default point *A*, shift it, and print the original and new coordinates:

```
point A = point();
A.print();
A.move(-0.2, 0.4);
A.print();
```

- Define point B, shift it, and print the original and new coordinates:

```
point B = point(1, 2);
B.print();
B.move(0.3, 0.4);
B.print();
```

An alternative to the first statement is:

```
point B(1, 2);
```

- Print the coordinates of point (10, 15):

```
point(10, 15).print();
```

- Print the coordinates of the default point:

```
point().print();
```

- Set *a* equal to the *x* coordinate of point *A*:

```
double a = A.get_x();
```

- Set b equal to the y coordinate of point A:

```
double b = A.get_y();
```

- Print the coordinates of point A:

```
cout << A.get_x() << " " << A.get_y() << endl;
```

Note that the main function is not able to access directly the private variables x and y, and must rely on member functions to fetch them.

We can directly add two points A and B by overloading the $+$ operator. This is done by inserting the following declaration in the public section of the class:

```
point operator + (point);
```

and defining the algebra class addition function:

```
point point::operator + (point B)
{
point add;
add.x = x + B.x;
add.y = y + B.y;
return add;
}
```

Once this is done, we can state in the main program:

```
point C;
C=A+B;
```

We can refer to the class members by pointers, as discussed in Section 6.10. Thus, if A and Z are defined members, including in the main code the statements:

```
point * pntname;
pntname = &A;
cout << pntname << endl;
point Z = *pntname;
Z.print();
pntname->print();
```

prints on the screen:

```
0xbfed5168
0.3 0.4
0.3 0.4
```

Problems

6.11.1. (*a*) Overload the ++ operator such that a point is reflected with respect to the *y* axis. (*b*) Overload the − operator such that a point is reflected with respect to the *x* axis.

6.11.2. Define the class of all points in three-dimensional space by analogy to the class of points in the plane discussed in the text.

6.11.3. Define the class of complex numbers $x = x+iy$, where i is the imaginary unit, $i^2 = -1$. Implement member functions that carry out addition, subtraction, multiplication, and division.

6.12   The class of runners

An international sports competition has been subscribed by runners originating from all over the world. Each runner is recorded by his/her name, country of origin, and performance time. The runners are placed to the "runner" class that is defined as follows:

```
class runner
{
public:
  runner();
  runner(string runner_name, string runner_country,
             double runner_time);
  void read();
  string get_name() const;
  string get_country() const;
  double get_time() const;
void print() const;
private:
  string name;
  string country;
  double time;
};
```

The implementation of the default constructor is:

```
runner::runner()
{
name = "Euripides";
country = "Nigeria";
time = 9.9;
}
```

where 9.9 is a default time in seconds.

The implementation of the parametered constructor is:

```
runner::runner(string runner_name, string runner_country,
               double runner_time)
{
name = runner_name;
country = runner_country;
time = runner_time;
}
```

The purpose of the parametered constructor is to evaluate the private fields "name", "country", and "time" describing each runner.

The implementation of the "read" function is:

```
void runner::read()
{
cout << " Please enter the runner's name:   ";
getline (cin, name);
cout << " Please enter the runner's country:   ";
getline(cin, country);
cout << " Please enter the runner's time:   ";
cin >> time;
string remainder;
getline (cin, remainder);
}
```

The implementation of the "get_name" function is:

```
string runner::get_name() const
{
return name;
}
```

The implementation of the "get_country" function is:

```
string runner::get_country() const
{
return name;
}
```

The implementation of the "get_time" function is:

```
double runner::get_time() const
{
return time;
}
```

The implementation of the **print** function is:

```
void runner::print() const
{
cout << name << " Country:  " << country << " time:  " << endl;
}
```

The main function is allowed to make any of the following calls:

- Define a default runner R:

```
runner R=runner();
```

- Read the properties of runner A:

```
A.read();
```

- Print the properties of runner A:

```
A.print();
```

- Print the name of runner A and move to the next line:

```
cout << A.get_name() << endl;
```

- Set and print the properties of runner B:

```
runner B = runner("Abdul", "Ethiopia", 9.00);
B.print();
```

- Print the country and the performance time of runner B on different lines:

```
cout << B.get_country() << endl;
cout << B.get_time() << endl;
```

- Set the properties of runner C and print her time:

```
runner C("Dafela", "Ivory Coast", 9.40);
cout << C.get_time() << endl;
```

- Introduce the default runner D and print his time:

```
D = runner();
cout << D.get_time() << endl;
```

The following main function contained in the file *runner.cc* reads the properties of the runners from the keyboard, keeps a record of the fastest runner, and prints the fastest runner in the end:

```cpp
#include <iostream>
#include <string>
using namespace std;

int main()
{
runner fastest;                        // introduce the default runner
double fast_time = fastest.get_time(); // default time:
bool more = true;
string answer;

while(more) // repeat as long as more is true
  {
  runner member; // introduce the next runner
  member.read(); // evaluate the next runner named ''member''
  member.print(); // print the properties of ''member''

  if(member.get_time() < fast_time)
  { fastest = member;
  fast_time = member.get_time();
  }

  cout << " More runners?  (y/n)"; // inquire for more runners
  getline (cin, answer);
  if(answer != "y") more = false;
  }

cout << endl << " Fastest runner:" << endl;
cout <<        " ---------------" << endl;
fastest.print(); // print the properties of the fastest runner

return 0;
}
```

If we want to keep a table of the runners, we can introduce the vector "member[i]" whose entries are objects of the "runner" class. The following main function contained in the file *runner_fast.cc* reads the properties of the runners from the keyboard, keeps track of the fastest runner, and prints the fastest runner in the end:

```cpp
#include <iostream>
#include <string>
#include "cl_runner.h"

using namespace std;
```

```
int main()
{
runner member[200]; // will hold up to 200 runners

runner fastest; // introduce the fastest runner
double fast_time = fastest.get_time(); // default time
bool more = true;
string answer;
int Ic = 0; // member counter

while (more)
{
Ic=Ic+1;
member[Ic].read(); // enter the next runner
member[Ic].print(); // print the properties of the next runner
if(member[Ic].get_time() < fast_time)
    {
    fastest = member[Ic];
    fast_time = member[Ic].get_time();
    }

cout << " More runners?  (y/n)"; // inquire for additional runners
getline(cin, answer);
if(answer != "y") more = false;
}

int runners = Ic; // number of runners

cout << endl << " List of runners:" << endl;
cout << " ----------------" << endl;

for(int i=1;i<=runners;i++) member[i].print();

cout << endl << " Fastest runner:" << endl;
cout << " ---------------" << endl;

fastest.print(); // print the properties of the fastest runner

return 0;
}
```

Problems

6.12.1. What is the output of the following code?

```
E = runner();
cout << E.get_name() << endl;
```

6.12.2. Endow the runners with an additional integer field expressing their birth year.

6.12.3. Modify the code "runner" to count the number of countries entered.

6.13   Header files and projects

We want to place the user-defined functions, class declarations, and class member functions in separate source files that can be compiled individually and then linked to form the executable.

Let us assume that a main function uses the "runner" class. In this case, we generate the following three source files.

File "runner_fast.cc" contains the main function:

```
#include <iostream>
#include <string>
#include "cl_runner.h"
using namespace std;

int main()
{
    ...
return 0;
}
```

where the three dots denote additional lines of code.

The header file "cl_runner.h" contains the class definition:

```
#ifndef CL_RUNNER_H
#define CL_RUNNER_H

#include <iostream>
#include <string>
using namespace std;

class runner
{
public:
...
private:
...
};

#endif
```

The source file "cl_runner.cc" contains the class implementation:

```
#include <iostream>
#include <string>
using namespace std;

//--- CLASS DEFINITION

class runner
{
public:
...
private:
...
};

//--- CLASS IMPLEMENTATION

runner::runner()
{
time = 2000.0;
}
...
double runner::get_time() const
{
return time;
}
```

A makefile that compiles separately the main function and the class, and then links the object files to generate the executable is structured as follows:

```
runner_fast:  cl_runner.o runner_fast.o
    c++ -o runner_fast cl_runner.o runner_fast.o
runner_fast.o:  runner_fast.cc
    c++ -c runner_fast.cc
cl_runner.o:  cl_runner.cc cl_runner.h
    c++ -c cl_runner.cc
```

To compile the program and create the executable named "runner_fast", we issue the command:

```
make runner_fast
```

and then hit the <Enter> key.

Note that the "include" statement:

```
#include "cl_runner.h"
```

appears both in the main function and class implementation.

The union of the source files, header files, and the makefile constitutes a project.

Problem

6.13.1. Split the algebra class and main program discussed in Section 6.8 into separate files.

6.14   Inheritance

In C++, we can generate a hierarchy of derived classes that inherit the attributes and functions of their ancestors and are endowed with added features. In this way, the class of equilateral triangles can be derived from the class of all triangles, and the class of roses can be derived from the class of flowers. The class of flowers is the base-class or super-class, and the class of roses is the derived class.

A derived class inherits all functions of the base class except for its constructor and destructor, the members of the assignation (=) class operator, and the inherited function friends. A cynic defines friends as people with common enemies.

As an example, we consider the class of all flowers available in a flower shop, defined by the type (annual or perennial), color, and price. The flower class definition is:

```
#include <iostream>
using namespace std;

//--- FLOWER CLASS DEFINITION

class flower
{
public:
      flower(); // default constructor
      flower(string, string, float); // parametered constructor
      string get_type() const;
      string get_color() const;
      float get_price() const;
      void print() const;
protected:
      string type;
      string color;
      float price;
};
```

The only new feature is that we have replaced the statement:

private:

with the statement:

protected:

in anticipation of inheritance.

The flower class implementation is:

```
//--- FLOWER CLASS IMPLEMENTATION

flower::flower()
{
type = "tulip";
color = "black";
price = 4.99;
}

flower::flower(string ftype, string fcolor, float fprice)
{
type = ftype;
color = fcolor;
price = fprice;
}

string flower::get_type() const
{
return type;
}

string flower::get_color() const
{
return color;
}

float flower::get_price() const
{
return price;
}

void flower::print() const
{
cout << type <<" "<< color <<" "<< "$"<<price << endl;
}
```

Roses are flowers

Next, we define the derived class of roses, which can be either garden or long-stem roses. The rose class definition is:

```
class rose :  public flower
{
public:
  rose(string, string, string, float); // parametered constructor
  void print() const;
private:
  string rose_type;
};
```

Since roses derive from flowers, there is no need to repeat the flower attributes or functions, and we simply add to them. The rose class implementation includes the parameter constructor and the new function print whose name is identical to that of a function in the flower class as an illustration of polymorphism:

```
rose::rose(string ftype, string rtype, string fcolor, float fprice)
{
type = ftype;
rose_type = rtype;
color = fcolor;
price = fprice;
}

void rose::print() const
{
cout << type <<" "<<rose_type<<" "<< color
  <<" "<< "$"<<price << endl;
}
```

Now consider the main program:

```
int main()
{
flower A = flower();
A.print();

flower B = flower("annual", "red", 6.0);
string type=B.get_type();
string color=B.get_color();
float price=B.get_price();
cout << type << " " << color << " flower for $" << price << endl;
rose W = rose("perennial", "garden", "yellow", 9.39);
W.print();
return 0;
}
```

Running the program prints on the screen:

```
tulip black $4.99
annual red flower for $6
perennial garden yellow $9.39
```

Note that a flower uses the flower-class `print` function, and a rose uses the rose-class `print` function.

To further illustrate this distinction, we endow the flower class with the function:

```
void flower::print_price() const
{
cout <<"PRICE: $"<< price << endl;
}
```

and the derived rose class with the same-named function:

```
void rose::print_price() const
{
cout << "OUR PRICE: $" << price << endl;
}
```

We may then state in the main code:

```
flower A = flower();
A.print_price();
rose W = rose("perennial", "garden", "yellow", 9.39);
W.print_price();
```

Running the code produces on the screen:

```
PRICE: $4.99
OUR PRICE: $9.39
```

If we had implemented the `print_price` function only in the flower class and not the `print_price` function in the rose class, the output of the code would have been:

```
PRICE: $4.99
PRICE: $9.39
```

Problems

6.14.1. Introduce the class of countries defined by the host continent, size, population, and official language, and then define the derived class of countries with two official languages.

6.14.2. Introduce the class of polygons defined by their vertices, and then define the derived classes of triangles and quadrilaterals incorporating respective functions that compute the area.

6.15   Pointers and virtual functions

In Section 6.10, we introduced pointers to class members. We can represent a member of the flower class, F, and a member of the rose class, R, with pointers that can be declared and initialized as:

```
flower * pointer = &F;
```

and

```
rose * pointer1 = &R;
flower * pointer2 = &R;
```

If we print `pointer1` and `pointer2`, they will be identical. This example illustrates that a pointer of a derived class is type-compatible with a pointer of its base class.

However, the type-compatibility is a mixed blessing, as the statements:

```
pointer1 -> print();
pointer2 -> print();
```

are *not* equivalent, even though the values of the two pointers are identical! The first statement uses the `print` function of the derived class, whereas the second statement uses the `print` function of the base class. The first statement is equivalent to

```
R.print();
```

whereas the second statement cannot be implemented in terms of R. Thus, if a flower pointer is issued for a rose, use of this pointer deprives us from using rose functions whose names duplicate flower functions.

To make matters worse, we endow the rose class with the function:

```
void rose::print_rtype() const
{
cout << "Rose type:  "<< rose_type << endl;
}
```

and issue the statement:

```
pointer2 -> print_rtype();
```

only to be greeted with the compiler error:

```
'class flower has no member named print_rtype'
```

In contrast, the statement

```
pointer1 -> print_rtype();
```

is perfectly acceptable. Thus, if a flower pointer is issued for a rose, use of this pointer deprives us from using exclusive rose functions.

Virtual functions

A derived class inherits all parental functions. Can a derived class also define, implement, and ultimately override parental functions? The answer is affirmative, thanks to the concept of virtual functions.

In our example, we include in the public section of the flower class the virtual function `print_rtype` implementation:

```
virtual void print_rtype() const {};
```

which renders the statement:

```
pointer2 -> print_rtype();
```

perfectly acceptable. Because `pointer2` points to a rose, when this statement is executed, the function `print_rtype` of the rose class is invoked. Note that we have entered nothing inside the curly brackets of the flower class function `print_rtype`, thus rendering this function idle. Alternatively, we could have stated:

```
virtual void print_rtype() const =0;
```

If instead we include in the public section of the flower the non-virtual function `print_rtype` implementation:

```
void print_rtype() const { };
```

then the statement

```
pointer2 -> print_rtype();
```

will invoke the `print_rtype` function of the flower class, which is idle.

When a virtual function is declared, a v-table is constructed for the class consisting of addresses to the virtual functions for classes and pointers to the functions from each of the objects of the derived class. Whenever a function call is made to the virtual function, the v-table is used to resolve to the function address by way of *dynamic binding*.

Virtual functions exemplify intriguing concepts underlying the notion of object-oriented programming. A class that declares or inherits virtual functions is called a *polymorphic*.

Student tuition

The following code exemplifies the use of virtual functions with a base class of students and two derived classes of resident and non-resident students. For convenience, the class definition and implementation are consolidated. The base class is defined and implemented as:

```
#include <iostream>
using namespace std;

//--- STUDENT CLASS

class student
{
public:
        virtual void payment()=0;
};
```

Note that the base class is endowed with only one idle virtual function, and lacks a constructor. A class with such minimum functionality is called an *abstract base class*.

The resident class is defined and implemented as:

```
//--- RESIDENT CLASS

class resident :  public student
{
public:
    void payment()
    {
    tuition = 2567.65;
    cout << " Resident tuition:   " << tuition << endl;
    };
private:
    float tuition;
};
```

Note that the resident class is endowed with only one function and lacks a constructor.

The non-resident class is defined and implemented as:

```
//--- NONRESIDENT CLASS

class nonresident :  public student
{
public:
void payment()
    {
    tuition = 4879.99;
    cout << " Non-resident tuition:   " << tuition << endl;
    };
private:
    float tuition;
};
```

Note that the non-resident class is also endowed with only one function and lacks a constructor.

The following main program declares students and pays their tuition directly or through pointers:

```
int main()
{
resident R;
R.payment();

nonresident N;
N.payment();
```

```
                    student * pntR = &R;
                    student * pntN = &N;

                    pntR->payment();
                    pntN->payment();

                    return 0;
                    }
```

Running this program prints on the screen:

```
            Resident tuition:  2567.65
            Non-resident tuition:  4879.99
            Resident tuition:  2567.65
            Non-resident tuition:  4879.99
```

Note that pointers of residents and non-residents are defined on the base student class. Thanks to the virtual function declaration, these pointers assume a proper identity when interacting with functions of their respective derived class.

Problems

6.15.1. Add to the student, resident, and nonresident classes constructors to specify the student names.

6.15.2. Add to the student, resident, and nonresident classes a second virtual function of your choice.

6.16   Class templates

In Section 4.10, we defined function templates with the objective of consolidating code. If a function operates on integers and the same function operates on real numbers, we can consolidate the two functions into a template that does both. Class templates are designed with a similar goal in mind.

In Section 6.11, we discussed the class of points in the xy plane. The following code generalizes this class into a template. The class definition is:

```
    /*--------------------------------------------------
    This program illustrates the use of class templates
    ---------------------------------------------------*/

    #include <iostream>
    using namespace std;
```

```
//--- CLASS DEFINITION

template <class T>
class point
{
public:
     point();    // default constructor
     point(T value_x, T value_y);
     T get_x() const;
     T get_y() const;
     void print() const;
     void move(T dx, T dy);
     point<T> operator + (point<T>); // overload +
private:
     T x;
     T y;
};
```

Note that the class definition includes the overloading of the + operator. Replacing T with a regular data type such as double yields familiar code.

The class implementation is:

```
template <class T>
point<T>::point(T value_x, T value_y)
{
x = value_x;
y = value_y;
}

template <class T>
T point<T>::get_x() const
{
return x;
}

template <class T>
T point<T>::get_y() const
{
return y;
}

template <class T>
void point<T>::print() const
{
cout << x << " " << y << endl;
}

template <class T>
```

```
void point<T>::move(T dx, T dy)
{
x=x+dx; y=y+dy;
}

// overload + :

template <class T>
point<T> point<T>::operator + (point<T> param)
{
point<T> add;
add.x = x + param.x;
add.y = y + param.y;
return add;
}
```

The following main code uses the point class template:

```
int main()
{
point<int> A = point<int>(1, 2);
A.print();
A.move(4, -5);
A.print();

point<float>B(3.2, 4.9);
cout << B.get_x() << " " << B.get_y() << endl ;

point<string> C("day", "young");
C.print();
C.move("s","ster");
C.print();

point<string> D("viet", "kambo");
point<string> E("nam", "dia");
point<string> F=D+E;
F.print();

return 0;
}
```

Running the code produces on the screen:

```
1 2
5 -3
3.2 4.9
day young
days youngster
vietnam kambodia
```

Problems

6.16.1. Generalize the algebra class discussed in Section 6.8 into a template.

6.16.2. Generalize the class of points in a plane discussed in Section 6.11 into a template.

Graphics Programming with VOGLE

7

The basic Input/Output system (BIOS) installed on the motherboard by the manufacturer and the kernel of the operating system (OS) installed on the hard drive are able to display characters on the screen, but are unable to draw pictures. Additional graphics libraries are needed to generate icons and menus, display windows, and launch graphics applications. These graphics libraries are built on a succession of layers.

On Unix systems, the X11 server provides graphics functionality at the lowest possible level. Higher-level libraries provide application programming interfaces (API) in the form of C or C++ code that can be compiled and linked statically or dynamically with user-defined functions. For example, an API may encapsulate functions to generate a window on the desktop, or monitor the mouse and keyboard.

The Very Ordinary Graphics Learning Environment implemented in the VOGLE library for the X11 server is ideally suited for learning the fundamentals of graphics programming and developing small or private applications.

The VOGLE library is written in C and includes FORTRAN 77 and PASCAL interfaces.[1] Drivers are available for a variety of devices to generate graphs and images suitable for display and printing in black and white or color format.

The source code, the compiled binary file for several Unix systems including the *cygwin* environment running inside Windows, and the necessary header files, can be downloaded from this book's Internet site. An informative reference manual can be found at `http://dehesa.freeshel.org/vogle`. A summary of the VOGLE functions is given in Appendix B.

To run VOGLE on Windows, we launch the cygwin environment by clicking on the cygwin shell icon, and then issue the command:

```
startx
```

---

[1]Implementation in C++ is possible thanks to a header file written by Tim Love of Cambridge, U.K.

■

At the time the VOGLE project get under way, the wife of one of the developers was working for a library and an article about a group of European Zoologists who came out to study Australian native animals happened to cross her desk. Unfortunately, the title of this worthy piece of science is currently lost, however, by way of summary, we are sad to report that the intention of the investigation (at least originally) was to demonstrate that since Australian native animals are, in a sense, less evolved than their European counterparts they are also less intelligent. It happened that one of the animals helping the scientists in their investigations was an echidna and it was given the task of learning a maze on the basis of receiving a reward by pushing a button on a machine at the other end of the maze. Having demonstrated that it was quite capable of learning a maze, the scientists were then faced with finding the answer to the next question. If we take the food out of the machine, how will the echidna react? Will it be dumb enough to keep running through the maze again and again? What will it do? So they took the food out of the machine. And this is what happened. The echidna ran through the maze, pushed the button on the machine, no food came out. The echidna pushed the button again, again no food came out. It then turned and looked up at the observers giving them what was described as a "filthy look" and proceeded not only to destroy the food dispensing machine, but to introduce the observers to how one can traverse a maze in a straight line by pushing the walls down! It is to the memory of this echidna (which we dubbed Eric H. Echidna), this software is duly dedicated.

Testimonial: Taken from the VOGLE Internet site dedicated to Eric H. Echidna (`http://bund.com.au/dgh/eric`).

■

This will start the X11 server that allows us to display VOGLE graphics on the Windows desktop.

In this chapter, we demonstrate the usage of the VOGLE library and discuss simple and advanced applications that illustrate the basic concepts of graphics programming, including animation and user control by the mouse and keyboard. Further examples can be found in the directory *examples* of the VOGLE distribution. A extensive collection of applications in Computational Fluid Dynamics (CFD) through FORTRAN 77 code can be found in the library CFDLAB; see `http://dehesa.freeshel.org/CFDLAB`

7.1 Compilation

To compile a C++ program named *oliver.cc* residing in a certain directory of a Linux system, we compose the makefile:

```
oliver:  oliver.cc
        c++ -o oliver oliver.cc -lX11 VOGLE/vogle_linux_ansi.a
```

and issue the command:

```
make oliver
```

The compiler options shown in the second line of the makefile have the following meanings:

- The option -o oliver requests that the binary executable file named "oliver" be generated after compilation.

- The option -lX11 requests that the library *libX11.so* be linked with the object file of the oliver.cc code when producing the executable.

  More generally, the compiler option -l*pindos* requests that a library named *libpindos.a* or *libpindos.so* be linked with the object of the source code. The suffix "a" denotes an archival static library, and the suffix "so" denotes a dynamically shared object. The search directories during linking include several standard system directories listed in the system archive *liblibrary.a*

- The entry VOGLE/volge_linux_ansi.a requests that the VOGLE library *vogle_ansi.a* be linked with the object file of the oliver.cc code to form the executable.

  It has been assumed that *vogle_ansi.a* has been placed in the subdirectory *VOGLE* of the current working directory. This directory location is arbitrary and can be replaced by any other convenient location, provided that access permissions have been granted.

In summary, the object file of our source code will be linked statically with the VOGLE library and dynamically with the X11 library. An equivalent makefile is:

```
oliver:  oliver.cc
        c++ -o oliver oliver.cc -lX11 -lvogle_linux_ansi -LVOGLE
```

The compiler option -LVOGLE adds the VOGLE directory to the list of library search directories.

In the cygwin environment inside Windows, we use the makefile:

```
oliver:  oliver.cc
        c++ -o oliver oliver.cc VOGLE/vogle_cygwin_ansi.a \
        -lX11 -lm -L/usr/X11R6/lib
```

(a)   (b)

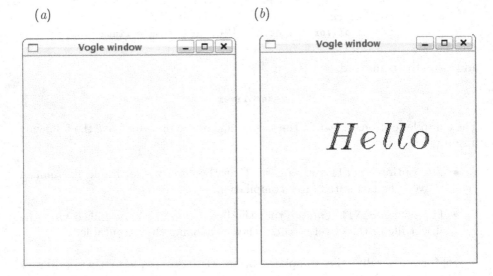

Figure 7.2.1. (a) A blank VOGLE window, and (b) a greeting VOGLE window.

where the backslash is a line continuation mark.

Throughout this chapter, we shall assume that the VOGLE C++ header file *vogle_c++.h* resides in the subdirectory *VOGLE* of the current working directory.

7.2 Getting started with Vogle

The following code contained in the file *window.cc* generates the red graphics window shown in Figure 7.2.1(a):

```
#include "VOGLE/vogle_c++.h"
using namespace std;

int main()
{
prefposition (600,200);      // window position
prefsize(300, 300);          // window size
vinit("X11");                // initialize the screen
color (RED);
clear();
getkey();
return 0;
}
```

The code features the following implementations:

- The graphics window position and size are first defined in screen pixel units.

- The VOGLE device is initialized as "X11" to draw on the screen.

- The background color is set to RED, and the window is cleared. The menu of available colors is given in Appendix B.

- The VOGLE function `getkey` monitors the keyboard; When the window is selected and a key is pressed, the session terminates.

Hello

The following code contained in the file *hello.cc* generates a graphics window and prints the greeting "Hello", as shown in Figure 7.2.1(*b*):

```
/*-------------
VOGLE to greet
-------------*/

#include<iostream>
#include "VOGLE/vogle_c++.h"

using namespace std;

int main()
{

//--- Graphics window position and size in pixel units:

prefposition (600,200); // window position
prefsize (300, 300); // window size

//--- Initialize graphics device to be the screen:

vinit("X11");
color (YELLOW);
clear();

//--- Move to a position defined by default coordinates
//--- ranging from -1 to 1 in the x and y direction

move2 (-0.4, 0.0);

//--- Prepare to write:
```

```
color(BLACK);
font("/tmp/hfonts/times.ib");
textsize(0.4,0.4);

//--- Draw a string:

drawstr("Hello");

//--- Press key to finish:

getkey();
vexit();

return 0;
}
```

The code features the following new implementations:

- The *move2* function moves the pen to a point specified by the coordinates. By default, the horizontal and vertical coordinates x and y vary from -1 to 1.

- The text color and font are selected, the text size is defined, and a string of characters is drawn using the **textstr** VOGLE function. The font files are located in the */tmp/hfonts* directory.

Fonts

The *hfont* directory containing the fonts should be copied from the directory *07/VOGLE* of the software distribution accompanying this book to the */tmp* directory of the operating system. Because all users have "read" and "write" permissions for this directory, they do not have to buy gifts for the system administrator. However, because this directory is routinely cleaned, the font directory must be periodically recopied.

The menu of available fonts includes the following:

```
astrology   futura.m    greek      math.upp     symbolic   times.r
cursive     gothic.eng  japanese   meteorology  times.g    times.rb
cyrillic    gothic.ger  markers    music        times.i
futura.l    gothic.ita  math.low   script       times.ib
```

The suffix *i* stands for italic, *b* stands for bold, *r* stands for roman, and *l* stands for low.

Graphics files

To generate a file containing the graphics, instead of initializing the graphics device to X11, we initialize it to a different device. Postscript files are generated by choosing the devices:

> postscript   ppostscript   cps   pcps

where the prefix "p" stands for "portrait" and the prefix "c" stands for "color". The name of the graphics file is defined by inserting the vogle command:

```
voutput ("filename");
```

where *filename* is a chosen graphics file name. If we do not include this statement, the postscript file will be printed on the screen as a text.

For example, to generate a postscript graphics file named *hello.ps*, we replace the statement `vinit("X11")` with the two statements:

```
voutput ("hello.ps");
vinit("pcps");
```

written in this particular order. After execution, the file *hello.ps* will appear in the current directory.

VOGLE allows us to initialize the graphics device to one type, and then change it to a different type, as will be discussed in later sections. This feature allows us to draw a graph on the screen and, if approved, print it in a graphics file.

The postscript file can be transformed into an encapsulated postscript (eps) file using, for example, the *ps2epsi* facility in Unix. The eps file may then be inserted in a document, as was done in the typesetting of this book.

World coordinates

In the default screen coordinates, the horizontal and vertical variables x and y vary in the range $(-1, 1)$ over the graphics window. To change the screen coordinates into world coordinates that vary over a specified range, we use the *ortho2* function.

The following code implemented in the file *elaiolado.cc* introduces world coordinates, and then prints and underlines olive oil in Greek:

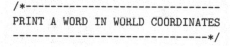

```
/*--------------------------------
PRINT A WORD IN WORLD COORDINATES
------------------------------*/
```

```
#include "VOGLE/vogle_c++.h"
using namespace std;

int main()
{
prefposition (600,200);          // window position
prefsize (300, 300);             // window size
vinit("X11");                    // initialize on the screen
color (YELLOW);                  // background color
clear();                         // clear the screen

ortho2 (0.0,2.0, 0.0,6.0);       // world coordinates for x and y

color(RED);                      // print the word
move2(0.1, 3.0);
font("/tmp/hfonts/greek");
textsize(0.3,0.9);
drawstr("Elaiolado");

move2(0.1,3.0);                  // underline the word
draw2(1.6,3.0);

//--- Press key to finish:

getkey();
vexit();
return 0;
}
```

In this code, the "move to"(move2) and "draw to" (draw2) Vogle functions have been used to move the pen lifted or pressed down. The generated graphics window is shown in Figure 7.2.2(a).

Shapes

The following code contained in the file *shapes.cc*, adapted from an example given in the Vogle distribution, illustrates the use of further Vogle drawing functions:

```
/*------------------------------------------------
DRAW A VARIETY OF SHAPES USING VOGLE FUNCTIONS
-------------------------------------------------*/

#include "VOGLE/vogle_c++.h"
using namespace std;
```

(a)   (b)

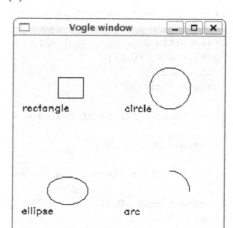

Figure 7.2.2. (a) A VOGLE window printing and underlining a Greek word in world
    coordinates. (b) A VOGLE window with several shapes created by changing
    the viewport.

```
int main()
{
prefposition (600,200); // window position
prefsize (300, 300); // window size
vinit("X11"); // initialize on the screen
color (BLACK);
clear();

ortho2 (-1.0,1.0, -1.0,1.0);

//--- Prepare to write:

font("/tmp/hfonts/futura.m");
textsize(0.2,0.2);

//--- Define a viewport in the top left corner and draw a rectangle:

viewport(-1.0, 0.0, 0.0, 1.0);

move2(-0.9, -0.5); /* write out a heading */
color(MAGENTA);
drawstr("rectangle");
rect(-0.2, -0.2, 0.3, 0.2);
```

```
//--- Define a viewport in the top right corner and draw a circle:

viewport(0.0, 1.0, 0.0, 1.0);
move2(-0.9, -0.5);
color(BLUE);
drawstr("circle");

//--- draw a circle of radius 0.4 centered at the point (0.0, 0.0)

circle(0.0, 0.0, 0.4);

//--- Define a viewport in the bottom left corner and draw an ellipse:

viewport(-1.0, 0.0, -1.0, 0.0);
move2(-0.9, -0.5);
color(GREEN);
drawstr("ellipse");

/* To draw an ellipse, we change the aspect ratio so it is no longer
equal to one and call circle.  In this case we use ortho2 to make
the square viewport appear rectangular.

The call to pushmatrix saves the current viewing transformation.
After the ortho2 is done, we restore the current viewing
transformation with a call to popmatrix.  Otherwise everything
after the call to ortho would come out looking squashed as the
world aspect ratio is no longer 1.  */

pushmatrix();
ortho2(-1.0, 1.0, -1.0, 2.0);
circle(0.0, 0.5, 0.4);
popmatrix();

//--- Define a viewport in the bottom right corner and draw an arc:

color(RED);
viewport(0.0, 1.0, -1.0, 0.0);
move2(-0.9, -0.5);
drawstr("arc");

/* Draw an arc centered at (0.0, 0.0), radius of 0.4.  The start
angle is 0.0 and the end angle is 90 degrees.  */

arc(0.0, 0.0, 0.4, 0.0, 90.0);

//--- Done:

getkey();
```

```
vexit();

return 0;
}
```

Figure 7.2.2(*b*) shows the generated graphics window. We see that the *viewport* function combined with the *pushmatrix* and *popmatrix* functions considerably facilitates the drawing of composite shapes.

VOGLE distribution codes

The VOGLE distribution contains the following C programs: *trivial.c text.c, simple.c, slant.c, shapes.c, poly.c, views.c, circtxt.c, moretxt.c, getstr.c, jtext.c, lstyles.c, curves.c, patches.c, balls.c, objvws.c, world.c, cube.c, licosa.c, tetra.c, loc.c, lcube.c, beer.c, teapot.c.*

These codes have been copied into the directory *07/VOGLE_C_examples* of the software distribution accompanying this book. Translation into C++ is both instructive and straightforward.

Problems

7.2.1. Generate a VOGLE window and print a word of your choice using a font and color of your choice.

7.2.2. Generate a VOGLE window and draw the outline of a musical instrument or your choice working in world coordinates.

7.2.3. Generate a VOGLE window and paint different colors at the four quadrants.

7.2.4. Translate into C++ a VOGLE distribution code of your choice.

7.3   Animation

To perform animation, we use two memory spaces holding the graphics, one called the *back buffer* and the second called the *primary* or *active buffer*. The computer displays the content of the primary buffer, and then the two buffers are swapped in a process dubbed *double buffering*.

A rotating polygon

The following code contained in the file *poly_2d.cc* displays a rotating polygon in animation:

```
/*--------------------------------
Animation of a rotating polygon
using VOGLE
---------------------------------*/

#include<iostream>
#include<cmath>
#include "VOGLE/vogle_c++.h"
using namespace std;

int main()
{
//--- Window plotting limits:

float xmin=0.0; float xmax=1.0; // plotting limits
float ymin=0.0; float ymax=1.0;
float xmarg = 0.2*(xmax-xmin); // plotting margins
float ymarg = 0.2*(ymax-ymin);

//--- Polygon variables:

const int n = 5; // number of vertices
float points[n][2]; // plotting array
float omega = 0.1; // angular velocity
float t=0; // time
float Dt = 0.01; // time step
float xc_rot = 0.5; // rotation center
float yc_rot = 0.5; // rotation center

//--- Initial polygon vertices:

float x[n] = {0.80, 0.90, 0.90, 0.80, 0.80};
float y[n] = {0.50, 0.50, 0.88, 0.88, 0.50};

//--- Prepare the graphics:

prefposition (500,100); // window position
prefsize (300, 300); // window size
char device[]="X11"; // initialize on the screen
vinit(device);

//--- Define the plotting units

ortho2 (xmin-xmarg, xmax+xmarg, ymin-ymarg, ymax+ymarg);

//--- Polygon plotting option:

bool fill = true; // fill the polygon
polyfill (fill);
```

```
//--- Animation loop:

backbuffer(); // draw in the back buffer

repeat:

color(BLUE);
clear();

float dot = omega*Dt;
float cs = cos(dot);
float sn = sin(dot);

//--- Rotate the polygon by the angle dot around the rotation center:

for (int i=0; i<n; i++)
   {
   float xtemp = x[i]-xc_rot;
   float ytemp = y[i]-yc_rot;
   x[i] = xtemp*cs + ytemp*sn + xc_rot;
   y[i] = -xtemp*sn + ytemp*cs + yc_rot;
   points[i][0]=x[i];
   points[i][1]=y[i];
   }

//--- Paint the polygon:

color (RED);
poly2 (n,points);

//--- Swap the buffers:

swapbuffers();

//--- check the keyboard:

char kbd = char(checkkey()); // any key pressed?

//--- If s is pressed, wait for another key:

if(kbd == 's')
{
char kbd1 = char(getkey());
}

//--- If q is pressed, quit:

if(kbd == 'q')
```

(a)   (b)

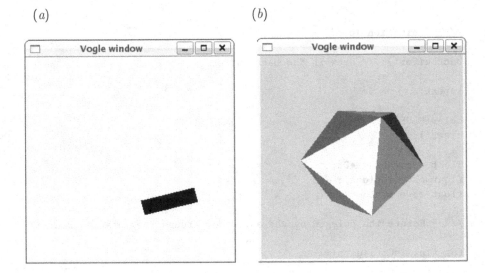

Figure 7.3.1. Snapshot of (a) an animated rotating polygon produced by the code *poly_2d*, and (b) icosahedron produced by the code *licosa*.

```
{
vexit();
exit(1);
}

t=t+Dt; // update time

goto repeat;

//--- Done

return 0;
}
```

Figure 7.3.1(a) shows a snapshot of the animation. The code features the following implementations:

- When the cursor is on the graphics window and the "q" key is pressed, the execution terminates.

- When the cursor is on the graphics window and the "s" key is pressed, the execution halts and resumes when another key is pressed.

We see that only a handful of simple graphics commands are necessary to program animation, and this is generally true for most applications. However, in Chapter 8 we will see that the menu of available graphics functions and system dependencies increases considerably with the size and sophistication of the graphics library.

Interactive drawing of an icosahedron

An icosahedron is a polyhedron with twenty triangular faces defined by twelve unique vertices. The mapping of faces to vertices is mediated through a connectivity table.

The following code contained in the file *licosa.cc* and adapted from an example given in the VOGLE distribution draws an icosahedron and uses the mouse and keyboard to implement interactive rotation and translation:

```
include<iostream>
#include "VOGLE/vogle_c++.h"

#define TRANS 0.06

void drawshape(int fill);

//--- main

int main()
{
char device[10];
float x, y, tdir = TRANS;
int but, nplanes;
int i;

//--- Initiate the graphics window:

prefposition(50, 50);
prefsize(300, 300);
vinit("X11");
nplanes = getdepth(); // color depth
window(-1.0, 1.0, -1.0, 1.0, -1.0, 1.0);
lookat(0.0, 0.0, 2.1, 0.0, 0.0, 0.0, 0.0);
textsize(0.15, 0.3);
backface(1);
backbuffer();

//--- Green color map:

for (i=1; i<=20; i++)
{
mapcolor(i, 20, 20+i*10, 20);
}
```

```
//--- Loop indefinitely:

while((but=slocator(&x, &y)) != 44)

{
pushmatrix();
rotate(120.0 * x, 'y');
rotate(120.0 * y, 'x');
color(BLACK);
clear();
color(20);
drawshape(1);
if (nplanes == 1)
  {
  drawshape(0);
  }
popmatrix();
swapbuffers();

//--- Check the keyboard:

switch (but = checkkey())
{
  case 'p':
        voutput("licosa.ps");
        vnewdev("postscript");
        pushmatrix();
        rotate(100.0 * x, 'y');
        rotate(100.0 * y, 'x');
        color(BLACK);
        clear();
        drawshape(1);
        if (nplanes == 1)
        drawshape(0);
        popmatrix();
        vnewdev(device);
        break;
    case 'x':
        translate(tdir, 0.0, 0.0);
        break;
    case 'y':
        translate(0.0, tdir, 0.0);
        break;
    case 'z':
        translate(0.0, 0.0, tdir);
        break;
    case '-':
        tdir = -tdir;
```

```
            break;
    case '+':
            tdir = TRANS;
            break;
    case 27:   /* ESC */
    case 'q':
            vexit();
            exit(0);
    }
}

//--- Done:

vexit();

return(0);
}

//--- vertices

static float xyz[12][3]
    = {
    {0.000000, 0.000000, 1.0 },
    {0.809017, -0.587785, 0.500000 },
    {0.809017, 0.587785, 0.500000 },
    {-0.309017, 0.951057, 0.500000 },
    {-1.000000, 0.000000, 0.500000 },
    {-0.309017, -0.951057, 0.500000 },
    {1.000000, 0.000000, -0.500000 },
    {0.309017, 0.951057, -0.500000 },
    {-0.809017, 0.587785, -0.500000 },
    {-0.809017, -0.587785, -0.500000 },
    {0.309017, -0.951057, -0.500000 },
    {0.000000, 0.000000, -1.0 }
    };

//--- connectivity table

static int ncon[20][3]
    = {
    {1, 2, 3},{1, 3, 4},{1, 4, 5},{1, 5, 6},
    {1, 6, 2},{2, 7, 3},{3, 8, 4},{4, 9, 5},
    {5, 10, 6},{6, 11, 2},{7, 8, 3},{8, 9, 4},
    {9, 10, 5},{10, 11, 6},{11, 7, 2},{7, 12, 8},
    {8, 12, 9},{9, 12, 10},{10, 12, 11},{11, 12, 7}
    };

//--- drawshape
```

```
void drawshape(int fill)

{
polyfill(fill);

if (!fill)

  for (int i=0; i<20; i++)
  {
  if (fill)
    {
    color(i+1);
    }

  makepoly();
  move(xyz[ncon[i][0]-1][0], xyz[ncon[i][0]-1][1], xyz[ncon[i][0]-1][2]);
  draw(xyz[ncon[i][1]-1][0], xyz[ncon[i][1]-1][1], xyz[ncon[i][1]-1][2]);
  draw(xyz[ncon[i][2]-1][0], xyz[ncon[i][2]-1][1], xyz[ncon[i][2]-1][2]);
  closepoly();
  }
}
```

Figure 7.3.1(b) shows a snapshot of the animation. The code features the following implementations:

- A function is used to draw the icosahedron based on hard-coded data for the vertex coordinates and a connectivity table relating faces to vertices.

- When the "p" key is pressed, a postscript file of the current shape is produced.

- When the "x", "y", or "z" key is pressed, the icosahedron translates by a specified shift in the respective directions. When the "-" key is pressed, the direction of translation is reversed, and when the "+" key is pressed, the direction of translation is reinstated.

- When either the Escape or the "q" key is pressed, the execution terminates.

Problems

7.3.1. Modify the polygon animation code to implement a rotating regular hexagon.

7.3.2. Modify the polygon animation code to insert a second rotating polygon.

7.3.3. Translate into C++ a Vogle distribution animation code of your choice.

7.4 Plotting a line

Next, we build a code that draws the graph of a line in the xy plane defined by a group of data points. The code will offer an option for drawing markers at the data points, including circles, squares, and diamonds. The application will employ two ancillary functions that use basic VOGLE commands to move the cursor and draw straight segments:

1. Function draw_marker_2d draws a marker at a specified location.

2. Function draw_line_2d draws the graph of a line defined by a group of points inside a specified window.

We will discuss these functions individually and then illustrate their usage in a plotting code.

Function draw_marker_2d

The implementation of the marker drawing function draw_marker_2d is:

```
/*------------------------------------------------
void draw_marker_2d

Draw a symbol at the location (x, y) according
to the value of the integer variable marker:

marker:

0 :  no symbol
1 :  circle
2 :  triangle
3 :  square
4 :  diamond
5 :  dot
---------------------------------------------- */

#include "VOGLE/vogle_c++.h"

using namespace std;

void draw_marker_2d (float x, float y, int marker
                ,float xmin, float xmax
                ,float ymin, float ymax)
  {
float xrange = xmax-xmin; // plotting range
float yrange = ymax-ymin;

float xsize = 0.02*xrange; // marker size
```

```
    float ysize = 0.02*yrange;

    // move to the point:

    move2(x, y);

    if (marker==1)
         circle (x,y,0.005*xrange) ; // circle

    else if(marker==2) // triangle
         {
         rmove2 (0.0,0.5*ysize);
         rdraw2 (-0.4*xsize,-0.75*ysize);
         rdraw2 (0.8*xsize,0.0);
         rdraw2 (-0.4*xsize,0.75*ysize);
         rmove2 (0.0,-0.5*ysize);
         }

    else if(marker==4) // square
    {
         rmove2 (0.25*xsize,0.25*ysize);
         rdraw2 (-0.5*xsize,0.0);
         rdraw2 (0.0, -0.5*ysize);
         rdraw2 (0.5*xsize,0.0);
         rdraw2 (0.0, 0.5*ysize);
         rmove2 (-0.25*xsize,-0.25*ysize);
         }

    else if(marker==5)
         {
         rmove2 (0.0,0.5*ysize);
         rdraw2 (-0.5*xsize,-0.5*ysize);
         rdraw2 (0.5*xsize,-0.5*ysize);
         rdraw2 (0.5*xsize,0.5*ysize);
         rdraw2 (-0.5*xsize,0.5*ysize);
         rmove2 (0.0,-0.5*ysize);
         }

    else if(marker==6)
         circle (x,y,0.00001*xrange);
    }
```

Note that the "move to"(move2) and "draw to" (draw2) VOGLE functions have been used to move the pen lifted up or pressed down.

Function draw_line_2d

The implementation of the line drawing function draw_line_2d is:

```
/*---------------------------------------------
void draw_line_2d

Draw a polygonal line defined by a set of points
and put symbols at the points

If a segment crosses the boundaries of the plotting
window, interpolate for the crossing point

SYMBOLS
--------
n:   number of points to be plotted
x,y:  coordinates of the points
xmin,xmax:  x plotting window
ymin,ymax:  y plotting window
tol:  tolerance for window crossing
Icheck:  1 to perform crossing checks
------------------------------------------- */

#include "VOGLE/vogle_c++.h"

using namespace std;

void draw_line_2d (int n, float x[], float y[]
                 ,float xmin, float xmax
                 ,float ymin, float ymax, int Icheck)
{
float xrange = xmax-xmin;
float yrange = ymax-ymin;
float xp, yp, xpp, ypp; // temporary positions
float xint, yint; // interpolation variables
float tol=0.000001; // tolerance

//--- Move to the first point:

xp=x[0]; yp=y[0];
move2 (xp,yp);

/*-----------------------------------------
If both the current and the previous point
lie outside the window, do not draw the line
If a segment crosses the borders, draw up to
the interpolated crossing points
----------------------------------------- */

for (int i=1; i<n; i++)   // closes at sousami
{
xpp=x[i-1];
ypp=y[i-1];
```

```
xp=x[i];
yp=y[i];

if(Icheck==1) // perform crossing checks
{

  if( (xp>xmax && xpp>xmax) // both points are
  ||(xp<xmin && xpp<xmin) // outside the plotting
  ||(yp>ymax && ypp>ymax) // window:  move
  ||(yp<ymin && ypp<ymin)) // but do not draw
  {
  move2 (xp,yp); continue; // consider the next value of i
  }

  float crossxmax = (xp-xmax)*(xpp-xmax); // crossing test

  if (crossxmax<tol)
  {
  xint = xmax-0.001;
  yint = ((xint-xpp)*yp-(xint-xp)*ypp)/(xp-xpp);
  if(xpp>=xmax)
    {
    xpp = xint; ypp = yint;
    move2 (xpp,ypp);
    }
  else
    {
    xp=xint; yp=yint;
    }
  }

  float crossxmin = (xp-xmin)*(xpp-xmin);

  if (crossxmin<tol)
  {
  xint = xmin+0.001;
  yint = ((xint-xpp)*yp-(xint-xp)*ypp)/(xp-xpp);
  if(xpp<=xmin)
    {
    xpp = xint; ypp = yint;
    move2 (xpp,ypp);
    }
  else
    {
    xp=xint; yp=yint;
    }
  }

  float crossymax = (yp-ymax)*(ypp-ymax);
```

```
      if (crossymax<tol)
      {
      yint = ymax-0.001;
      xint= ((yint-ypp)*xp-(yint-yp)*xpp)/(yp-ypp);
      if(ypp>=ymax)
          {
        xpp = xint; ypp = yint;
        move2 (xpp,ypp);
          }
      else
          {
        xp=xint; yp=yint;
          }
      }

      float crossymin = (yp-ymin)*(ypp-ymin);

      if (crossymin<tol)
      {
      yint = ymin+0.001;
      xint= ((yint-ypp)*xp-(yint-yp)*xpp)/(yp-ypp);
      if(ypp<=ymin)
          {
        xpp = xint; ypp = yint;
        move2 (xpp,ypp);
          }
      else
          {
        xp=xint; yp=yint;
          }
      }
      }

   draw2 (xp,yp);

   }    // sousami

   }
```

An important feature of the code is that, if a plotted line exits the plotting window, it is chopped off and the marginal values are computed by linear interpolation.

Code plot_2d_simple

The following code contained in the file *plot_2d_simple.cc* defines and plots data points based on the two functions we have constructed:

```
/*----------------
plot_2d_simple

plot a line
-----------------*/

#include<cmath>
#include "VOGLE/vogle_c++.h"
#include "draw_marker_2d.h"
#include "draw_line_2d.h"

using namespace std;

int main()
{

//--- Define the data :

const int n=512;
float xd[n], yd[n];

for (int i=0; i<n; i++)
{
  xd[i]=-0.3+4.0*(i-1.0)/n;
  yd[i]=0.5+0.3*sin(35.0*xd[i])*exp(xd[i]);
}

//--- Set plotting limits:

float xmin=0.0; float xmax=1.0;
float ymin=0.0; float ymax=1.0;

// Set plotting margins:

float xmarg = 0.2*(xmax-xmin);
float ymarg = 0.2*(ymax-ymin);

//--- Launch the graphics:

prefposition (500,100);
prefsize (500,500);
char device[]="X11"; // initialize on the screen
vinit(device);

ortho2 (xmin-xmarg,xmax+xmarg,ymin-ymarg,ymax+ymarg);
color (YELLOW); // yellow background
clear();

//--- Draw markers at the data points:
```

```
        color (BLACK);
        int marker = 3;

        for(int i=0; i<n; i++)
        {
        if( xd[i]>xmin && xd[i]<xmax && yd[i]>ymin && yd[i]<ymax)
        draw_marker_2d (xd[i],yd[i],marker,xmin,xmax,ymin,ymax);
        }

        //--- Plot the data:

        int Icheck=1;
        draw_line_2d (n,xd,yd,xmin,xmax,ymin,ymax,Icheck);

        //--- Draw a box:

        move2 (xmin,ymin);
        draw2 (xmax,ymin);

        draw2 (xmin,ymin);

        //--- Wait until a key is pressed:

        char kbd = char(getkey());

        return 0;
        }
```

The graphics output of the code is shown in Figure 7.4.1.

Problems

7.4.1. Modify the function *draw_marker_2d* to include an option for drawing (*a*) a solid circle, and (*b*) a filled triangle with a color of your choice.

7.4.2. Modify the code *plot_2d_simple.cc* so that the data points are (*a*) generated in a function, or (*b*) read from a file.

7.4.3. Modify the code *plot_2d_simple.cc* so that the graph is printed in a graphics file.

7.5 A graph with axes

To plot scientific data, we require axes with tick marks, corresponding numerical labels, and axis labels.

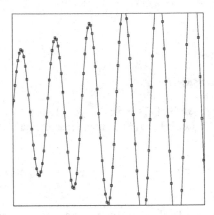

Figure 7.4.1 Graphics display of code *plot_2d_simple* showing a line with markers at the data points.

Function draw_2d_axes

Drawing and formatting axes is done through a sequence of operations for defining and plotting ticks and underlying labels, as implemented in the function *draw_2d_axes.cc*:

```
/*---------------------
draw_2d_axes.cc

Draw axes,
Label axes,
Put labels on the plot
---------------------- */

#include <iostream>
#include <iomanip>
#include <fstream>
#include "VOGLE/vogle_c++.h"

using namespace std;

void draw_axes_2d (float xmin, float xmax // x plotting limits
              ,float ymin, float ymax // y plotting limits
              ,int ntc_x // number of ticks on the x axis
              ,int ntc_y // number of ticks on the y axis
              ,int Ilabel_ax // 1 to label axes; 0 for no labels
              ,int ax_c // axis color
              ,int lb_c // label color
              ,char label_x[] // x-axis label
```

```
                        ,char label_y[] // y-axis label
                        ,char title1[] // first plot title
                        ,char title2[] // second plot title
                        ,char title3[] // third plot title
                        )
{

//--- Prepare:

float xrange = xmax-xmin;
float yrange = ymax-ymin;

float xmargin = 0.1*xrange;
float ymargin = 0.1*yrange;

float rtic_x = xrange/ntc_x; // x tick distance
float rtic_y = yrange/ntc_y; // y tick distance

float tch_x = 0.1*xmargin; // x tick height
float tch_y = 0.1*ymargin ; // y tick height

//--- Draw x and y axes:

color (ax_c);
move2 (xmin,ymin);

draw2 (xmax,ymin);
move2 (xmin,ymin);
draw2 (xmin,ymax);

//--- Print axes labels at the end of the axes:

move2 (xmax+0.5*rtic_x, ymin-0.1*ymargin);
drawstr (label_x);

move2 (xmin-0.8*xmargin, ymax+0.3*ymargin);
drawstr (label_y);

/*---------------------------
Prepare to draw axes ticks
Generate tick labels
Print them in file "xyunit"
Read them as characters into arrays:  xunit, yunit
-------------------------------*/

if(Ilabel_ax==1)
{
ofstream file1;
file1.open("xyunit");
```

```
file1<< setiosflags(ios::fixed | ios::showpoint);
for (int i=0; i<=ntc_x; i++){
float xprint = xmin + i*rtic_x;
file1 << setprecision(3) << setw(6) << xprint << endl;}
for (int i=0; i<=ntc_y; i++){
float yprint = ymin + i*rtic_y;
file1 << setprecision(3) << setw(6) << yprint << endl;}
file1.close();
float textsz_x = 0.3*xmargin; // text size
float textsz_y = 0.3*ymargin; // text size
textsize (textsz_x,textsz_y);
}


ifstream file2;
file2.open("xyunit");
char xunit[6];
char yunit[6];

//--- Draw the x tick marks:

for (int i=0; i<=ntc_x; i++)
{
float xgo = xmin+i*rtic_x;
move2 (xgo, ymin);
rmove2 (0.0, tch_y);
rdraw2 (0.0,-tch_y);

if(Ilabel_ax==1)
  {
  move2(xgo-0.4*rtic_x, ymin-0.4*ymargin);
  file2 >> xunit;
  drawstr (xunit);
  }
}

//--- Draw the y tick marks:

for (int i=0; i<=ntc_y; i++)
{
float ygo = ymin+i*rtic_y;
move2 (xmin, ygo);
rmove2 (tch_x, 0.0);
rdraw2 (-tch_x, 0.0);

if(label_ax==1)
  {
  move2 (xmin-0.9*xmargin,ygo-0.1*ymargin);
  file2 >> yunit;
  drawstr (yunit);
```

```
      }
    }

    //--- Complete the axes box:

    move2 (xmax,ymin);
    draw2 (xmax,ymax);
    draw2 (xmin,ymax);

    //--- Print plot titles:

    color (lb_c);
    xmargin = 0.2*xrange;
    ymargin = 0.2*yrange;

    //--- First plot title:

    font("/tmp/hfonts/futura.l");
    float textsz_x = 0.4*xmargin; // text size
    float textsz_y = 0.4*ymargin; // text size
    textsize (textsz_x,textsz_y);
    move2 (xmin+0.3*xrange,ymax+0.6*ymargin);
    drawstr(title1);

    //--- Second plot title:

    font("/tmp/hfonts/times.ib");
    textsz_x = 0.35*xmargin; // text size
    textsz_y = 0.35*ymargin; // text size
    textsize (textsz_x,textsz_y);
    move2 (xmin+0.3*xrange,ymax+0.4*ymargin);
    drawstr(title2);

    //--- Third plot title:

    font("/tmp/hfonts/times.i");
    textsz_x = 0.30*xmargin; // text size
    textsz_y = 0.30*ymargin; // text size
    textsize (textsz_x,textsz_y);
    move2 (xmin+0.3*xrange,ymax+0.2*ymargin);
    drawstr(title3);

}
```

Code plot_2d

The following program contained in the file *plot_2d.cc* defines and plots data points:

```
*------------------------
plot_2d
Plot a line with axes
------------------------*/

#include<cmath>
#include "VOGLE/vogle_c++.h"
#include "draw_marker_2d.h"
#include "draw_line_2d.h"
#include "draw_axes_2d.h"

using namespace std;

int main()
{

//--- Define the data:

const int n=512;
float xd[n], yd[n];

for (int i=0; i<n; i++)
{
xd[i]=-0.3+4.0*(i-1.0)/n;
yd[i]=0.5+0.3*sin(35.0*xd[i])*exp(xd[i]);
}

//--- Define the plotting parameters:

float xmin=0.0, xmax=1.0; // plotting limits
float ymin=0.0, ymax=1.0; // plotting limits
int ntc_x =10; // number of ticks on the x axis
int ntc_y =10; // number of ticks on the y axis
int Ilabel_ax =1; // 1 to label axes; 0 for no labels
int ax_c = BLACK; // axis color
int lb_c = RED; // label color
char label_x[] = "x-axis"; // x-axis label
char label_y[] = "y-axis"; // y-axis label
char title1[] ="vogle graphics"; // first plot title
char title2[] ="Eric H Echidna"; // second plot title
char title3[] ="Beerware"; // third plot title

//--- Launch the graphics:

float xmarg = 0.2*(xmax-xmin); // plotting margin
float ymarg = 0.2*(ymax-ymin);

prefposition (500,100);
prefsize (500,500);
```

```
char device[]="X11"; // initialize on the screen
vinit(device);
ortho2 (xmin-xmarg,xmax+xmarg,ymin-ymarg,ymax+ymarg);
color (WHITE);
clear();

//--- Draw markers:

color (BLACK);
int marker = 3;

for(int i=0; i<n; i++)
{
if( xd[i]>xmin && xd[i]<xmax
&& yd[i]>ymin && yd[i]<ymax)
draw_marker_2d (xd[i], yd[i], marker
,xmin, xmax,ymin, ymax);
}

//--- Prepare the graph:

color (BLUE);
int Icheck=1;
draw_line_2d (n,xd,yd,xmin,xmax,ymin,ymax,Icheck);

//--- Draw axes:

draw_axes_2d

(xmin,xmax

,ymin,ymax
,ntc_x,ntc_y
,Ilabel_ax // 1 to label axes; 0 for no labels
,ax_c // axis color
,lb_c // label color
,label_x // x-axis label
,label_y // y-axis label
,title1 // first title
,title2 // second title
,title3 // third title
);

//--- Wait to finish:

char kbd = char(getkey());

return 0;
}
```

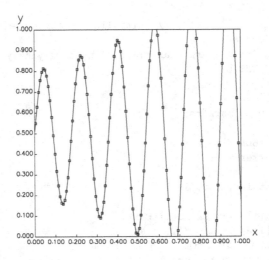

Figure 7.5.1 Graphics display produced by code *plot_2d* showing a line with markers at the data points and complete axes.

The graphics output of the code is shown in Figure 7.5.1.

Preparing a postscript file

Now we would like to see a graph on the screen and, if approved, produce a postscript file that can be sent to a printer or included in a document. VOGLE allows us to do this efficiently by repeating the graph with "postscript" as the output device and a specified file name as the recipient. The necessary modifications are shown in the following code:

```
/*------------------------
plot_2d
Plot a function with axis
and generate a postscript file
------------------------*/

#include<iostream>
#include<cmath>
#include "VOGLE/vogle_c++.h"
#include "draw_marker_2d.h"
#include "draw_line_2d.h"
#include "draw_axes_2d.h"
using namespace std;

char kbd;
```

```
int main()
{
float points[4][2];

//--- Define the data to be plotted:

...

//--- Define plotting parameters:

...

//--- Graphics:

float xmarg = 0.2*(xmax-xmin); // plotting margin
float ymarg = 0.2*(ymax-ymin);
int Icheck;

again:

prefposition (500,100);
prefsize (500,500);
vinit ("X11");
short Itry = 0;
short Iplot = 0;

repeat:

ortho2 (xmin-xmarg,xmax+xmarg,ymin-ymarg,ymax+ymarg);
color (YELLOW);
clear();

//--- Repaint the plotting area:

if(Iplot==4 || Iplot==6)
{
points[1][1] = xmin;
points[1][2] = ymin;
points[2][1] = xmax;
points[2][2] = ymin;
points[3][1] = xmax;
points[3][2] = ymax;
points[4][1] = xmin;
points[4][2] = ymax;
poly2 (4,points);
}

//--- draw markers
```

```
...

//--- Prepare the graph:

...

//--- Draw axes:

...

//-------------------------------
if(Itry==1)
{
vexit();
goto again;
};
//-------------------------------

cout << "Press p to print a postscript file" << endl;
cout << " any other key to finish" << endl;
kbd = char(getkey());

if(kbd =='p')
   {
   char outfile[1];
   cout << " Please enter the name of the postscript file " <<endl;
   cin >> outfile;
   cout << "Please enter:" << endl << endl;
   cout <<" 1 for a black/white plot" << endl;
   cout <<" 2 for a black/white plot in portrait" << endl;
   cout <<" 3 for a color plot" << endl;
   cout <<" 4 for a color plot with background color" << endl;
   cout <<" 5 for a color plot in portrait" << endl;
   cout <<" 6 for a color plot in portrait with background color" << endl;
   short Iplot;
   cin >> Iplot;

   voutput (outfile);

   if(Iplot==1) vnewdev("postscript");
   if(Iplot==2) vnewdev("ppostscript");
   if(Iplot==3) vnewdev("cps");
   if(Iplot==4) vnewdev("cps");
   if(Iplot==5) vnewdev("pcps");
   if(Iplot==6) vnewdev("pcps");

   Itry = 1;
   goto repeat;
   }
```

```
    return 0;
    }
```

The three dots indicate previously listed blocks of code.

When the graph is drawn on the screen, the program waits for a key to be pressed *while the cursor is on the graphics window.* When the "q" key is pressed, the program issues a prompt for postscript drawing options and file name. If any other key is pressed, the execution quits.

Problems

7.5.1. Run code *plot_2d* to produce a postscript file containing the graph of a function of your choice.

7.5.2. Modify code *plot_2d* to allow for multiple functions printed on the same graph with different colors.

7.6   Graph animation

As a further application, we discuss a code contained in the file *graph_2d_anm.cc* that animates a specified time-dependent function:

```
/*------------------------
graph_2d_anm.cc

Animate an evolving function
------------------------*/

#include<iostream>
#include<cmath>
#include "VOGLE/vogle_c++.h"
#include "draw_marker_2d.h"
#include "draw_line_2d.h"
#include "draw_axes_2d.h"

using namespace std;

char kbd;

int main()
{
float points[4][2];

//--- Define the data:

const int n=32;
```

```cpp
float xd[n], yd[n]; // data points
float t=0.; // time
float Dt=0.05; // time step

for (int i=0; i<n; i++)
{
xd[i]=(i-1.0)/n; // abscissas
}

//--- Plotting parameters:

float xmin=0.0, xmax=1.0; // plotting limits
float ymin=0.0, ymax=1.0;
int ntc_x =10; // number of ticks on the x axis
int ntc_y =10; // number of ticks on the y axis
int Ilabel_ax =1; // 1 to label axes; 0 for no labels
int ax_c = BLACK; // axis color
int lb_c = RED; // plot label color
char label_x[] = "x"; // x-axis label
char label_y[] = "y"; // y-axis label
char title1[] =" "; // // first plot label
char title2[] =" "; // // second plot label
char title3[] =" ";// // third plot label

//--- Graphics:

float xmarg = 0.2*(xmax-xmin); // plotting margin
float ymarg = 0.2*(ymax-ymin);
int Icheck;

again:

prefposition (500,100);
prefsize (500,500);
vinit ("X11");
backbuffer();
short Itry = 0;
short Iplot = 0;

repeat:

ortho2 (xmin-xmarg,xmax+xmarg,ymin-ymarg,ymax+ymarg);
color (WHITE);

clear();

//--- Repaint the plotting area:

if(Iplot==4 || Iplot==6)
```

```
{
points[1][1] = xmin;
points[1][2] = ymin;
points[2][1] = xmax;
points[2][2] = ymin;
points[3][1] = xmax;
points[3][2] = ymax;
points[4][1] = xmin;
points[4][2] = ymax;

poly2 (4,points);
}

//--- Data:

for (int i=0; i<n; i++)
{
yd[i] = 0.5+ 0.2*sin(6*xd[i]-0.3*t);
}

//--- Markers:

color (BLACK);
int marker = 0;

for(int i=0; i<n; i++)
{
if( xd[i]>xmin && xd[i]<xmax
&& yd[i]>ymin && yd[i]<ymax)
draw_marker_2d (xd[i], yd[i], marker
xmin, xmax,ymin, ymax);
}

//--- Prepare the graph:

color (BLUE);
Icheck=1;
draw_line_2d (n,xd,yd,xmin,xmax,ymin,ymax,Icheck);

//--- Draw draw axes:

draw_axes_2d
(xmin,xmax
,ymin,ymax
,ntc_x,ntc_y
,Ilabel_ax // 1 to label axes; 0 for no labels
,ax_c // axis color
,lb_c // label color
,label_x // x-axis label
```

```
,label_y // y-axis label
,title1 // first plot label
,title2 // second plot label
,title3 // third plot label
);

//----------------------------
if(Itry==1)
{
vexit();
goto again;
};
//----------------------------

swapbuffers();

//--- Check the keyboard:

kbd = char(checkkey());

if(kbd=='q') exit(1); // quit

if(kbd=='s')
{
cout << "Press p to print a postscript file" << endl;
cout << " any other key to finish" << endl;
kbd = char(getkey());
}

if(kbd =='p')
{
char outfile[1];
cout << " Please enter the name of the postscript file " <<endl;
cin >> outfile;
voutput (outfile);

cout << "Please enter:" << endl << endl;
cout <<" 1 for a black/white plot" << endl;
cout <<" 2 for a black/white plot in portrait" << endl;
cout <<" 3 for a color plot" << endl;
cout <<" 4 for a color plot with background color" << endl;
cout <<" 5 for a color plot in portrait" << endl;
cout <<" 6 for a color plot in portrait with background color" << endl;

short Iplot;
cin >> Iplot;

if(Iplot==1) vnewdev("postscript");
if(Iplot==2) vnewdev("ppostscript");
```

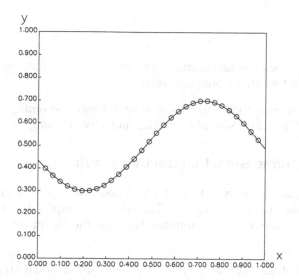

Figure 7.6.1 Snapshot of a traveling wave produced by the VOGLE animation code
graph_2d_anm.cc.

```
if(Iplot==3) vnewdev("cps");
if(Iplot==4) vnewdev("cps");
if(Iplot==5) vnewdev("pcps");
if(Iplot==6) vnewdev("pcps");

Itry = 1;
goto repeat;
}

t = t+Dt;

goto repeat;

//--- Done

return 0;
}
```

A snapshot of the animation is shown in Figure 7.6.1.

When the cursor is on the graphics window and the "q" key is pressed,
the application quits. When the "s" key is pressed, the application stops and
asks whether a postscript file should be printed.

Problems

7.6.1. Modify the code *graph_2d_anm* to display (*a*) a traveling square wave, and (*b*) a traveling triangular wave.

7.6.2. Write a code that animates a rolling wheel containing seven rotating spokes. The wheel should be rolling, not idly spinning.

7.7   Three-dimensional interactive graph

In the most ambitious project, we build a code that plots a group of three-dimensional lines in the *xyz* space. The code will employ two ancillary functions that use basic VOGLE commands to move the cursor and draw straight segments:

1. Function `draw_plot_3d` prepares the three-dimensional graph.

2. Function `plot_3d_trans` transforms the graph by rotating the axes and zooming in and out. In addition, it offers an option for printing and resetting the plotting parameters.

We discuss these two functions individually and then illustrate their use in a plotting code.

Function draw_plot_3d

The implementation of the function `draw_plot_3d` is:

```
/*-----------------------
draw_plot_3d
Draw a three-dimensional plot with axes
------------------------*/

#include<fstream>
#include<iostream>
#include<iomanip>
#include<cmath>
#include "VOGLE/vogle_c++.h"
#include "plot_3d_globals.h"

using namespace std;

void draw_plot_3d ()
{

//--- Prepare:
```

```
float xrange = xmax-xmin;
float yrange = ymax-ymin;
float zrange = zmax-zmin;

float xmargin = 0.1*xrange;
float ymargin = 0.1*yrange;
float zmargin = 0.1*zrange;

ortho (xmin-0.50*xrange, xmax+0.50*xrange
,ymin-0.50*yrange, ymax+0.50*yrange
,zmin-0.50*zrange, zmax+0.50*zrange);

//--- Graphics:

color (bg_c);
clear ();

lookat (vx,vy,vz,0.0,0.0,0.0,twist);
rotate (angx, 'x');
rotate (angy, 'y');
rotate (angz, 'z');
scale (zoom,zoom,zoom);

/*--------------------
Draw axes and labels
--------------------*/

if(Iaxes==1)
{
color (ax_c);
move (xmin,ymin,zmin);
draw (xmax,ymin,zmin);
move (xmin,ymin,zmin);
draw (xmin,ymax,zmin);
move (xmin,ymin,zmin);
draw (xmin,ymin,zmax);

//--- Print axes labels:

font ("/tmp/hfonts/futura.1");

textsize(0.9*xmargin,0.9*ymargin);

float tic_x = xrange/ntc_x; // x tick distance
float tic_y = yrange/ntc_y; // y tick distance
float tic_z = yrange/ntc_y; // z tick distance

move (xmax+0.5*tic_x, ymin-0.1*ymargin,zmin);
drawstr(label_x);
```

```cpp
move (xmin, ymax+0.3*ymargin,zmin-0.8*zmargin);
drawstr(label_y);
move (xmin-0.8*xmargin, ymin, zmax+0.50*tic_z);
drawstr(label_z);

//--- Draw ticks:

if(Itick==1)
{

float tch_x = 0.4*xmargin; // x tick height
float tch_y = 0.4*ymargin; // y tick height
float tch_z = 0.4*zmargin; // z tick height

//--- Produce tick labels:

ofstream file1("xyzunit");

file1<< setiosflags(ios::fixed | ios::showpoint);

const int ndig = 6;
const int nprc = 3;

for (int i=0; i<=ntc_x; i++)
{
float xprint = xmin + i*tic_x;
file1 << setprecision(nprc) << setw(ndig) << xprint << endl;
}
for (int i=0; i<=ntc_y; i++)
{
float yprint = ymin + i*tic_y;
file1 << setprecision(nprc) << setw(ndig) << yprint << endl;
}
for (int i=0; i<=ntc_z; i++)
{
float zprint = zmin + i*tic_z;
file1 << setprecision(nprc) << setw(ndig) << zprint << endl;
}
file1.close();

//--- Read the tick labels

ifstream file2("xyzunit");
char xunit[ndig];
char yunit[ndig];
char zunit[ndig];

float csizex=0.5*xmargin;
float csizey=0.5*ymargin;
```

```
textsize(csizex,csizey);

// ..x axis ticks.../

for (int i=1; i<=ntc_x+1; i++)
{
float xgo = xmin+(i-1.0)*tic_x;
move (xgo, ymin, zmin);
rmove (0.0, tch_x, 0.0); // ticks parallel to the y axis
rdraw (0.0,-tch_x, 0.0);
rmove (0.0, 0.0, tch_x); // ticks parallel to the z axis
rdraw (0.0, 0.0,-tch_x);
file2 >> xunit;
color (lb_c);
move (xgo-csizex, ymin-2.0*csizex, zmin);
if(xunit[0]=='-')
{
move (xgo-2*csizex, ymin-2.0*csizex, zmin);
}

// ..y axis ticks.../

for (int i=1; i<=ntc_y+1; i++)
{
float ygo = xmin+(i-1.0)*tic_y;
move (xmin, ygo, zmin);
rmove ( tch_y, 0, 0); // ticks parallel to the x axis;
rdraw (-tch_y, 0, 0 );
rmove (0, 0, tch_y); // ticks parallel to the z axis;
rdraw (0, 0,-tch_y);
file2 >> xunit;
color (lb_c);
move (xmin-ndig*csizex/2, ygo, zmin);
if(xunit[0]=='-')
{
move (xmin-(ndig/2+1)*csizex, ygo, zmin);
}

// ..z axis ticks.../

for (int i=1; i<=ntc_z+1; i++)
{
float zgo = zmin+(i-1.0)*tic_z;
move (xmin, ymin, zgo);
rmove ( tch_z, 0.0, 0.0); // ticks parallel to the x axis;
rdraw (-tch_z, 0.0, 0.0);
rmove (0.0, tch_z, 0.0); // ticks parallel to the y axis;
rdraw (0.0,-tch_z, 0.0);
```

```
file2 >> zunit;
color (lb_c);
move (xmin-3*csizex, ymin-1.5*ymargin, zgo);
drawstr(zunit);
color (ax_c);
}

} // end of ticks

//--- Plot titles:

color (CYAN);
font ("/tmp/hfonts/futura.m");
textsize (0.8*xmargin,0.8*ymargin);
move (xmin+0.3*xrange,ymax+0.8*ymargin,zmin);
drawstr(title1);
textsize (0.6*xmargin,0.6*ymargin);
move (xmin+0.3*xrange,ymax+0.4*ymargin,zmin);
drawstr(title2);
textsize (0.5*xmargin,0.5*ymargin);
move (xmin+0.3*xrange,ymax+0.0*ymargin,zmin);
drawstr(title3);

} // end of axes

/*----------------
Draw nc curves
----------------*/

color (ln_c);

for(int i=1;i<=nc;i++) // over curves
{
    move (xd[i][1],yd[i][1],zd[i][1]);
    for(int j=2;j<=np[i];j++)
    {
    draw (xd[i][j],yd[i][j],zd[i][j]);
    }
} // over curves

if(Iswap==1) // for animation
{
swapbuffers();
}

//--- Done

return;
}
```

Function plot_3d_trans

The implementation of the function `plot_3d_trans` is:

```
/*-----------------------
plot_3d_trans

transform a 3D plot produced
by draw_plot_3d
------------------------*/

#include<fstream>
#include<iostream>
#include<iomanip>
#include<cmath>
#include "VOGLE/vogle_c++.h"
#include "draw_plot_3d.h"
#include "plot_3d_globals.h"

using namespace std;

void plot_3d_trans ()
{
char outfile[10];
float xaddr,yaddr;
int click;

//--- Initialize:

angx = angx_init;
angy = angy_init;
angz = angz_init;
zoom = zoom_init;

/*--------------------------------
loop over keys and buttons
until a key or button is pressed
--------------------------------*/

again:

//--- Check the keyboard:

char kbd = char(checkkey());

//--- If 'r' is pressed, reset:

if(kbd=='r')
{
```

```
angx = angx_init;
angy = angy_init;
zoom = zoom_init;
color (bg_c);
clear ();
draw_plot_3d();
}

//--- If 'p' is pressed, print in a file:

if(kbd=='p')
{
char outfile[1];
cout << " Please enter the name of the postscript file " <<endl;
cin >> outfile;
cout << "Please enter:" << endl << endl;
cout <<" 1 for a black/white plot" << endl;
cout <<" 2 for a black/white plot in portrait" << endl;
cout <<" 3 for a color plot" << endl;
cout <<" 4 for a color plot with background color" << endl;
cout <<" 5 for a color plot in portrait" << endl;
cout <<" 6 for a color plot in portrait with background color" << endl;
short Iplot;
cin >> Iplot;

voutput (outfile);

if(Iplot==1) vnewdev("postscript");
if(Iplot==2) vnewdev("ppostscript");
if(Iplot==3) vnewdev("cps");
if(Iplot==4) vnewdev("cps");
if(Iplot==5) vnewdev("pcps");
if(Iplot==6) vnewdev("pcps");

draw_plot_3d(); // print in file

vnewdev ("X11"); // redraw on the screen
color (bg_c);
clear ();
draw_plot_3d();

//--- Interactive:

cout << "Press q to quit" << endl;
cout << " p to print a postscript file" << endl;
cout << " r to reset" << endl;
cout << "Place cursor at the center of the graphics window" << endl;
cout << "and then click and move the:" << endl;
cout << " left-mouse button to rotate left-right" << endl;
```

```
cout << " right-mouse button to rotate up-down" << endl;
cout << " both buttons to zoom" << endl;

}

//--- If 'q' is pressed, quit:

if(kbd=='q')
{
vexit();
return;
}

//--- Check the mouse:

click = slocator (&xaddr, &yaddr);

//--- Not pressed:

if(click==0)
{
goto again;
}

//--- Ignore if cursor lies outside the plotting window

if( xaddr<-1 || xaddr > 1||yaddr<-1 || yaddr > 1)
goto again;

//--- Rotate if left button is pressed:

if(click==1)
{
angx = angx_init+200.0*yaddr;
color(bg_c);
clear();
draw_plot_3d();
}

//-- Rotate if right button is pressed:

if(click==4)
{
angy = angy_init+200.0*xaddr;
color(bg_c);
clear();
draw_plot_3d();
}
```

```
//--- Zoom if middle button is pressed:

if(click==2)
{
zoom = zoom_init*(xaddr+1.0);
color(bg_c);
clear();
draw_plot_3d ();
}

goto again;

//--- Done

return;
}
```

Code plot_3d

The following main program contained in the file *plot_3d.cc* defines and plots data points based on the two functions we have constructed:

```
/*------------------------
plot_3d
interactive 3-D plot
------------------------*/

#include<iostream>
#include<cmath>
#include "VOGLE/vogle_c++.h"
#include "draw_plot_3d.h"
#include "plot_3d_trans.h"

using namespace std;

//--- Global variables:

const float pi=3.1415926;

float xmin=0, xmax=1;
float ymin=0, ymax=1;
float zmin=0, zmax=1;
float vx=0.1, vy=0.1, vz=0.5*zmax;
float twist=0;
float angx=0; // rotation angle
float angy=0; // rotation angle
float angz=0; // rotation angle
```

```
float zoom=1.0; // zoom
float angx_init = angx;
float angy_init = angy;
float angz_init = angz;
float zoom_init = zoom;
int ntc_x=4; // number of ticks on the x axis
int ntc_y=4; // number of ticks on the y axis
int ntc_z=4; // number of ticks on the z axis
int bg_c=WHITE; // background color
int ax_c=RED; // axis color
int lb_c=GREEN; // label color
int ln_c=BLUE; // line color
int Iswap=1;
char label_x[]="x"; // x-axis label
char label_y[]="y"; // y-axis label
char label_z[]="z"; // y-axis label
char title1[12]="vogle"; // first title
char title2[12]="plot_3d"; // second title
char title3[12]="beerware"; // third title
int Iaxes; // draw axes?
int Itick; // ticks on axes?
int Itry; // repeat index for animation
int np[21];
float xd[21][128];
float yd[21][128];
float zd[21][128];
int nc=2; // number of curves

//------------main----------------

int main()
{

//--- Preferences:

Iaxes = 1; // draw axes
Itick = 1; // draw ticks
int Itry = 1; // for animation

//--- Initialize the device:

char device[] = "X11";
prefposition (500,100);
prefsize (500,500);
vinit (device);

if(backbuffer()==0)
  {
  vexit();
```

```cpp
    cout << "Device cannot support double-buffering" << endl;
    exit(1);
    }

//--- Generate data:

np[1] = 33;
np[2] = 49;

for(int i=1;i<=nc;i++)
{
for(int j=1;j<=np[i];j++)
{
float phase = (j-1)*2*pi/(np[i]-1);
if(i==1)
  {
  xd[i][j]=0.5+0.6*cos(phase)*sin(phase);
  yd[i][j]=0.5+0.2*cos(phase);
  zd[i][j]=0.2*sin(phase);
  }
else if(i==2)
  {
  xd[i][j]=0.3*cos(phase);
  yd[i][j]=0.4+0.2*cos(phase)*cos(phase);
  zd[i][j]=0.3*sin(phase);
  }
}
}

//--- Plot:

draw_plot_3d();
plot_3d_trans();

//--- Interactive:

cout << "Press q to quit" << endl;
cout << " p to print a postscript file" << endl;
cout << " r to reset" << endl;
cout << "Place cursor at the center of the graphics window" << endl;
cout << "and then click and move the:" << endl;
cout << " left-mouse button to rotate left-right" << endl;
cout << " right-mouse button to rotate up-down" << endl;
cout << " both buttons to zoom" << endl;

//--- Wait for the keyboard:

char kbd = char(getkey());
```

```
vexit();

return 0;
}
```

The plotting parameters are passed to the functions *draw_plot_3d.cc* and *plot_3d_trans.cc* as global variables through the header file `draw_plot_3d_globals.h`:

```
#ifndef DRAW_PLOT_3D_GLOBALS_H
#define DRAW_PLOT_3D_GLOBALS_H

extern float xmin, xmax;
extern float ymin, ymax;
extern float zmin, zmax;
extern float vx, vy, vz;
extern float twist;
extern float angx; // rotation angle
extern float angy; // rotation angle
extern float angz; // rotation angle
extern float zoom; // zoom
extern float angx_init;
extern float angy_init;
extern float angz_init;
extern float zoom_init;
extern int ntc_x; // number of ticks on the x axis
extern int ntc_y; // number of ticks on the y axis
extern int ntc_z; // number of ticks on the y axis
extern int bg_c; // background color
extern int ax_c; // axis color
extern int lb_c; // label color
extern int ln_c; // line color
extern int Iswap;
extern char label_x[]; // x-axis label
extern char label_y[]; // y-axis label
extern char label_z[]; // y-axis label
extern char title1[]; // first title
extern char title2[]; // second title
extern char title3[]; // third title
extern int Iaxes; // draw axes?
extern int Itick; // ticks on axes?
extern int Itry; // repeat index for animation
extern int nc;
extern int np[];
extern float xd[][128];
extern float yd[][128];
extern float zd[][128];

#endif
```

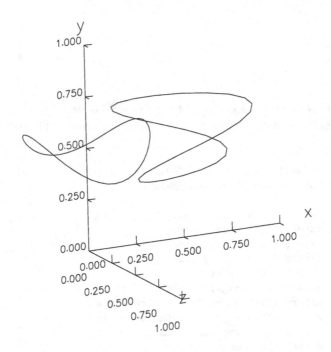

Figure 7.7.1 Graphics display of code *plot_3d*.

Since these variables are declared as external, their values are supplied from another code upon linking – in this case, from the main program. If these variables were defined and evaluated in the header file, multiple definitions would occur upon linking resulting in an exception, as discussed in Section 4.7.

The graphics output of the code is shown in Figure 7.7.1.

Problems

7.7.1. Run the code *plot_3d* to draw the wireframe of a sphere defined by azimuthal and meridional circles.

7.7.2. Modify the code *plot_3d* to animate the motion of a three-dimensional line.

7.8   Three-dimensional interactive object drawing

By a straightforward modification of the functions and main program discussed in Section 7.7 we are able to produce a code that draws an object in three dimensions. The object itself is defined by a collection of independently generated triangular elements, each defined by three nodes.

Function *draw_obj_3d* is identical to function *draw_plot_3d*, except that the drawing module reads:

```
/*----------------
Draw nc elements
----------------*/

int Ibcface = 1;
int Iclock = 0;

backface(Ibcface);
backfacedir(Iclock);

const int npoints = 4;
float points[npoints-1][3];

for(int j=1;j<=nc;j++)
{
points[0][0] = xd[j][1];
points[0][1] = yd[j][1];
points[0][2] = zd[j][1];
points[1][0] = xd[j][2];
points[1][1] = yd[j][2];
points[1][2] = zd[j][2];
points[2][0] = xd[j][3];
points[2][1] = yd[j][3];
points[2][2] = zd[j][3];
points[3][0] = xd[j][1];
points[3][1] = yd[j][1];
points[3][2] = zd[j][1];

color (CYAN); // paint the elements
bool fill = true;
polyfill (fill);
poly (npoints,points);

color (ln_c); // draw the element contours
fill = false;
polyfill (fill);
poly (npoints,points);

}
```

Function *obj_3d_trans* is a straightforward modification of function *obj_3d_trans* designed to handle element instead of line data.

The main program *obj_3d* is identical to program *plot_3d*, except that the data definition module reads:

```
int vertices;

ifstream file9("obj_3d.inp");

nc = 0; // count the number of elements

another:

file9 >> vertices; // number of vertices
if(vertices==0) {goto done;} // end of triangles

nc = nc+1;
np[nc]==vertices;
for(int i=1; i<=vertices;i++)
{
file9 >> xd[nc][i] >> yd[nc][i] >> zd[nc][i];
}

goto another; // read again
done:  // done reading

file9.close();
cout << nc;
```

The triangle vertices are recorded in the file *obj_3d.inp* in the following format:

```
3
    0.00000       0.00000       0.62573
    0.08762       0.00000       0.62272
    0.00000       0.17524       0.62272
  3
    0.08762       0.00000       0.62272
    ...
  3
    0.48196      -1.15671      -0.33737
    0.57835      -0.96392      -0.33737
    0.57174      -1.14349      -0.26681
  0
```

where the three dots denote further element blocks.

The graphics output of the code is shown in Figure 7.8.1.

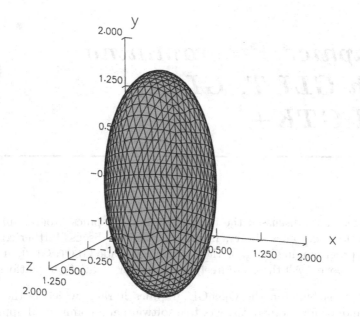

Figure 7.8.1 Graphics display of code *obj_3d* showing an object constructed of surface patches.

Problems

7.8.1. Run the code *obj_3d* to draw (*a*) a cube, and (*b*) a four-faced pyramid.

7.8.2. Modify the code *obj_3d* and supporting functions to draw an object defined by quadrilateral elements.

Graphics Programming with *GLUT, GLUI,* and *GTK+*

8

In Chapter 7, we discussed the fundamentals of graphics programming based on the VOGLE graphics library. In this chapter, we discuss further concepts of graphics programming based on the commercial-grade GLUT, GLUI, and GTK+ utility toolboxes. All three are freely available for a variety of platforms:

- GLUT is built on the OpenGL graphics library, which is the industry standard for a broad range of free software and commercial applications.

- GLUI is built on GLUT to provide a Graphical User Interface (GUI) equipped with controls such as buttons, check-boxes, and radio buttons.

- GTK+ is a popular widget toolbox.

Once we have mastered the functions implemented in these libraries, we can produce professional graphics displays and applications using C++ code that is portable virtually across any computer platform.

8.1   GLUT

The newest edition of GLUT is implemented in the FREEGLUT library, which includes the MESA library. The latter is the free implementation of OpenGL. An excellent manual of the GLUT functions and their usage can be found at several Internet sites including:

`http://pyopengl.sourceforge.net/documentation/manual/reference-GLUT`

`http://www.opengl.org/documentation/specs/glut`

To compile a C++ program named *phoebe.cc* and link it with the GLUT library in Unix, we use the makefile:

```
LIB = -I/usr/include/GL -I/usr/include/GL/freeglut -lX11 -lglut
phoebe:  phoebe.cc
      c++ -o phoebe phoebe.cc $(LIB)
```

The empty spaces in the third line must be generated by pressing the TAB key.

The first line defines the variable LIB as the union of the header files of (*a*) the OpenGL and freeglut libraries located in the system *include* directories, and (*b*) the X11 and *freeglut* libraries. The compiler option -Isomething adds the directory *something* to the top of the list of search directories.

To compile the program in Unix, we navigate to the working directory and issue the command:

```
make phoebe
```

To run the executable, we type:

```
./phoebe
```

Color and transparency

Color is defined as a mixture of fundamental components that can be separated by a prism. Color in GLUT is determined by the quadruplet of parameters:

Red   Blue   Green   Alpha

(RBGA), where "Alpha" determines the opacity. Each parameter varies between 0 and 1; Alpha=0 corresponds to transparent, and Alpha=1 corresponds to opaque.

A blank window

The following C++ code contained in the file *window.cc* consists of the main program and the user-defined function *blank*. The modest purpose of this code is to generate the empty graphics window shown in Figure 8.1.1(*a*):

```
#include <freeglut.h>
using namespace std;

void blank();

int main(int argc, char **argv)
{
glutInit(&argc, argv);
```

```
glutCreateWindow("GLUT window");
glClearColor(0.8,0.5,0.2,1.0);
glutDisplayFunc(blank);
glutMainLoop();
return 0;
}

//-- function blank

void blank()
{
glClear(GL_COLOR_BUFFER_BIT);
}
```

The code makes several GLUT (glut) and OpenGL (gl) calls according to a very specific protocol:

- The first command in the main program calls the GLUT function:

  ```
  glutInit(int &argc, char **argv);
  ```

  This function parses the window-specific parameters transmitted to the X11 server. Note that the first argument is the integer pointer, &argc.

- The last command in the main program calls the function:

  ```
  glutMainLoop();
  ```

  which launches the graphics display in an infinite loop that can be interrupted only by certain events.

  In OpenGL and GLUT programming, we first register the callbacks (graphics functions), then define the graphics object, and finally launch the graphics display by entering the main loop. *If we do not enter the main loop, nothing will happen.*

- The second command in the main program generates a graphics window and defines the title.

- The third command in the main program sets the background color painted when the window is cleared in the default RBGA mode.

- The fourth command in the main program calls the function:

  ```
  glutDisplayFunc(char function_name);
  ```

  This function launches the user-defined function stated in the argument.

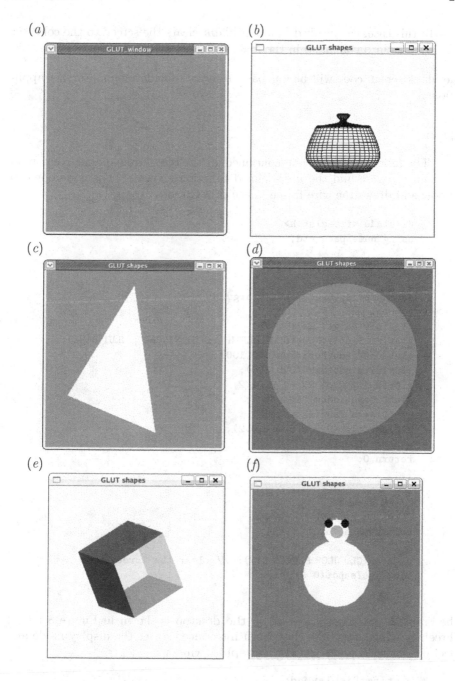

Figure 8.1.1 GLUT productions: (a) An empty window, (b) a teapot, (c) a triangle, (d) a disk, (e) a cube, and (f) a snowman.

In this case, the invoked function *blank* clears the screen to the color set by the third command in the main program.

The blank-screen code will be our basic template for developing further applications.

Teapot

The following C++ code contained in the file *glut_shapes.cc* consists of the main program and the user-defined function *showme*. The code opens a window and draws the wire-frame image of a teapot:

```
#include <freeglut.h>
using namespace std;

void disp(void);

int main(int argc, char **argv)
{
glutInit(&argc, argv);
glutInitDisplayMode(GLUT_DEPTH | GLUT_SINGLE | GLUT_RGBA);
glutInitWindowPosition(100,100);
glutInitWindowSize(320,320);
glOrtho(-1.2, 1.2, -1.2, 1.2, -1.2, 1.2);
glutCreateWindow("Teapot");
glutDisplayFunc(showme);
glClearColor(0.2,0.5,0.2,0.2);
glutMainLoop();
return 0;
}

//--- showme

void showme(void)
{
glClear(GL_COLOR_BUFFER_BIT); // clear the screen
glutWireTeapot(0.6);
}
```

The graphics output of the code on the desktop is shown in Figure 8.1.1(*b*). Three new GLUT functions have been introduced to set the display mode and specify the location and size of the graphics window:

```
glutInitDisplayMode
glutInitWindowPosition
glutInitWindowSize
```

In addition, the OpenGL function glOrtho was invoked to set the lower and

GLUT_RGBA	Select an RGBA mode window; default if neither GLUT_RGBA nor GLUT_INDEX are specified.
GLUT_RGB	Alias for GLUT_RGBA.
GLUT_INDEX	Color-index-mode window; overrides GLUT_RGBA.
GLUT_SINGLE	Single buffered window; default if neither GLUT_DOUBLE or GLUT_SINGLE is specified.
GLUT_DOUBLE	Double buffered window; overrides GLUT_SINGLE.
GLUT_ACCUM	Accumulation buffer.
GLUT_ALPHA	Alpha component to the color buffer(s).
GLUT_DEPTH	Depth buffer.
GLUT_STENCIL	Stencil buffer.
GLUT_MULTISAMPLE	Multisampling support.
GLUT_STEREO	Stereo window.
GLUT_LUMINANCE	"Luminance" color model.

Table 8.1.1 Directives of the the glutInitDisplayMode function.

upper limits of the x, y, and z axes.

- The **GLUT_DEPTH** directive of the glutInitDisplayMode function requests a color depth buffer, **GLUT_SINGLE** requests a single buffer, and **GLUT_RGBA** requests the RGBA color coding system. A list of possible directives is given in table 8.1.1.

- The first argument of the glutInitDisplayPosition function is the number of pixels from the left of the screen. The default value is -1, signifying that the window manager is free to choose where the window will appear. The second argument of the function is the number of pixels measured from the top of the screen.

- The first and second arguments of the glutInitWindowSize function are the window width and height, both measured in pixel units.

Graphics files

Obtaining a file or hard copy of the graphics window or display is easier said than done. Although some conversion software is available, the quick way out is to save a screen shot and obtain the desired image using an image manipulation application such as the **gimp**. The images shown in this chapter were extracted in this manner and then saved in the encapsulated postscript (eps) format.

Triangle

The following alternative user-defined function produces the triangle shown in Figure 8.1.1(c):

```
void showme(void)
{
glClear(GL_COLOR_BUFFER_BIT);
glBegin(GL_TRIANGLES);
     glVertex2f(-0.9,-0.5);
     glVertex2f( 0.3,-1.0);
     glVertex2f( 0.0, 1.0);
glEnd();
glFlush();
}
```

Note that the triangle is drawn using OpenGL functions alone. Initially, the triangle is put into the memory buffer. The `glFlush` function flushes the buffer and forces stored objects to be drawn.

OpenGL function names

Many OpenGL functions have the general name:

```
glNameNm(  ...   )
```

where N is 2 or 3 to indicate the number of function arguments, and m is f for float, d for double, s for signed short integer, us for unsigned short integer, i for signed integer, ui for unsigned integer, b for character, and ub for unsigned character.

Thus, the 2 in the name of the `glVertex2f` indicates two arguments, and the f indicates that the arguments will be floating-point numbers registered in single precision.

glBegin(TYPE) and glEnd()

The `glBegin(TYPE)` and `glEnd()` functions mark the beginning and end of a set of N vertices whose interpretation depends on TYPE. In the case of a triangle, TYPE is GL_TRIANGLES. A list of possible types follows:

GL_POINTS

Each vertex is a single point.

GL_POLYGON

Draws a convex N-sided polygon defined by the vertices.

GL_LINES

N must be even. Each pair of vertices defines a line segment.

GL_LINE_LOOP

Draws a closed polygonal line passing through the N vertices.

GL_TRIANGLES

Each consecutive triplet of vertices defines a triangle, for a total of $T = V/3$ triangles, where V is the number of vertices; V must be a multiple of three.

GL_TRIANGLE_STRIP

Draws a connected group of $N - 2$ triangles. A triangle is defined by any three successive vertices.

GL_TRIANGLE_FAN

Draws a connected group of $N - 2$ triangles. A triangle is defined by the first vertex and consecutive pairs of subsequent vertices.

GL_QUADS

Each consecutive quadruplet of vertices defines a quadrilateral, for a total of $Q = V/4$ elements, where V is the number of vertices; V must be a multiple of four.

GL_QUAD_STRIP

Draw a connected group of $Q = V/2 - 1$ quadrilaterals, where V is the number of vertices; V must be even. A quadrilateral is defined by any two successive vertex pairs. For example, when $V = 4$, one quadrilateral is drawn.

Functions defining vertices include, but are not limited to:

```
        glVertex2f      glVertex2d
        glVertex3f      glVertex3d
```

As an example, the following function draws the solid disk shown in Figure 8.1.1(*d*):

```
void disk()
{
int N=64;
float Dthet =2.0*3.1415926/N;
float centerx=0.0, centery=0.0;
float radius=1.0;

glClear(GL_COLOR_BUFFER_BIT);

glBegin(GL_TRIANGLE_FAN);
  glColor3f(0.8,0.5,0.2);
  glVertex2f(centerx,centery);
  for (int i=0; i<=N; i++)
  {
  float angle = i*Dtheta;
  glVertex2f(cos(angle)*radius,sin(angle)*radius);
  }
glEnd();

glFlush();
}
```

The disk is defined by a group of N triangles with one common vertex at the disk center.

Cube

Three-dimensional graphics can be drawn in similar ways. The following function paints the cube shown in Figure 8.1.1(*e*):

```
void cube(void)
{

glClear(GL_COLOR_BUFFER_BIT);

/* Introduce a transformation matrix.
All vertices will be multiplied by this matrix */

glLoadIdentity(); // introduce the identity matrix

glOrtho(-8.0, 8.0, -8.0, 8.0, -8.0, 8.0); // set the axes

glTranslatef(-0.5, 0.2, 0.1); // translate the identity matrix
glRotatef(-50, 1.0, 0.0, 0.0); // rotate by 50 deg about the x axis
glRotatef(50, 0.0, 1.0, 0.0); // rotate by 50 deg about the y axis
```

```
    glRotatef(30, 0.0, 0.0, 1.0); // rotate by 30 deg about the z axis

    //--- Paint three faces:

    glColor3f(1.0, 0.0, 1.0);
    glBegin(GL_QUAD_STRIP);
        glVertex3d(3, 3, -3);
        glVertex3d(3, -3, -3);
        glVertex3d(-3, 3, -3);
        glVertex3d(-3, -3, -3);
        glVertex3d(-3, 3, 3);
        glVertex3d(-3, -3, 3);
        glVertex3d(3, 3, 3);
        glVertex3d(3, -3, 3);
    glEnd();

    glColor3f(1.0, 1.0, 0.0); // Paint the individual faces
    glBegin(GL_QUADS);
        glVertex3d(-3, 3, 3);
        glVertex3d(-3, -3, 3);
        glVertex3d(3, -3, 3);
        glVertex3d(3, 3, 3);
    glEnd();
    glColor3f(0.0, 0.0, 1.0);
    glBegin(GL_QUADS);
        glVertex3d(-3, -3, -3);
        glVertex3d(3, -3, -3);
        glVertex3d(3, -3, 3);
        glVertex3d(-3, -3, 3);
    glEnd();
    glColor3f(0.0, 1.0, 1.0);
    glBegin(GL_QUADS);
        glVertex3d(-3, 3, -3);
        glVertex3d(3, 3, -3);
        glVertex3d(3, 3, 3);
        glVertex3d(-3, 3, 3);
    glEnd();
    glColor3f(0.2, 1.0, 0.0);
    glBegin(GL_QUADS);
        glVertex3d(3, 3, -3);
        glVertex3d(3, -3, -3);
        glVertex3d(-3,-3, -3);
        glVertex3d(-3, 3, -3);
    glEnd();
    glFlush();
}
```

The faces of the cube were painted with different colors using the glColor3f
function.

Transformations

The cube drawing code provides us with the opportunity to discuss transformations. Every point in space is represented by a position vector encapsulating the x, y, and z coordinates in a fixed (world or laboratory) frame. To implement translation, we call the function:

$$\texttt{glTranslatef(Dx, Dy, Dz)}$$

where the three arguments are the x, y, and z displacements.

Multiplying a position vector by a 3×3 transformation matrix gives a new position vector. In the cube code, the transformation matrix is introduced as the 3×3 identity matrix:

$$\begin{bmatrix} 1 & 0 & 0 \\ 0 & 1 & 0 \\ 0 & 0 & 1 \end{bmatrix}.$$

Multiplying a position vector by the identity matrix leaves the vector unchanged. To implement rotation around the axis defined by the direction cosines (ax, ay, az), we call the function:

$$\texttt{glRotatef(degrees, ax, ay, az)}$$

For example,

$$\texttt{glRotatef(48, 0, 0, 1);}$$

performs rotation by $48°$ around the z axis.

Prefabricated shapes

GLUT functions that display prefabricated shapes are shown in Table 8.1.2. In practice, these functions are used to construct composite objects from elementary geometries.

The following function produces the snowman wearing shades displayed in Figure 8.1.1(f):

```
void snowman(void)
{
glClear(GL_COLOR_BUFFER_BIT);

//--- Introduce a transformation matrix:

glLoadIdentity();
```

glutSolidSphere (double radius, int slices, int stacks)
glutWireSphere (double radius, int slices, int stacks)

glutSolidCone (double base, double height, int slices, int stacks)
glutWireCone (double base, double height, int slices, int stacks)

glutSolidCube (double size)
glutWireCube (double size)

glutSolidTorus (double innerRadius, double outerRadius,
                              int nsides, int rings)
glutWireTorus (double innerRadius, double outerRadius,
                              int nsides, int rings)
glutSolidDodecahedron()
glutWireDodecahedron()

glutSolidOctahedron()
glutWireOctahedron()

glutSolidTetrahedron()
glutWireTetrahedron()

glutSolidIcosahedron()
glutWireIcosahedron()

glutSolidTeapot (double size)
glutWireTeapot (double size)

Table 8.1.2 GLUT functions implementing prefabricated shapes.

```
//--- Body:

glColor3f(1.0f, 1.0f, 1.0f);
glutSolidSphere(0.5,20,20);

//--- Head:

glTranslatef(0.0,0.75,0.0);
glutSolidSphere(0.25,20,20);

//--- Eyes:

glPushMatrix();
```

```
glColor3f(0.0f,0.0f,0.0f);
glTranslatef(0.1, 0.10, 0.18);
glutSolidSphere(0.05,10,10);

glTranslatef(-0.2, 0.0, 0.0);
glutSolidSphere(0.05,10,10);

glPopMatrix();

//--- Nose:

glColor3f(1.0, 0.5 , 0.5);
glRotatef(0.0, 1.0, 0.0, 0.0);
glutSolidCone(0.08, 0.5, 10,2);

glFlush();
}
```

A transformation matrix can be temporary of permanent. In the first case, the old transformation matrix can be saved to be reinstated at a later time. The `glPushMatrix` function saves the current settings, and the `glPopMatrix` function reinstates the settings. The *snowman* code shows that these functions simplify the geometrical construction by allowing us to work in temporary coordinates that are properly translated or rotated with respect to fixed coordinates. When we are done, we revert to the original world coordinates.

Printing text on the screen

The following function contained in the file *the_end.cc* prints a character array on the screen:

```
void write()
{
glClear(GL_COLOR_BUFFER_BIT);
char protasi[] = "The Beginning";
int x=35, y=50;
int len, i;
glRasterPos2i(x, y);
len = (int) strlen(protasi);

for (i=0; i<len; i++)
  {
  glutBitmapCharacter(GLUT_BITMAP_HELVETICA_18, protasi[i]);
  }

glFlush();
}
```

The graphics display is shown in Figure 8.1.2(a). In this code, we have introduced the glRasterPos2i function to move the pen to a specified position, and the glutBitmapCharacter function to draw a character on the screen using a specified font.

The following function also contained in the file *the_end.cc* prints a character array using a different method:

```
void write1()
{
glClear(GL_COLOR_BUFFER_BIT);
char * ps = "The End";
int x = 35, y=50;

while(*ps)
    {
    glRasterPos2i(x,y);
    glutBitmapCharacter(GLUT_BITMAP_8_BY_13,*ps);
    x = x + 4;
    ps = ps+1;
    }

glFlush();
}
```

The graphics display is shown in Figure 8.1.2(b). In the second method, the individual characters of the array are identified by the pointer ps whose value is sequentially increased by one unit until the end of the array has been reached.

Available fonts include the following:

```
GLUT_BITMAP_8_BY_13
GLUT_BITMAP_9_BY_15
GLUT_BITMAP_HELVETICA_10
GLUT_BITMAP_HELVETICA_12
GLUT_BITMAP_HELVETICA_18
GLUT_BITMAP_TIMES_ROMAN_10
GLUT_BITMAP_HELVETICA_18
GLUT_BITMAP_TIMES_ROMAN_24
```

Spectacular designs

OpenGL allows us to manipulate the color with spectacular results seen in professional designs. The following function generates the design shown in Figure 8.1.3:

```
void spectacular()
{
```

```
int N=4;
float Dtheta = 2*3.1415926/N;
float centerx = 0.0, centery = 0.0;
float radius1 = 0.5;
float radius2 = 1.0;

glClear(GL_COLOR_BUFFER_BIT);
glBegin(GL_QUADS);

for (int i=1; i<= N; i++)
{
float angle1 = (i-1)*Dtheta;
float angle2 = i*Dtheta;
if(i==1)
{
centerx = 0.1;
centery = 0.1;
}
else if(i==2)
{
centerx = -0.1;
centery = 0.1;
}
else if(i==3)
{
centerx = -0.1;
centery = -0.1;
}
else
{
centerx = 0.1;
centery = -0.1;
}
glColor3f(0.2,0.5,0.2);
glVertex2f(centerx+cos(angle1)*radius1 ,centery+sin(angle1)*radius1);
glColor3f(0.8,0.5,0.2);
glVertex2f(centerx+cos(angle1)*radius2 ,centery+sin(angle1)*radius2);
glColor3f(0.8,0.5,0.2);
glVertex2f(centerx+cos(angle2)*radius2 ,centery+sin(angle2)*radius2);
glColor3f(0.2,0.5,0.2);
glVertex2f(centerx+cos(angle2)*radius1 ,centery+sin(angle2)*radius1);
}
glEnd();

glFlush();
}
```

Note that OpenGL allows us to set the vertex color, which is then automatically interpolated over the surface of a quadrilateral.

Problems

8.1.1. Program GLUT to open a blank window in a reddish color.

8.1.2. Program GLUT to draw a red square on a yellow background.

(a)   (b)

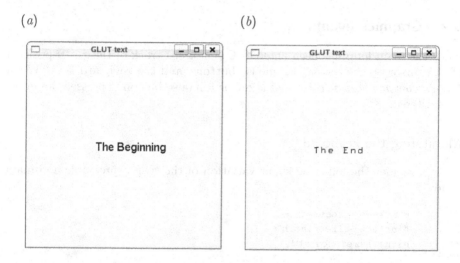

Figure 8.1.2 String of characters printed on a GLUT window using two methods.

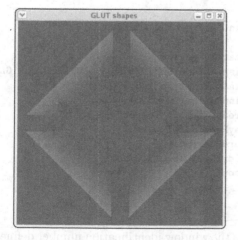

Figure 8.1.3 A spectacular color display generated by GLUT, printed here in gray scale.

8.1.3. Write a GLUT function that displays a four-sided pyramid.

8.1.4. Write a code that displays a bicycle.

8.1.5. Write a code that displays two lines of text.

8.1.6. Write a code that generates a spectacular color display of your choice.

8.2   Graphics events

Once the main loop has been entered, GLUT keeps track of the $x - y$ position of the cursor on the screen, the mouse buttons, and the keyboard keys. When *the window has been selected* and a key or a mouse button is pressed, an event is registered.

Monitoring the keyboard

Consider the following slight variation of the teapot preamble and main code:

```
#include <iostream>
#include <freeglut.h>
using namespace std;

void showme(void);
void quit(unsigned char, int, int);

int win;

int main(int argc, char **argv)
{
glutInit(&argc, argv);
glutInitDisplayMode(GLUT_DEPTH | GLUT_SINGLE | GLUT_RGBA);
glutInitWindowPosition(100,100);
glutInitWindowSize(620,620);
win=glutCreateWindow("Teapot");
glutDisplayFunc(disp);
glutKeyboardFunc(quit);
glClearColor(0.2,0.5,0.2,0.2);
glutMainLoop();
return 0;
}
```

The integer "win" is the window identification number defined in the main code. The user-defined function *quit* reads:

```
void quit(unsigned char key, int x, int y)
{
cout << "Key:   " << key << " pressed" << endl;
cout << "Cursor position:   " << x << " " << y << endl;
if(key == 'q')
   {
   glutDestroyWindow(win);
   exit(0);
   }
}
```

When a key is pressed, an event is registered and the function *quit* is executed. When the "q" key is pressed, the program stops as GLUT destroys the window.

Idle functions

What happens between events? We can have other tasks executed in the meanwhile. Consider the following main code:

```
#include <iostream>
#include <freeglut.h>
using namespace std;

void keyboard(unsigned char, int, int);
void mouse(int, int, int, int);
void add(void);
void showme(void);

int a=1; // global variable

//---- main:

int main(int argc, char **argv)
{
glutInit(&argc, argv);
glutInitDisplayMode(GLUT_DEPTH | GLUT_SINGLE | GLUT_RGBA);
glutCreateWindow("Prime");
glutDisplayFunc(showme);
glutIdleFunc(add);
glutKeyboardFunc(keyboard);
glutMouseFunc(mouse);
glutMainLoop();
return 0;
}
```

When the window is selected and a key pressed, the function *keyboard* is executed; when the mouse is clicked, the function *mouse* is executed; otherwise the function *add* keeps running. The implementation of these functions may be:

```
//--- keyboard:

void keyboard(unsigned char key, int x, int y)
{
cout <<"Please enter a number:"<<endl;
cin >> a;

//--- mouse:

void mouse(int button, int state, int x, int y)
{
a=-1000000;
}

//--- add:

void add(void)
{
a=a+1;
cout << a << endl;
}
```

Idle functions find important applications in window resizing and animation.

Event callbacks

Following is a summary of callbacks triggered by events:

`void glutDisplayFunc(void (*func)(void));`

This callback specifies the function to be executed when the window is shown for the first time, popped up, or otherwise redrawn.

`void glutPostRedisplay(void);`

This callback prompts the execution of the function defined by the `glutPostDisplayFunc` callback at the first available opportunity, signaling a need for redraw.

`void glutIdleFunc(void (*func)(void));`

This callback specifies the function to be executed between events and finds important applications in animation.

`void glutMouseFunc(void (*func)(int btn, int state, int x, int y));`

This callback specifies the function to be executed when a mouse button is clicked:

- If btn=GLUT_LEFT_BUTTON, the left button has been clicked.
- If btn=GLUT_RIGHT_BUTTON, the right button has been clicked.
- If btn=GLUT_MIDDLE_BUTTON, the middle button has been clicked.
- If state=GLUT_UP, the button has been pressed.
- If state=GLUT_DOWN, the button has been released.
- The variables x and y are the mouse coordinates.

```
void glutKeyboardFunc(void (*func)(unsigned char key,int x, int y));
```

This callback specifies the function to be executed when a key is pressed. The variables x and y are the mouse coordinates.

```
void glutMotionFunc(void (*func)(int x, int y));
```

This callback specifies the function to be executed when the mouse is moved while a button is pressed. The variables x and y arc the mouse coordinates.

```
void glutReshapeFunc(void (*func)(int width, int height));
```

This callback specifies the function to be executed when the window is being moved or resized. The arguments are the redrawn window width and height.

```
void glutTimerFunc(unsigned int msecs, void (*func)(int value), value);
```

This callback prompts the execution of the function stated in the second argument, called the "timer callback," after a maximum delay of msecs milliseconds.

The parameter value of the timer callback is the same as that in the third argument of the glutTimerFunc callback. It is possible to register multiple timer callbacks. Although a callback cannot be unregistered, it can be deactivated using the value parameter.

Timer callback

The following code implemented in the file *ascii.cc* generates a window and prints all ASCII characters in animation using a time callback:

```
#include <freeglut.h>
using namespace std;

void blank();
void print(int);
int delay=100; // in milliseconds

//--- main:

int main(int argc, char **argv)
{
int code=-1;
glutInit(&argc, argv);
glutInitDisplayMode(GLUT_DEPTH | GLUT_RGBA);
glutInitWindowPosition(100,100);
glutInitWindowSize(320,320);
glutCreateWindow("ASCII");
glOrtho(0, 100, 0, 100, 0, 100);
glClearColor(0.5,0.0,0.8,1.0);
glutDisplayFunc(blank);
glutTimerFunc(delay, print, code);
glutMainLoop();
return 0;
}

//--- Print:

void print (int code)
{
glClear(GL_COLOR_BUFFER_BIT);
char a = code++;
glRasterPos2i(50, 50);
glutBitmapCharacter(GLUT_BITMAP_8_BY_13, a);
glFlush();
glutTimerFunc(delay, print, code);
delay=delay+1;
}

//--- Blank screen:

void blank()
{
glClear(GL_COLOR_BUFFER_BIT);
}
```

Note that the glutTimerFunc function calls the user-defined function print, which in turn calls glutTimerFunc in an infinite loop. In this case, print also changes the delay.

Animation

To perform animation, we use two memory spaces holding the graphics, one called the *back buffer* and the second called the *primary* or *active buffer*. The computer displays the content of the primary buffer, then the two buffers are swapped in a process dubbed *double buffering*.

The following code animates the rotation of a circle drawn by a user-defined function:

```
#include <math.h>
#include <freeglut.h>

using namespace std;

const float radius = 1.0;
const int N=180;
const float Dtheta = 2*3.1415926/N;
const float radius = 1.0;
float angle=0.0;

void render_scene(void);
void drawCircle();

//--- main:

int main(int argc, char **argv)
{
glutInit(&argc, argv);
glutInitDisplayMode(GLUT_DEPTH | GLUT_DOUBLE | GLUT_RGBA);
glutInitWindowPosition(010,020);
glutInitWindowSize(256,256);
glutCreateWindow("GLUT Animation");
glutIdleFunc(render_scene);
glutMainLoop();
return 0;
}

//--- Render the scene:

void render_scene(void)
{
glClear(GL_COLOR_BUFFER_BIT | GL_DEPTH_BUFFER_BIT);
glPushMatrix();
glRotatef(angle,0.0,1.0,0.0);
drawCircle(radius);
glPopMatrix();
glutSwapBuffers();
angle=angle+0.1;
```

```
    }

    //--- Draw a circle:

    void drawCircle()
    {
    glBegin(GL_LINE_LOOP);
      for (int i=0; i <= N; i++)
      {
      float angle = i*Dtheta;
      glVertex2f(cos(angle)*radius,sin(angle)*radius);
      }
    glEnd();
    }
```

In this method, animation is performed using the `glutIdleFunc` callback. The code features the following implementations:

- Double buffering is ensured by including GLUT_DOUBLE in the argument of `glutInitDisplayMode`.

- It is mandatory to clear the depth buffer, otherwise the rendering will fail.

- The `glutSwapBuffers` function swaps the buffers.

A snapshot of the animation is shown in Figure 8.2.1(a).

(a)   (b)

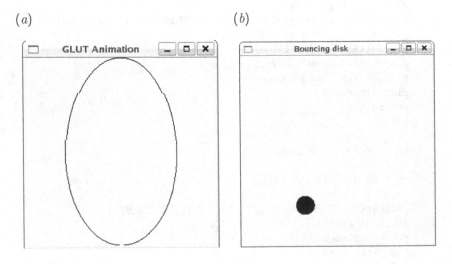

Figure 8.2.1 Snapshot of (a) a rotating circle, and (b) a bouncing disk.

To control the animation frequency, we use the `glutTimerFunc` callback. The following code contained in the file `bounce.cc` animates a bouncing disk:

```
#include <iostream>
#include <cmath>
#include <freeglut.h>

using namespace std;

void animate(int);
void disk();
void quit(unsigned char, int, int);

//--- Global variables:

int delay=10, N=64;
float Dtheta = 2*3.1415926/N;
float centerx = 0.0, centery = 0.0, radius = 0.1;
float Dx = 0.02, Dy=0.01;
int win;

//---------- main

int main(int argc, char **argv)
{
glutInit(&argc, argv);
glutInitDisplayMode(GLUT_DEPTH | GLUT_DOUBLE | GLUT_RGBA);
glutInitWindowPosition(500,100);
glutInitWindowSize(320,320);
win = glutCreateWindow("Bouncing disk");
glOrtho(-1.0, 1.0, -1.0, 1.0, -1.0, 1.0);
glClearColor(0.5,0.0,0.8,1.0);
glutKeyboardFunc(quit);
glutTimerFunc(delay, animate, 0);
glutMainLoop();
return 0;
}

//---------- animate

void animate(int code)
{
disk();
glutTimerFunc(delay, animate, 0);
glutSwapBuffers();
}

//-------- disk
```

```
void disk()
{
glClear(GL_COLOR_BUFFER_BIT | GL_DEPTH_BUFFER_BIT);
glColor3f(0.8,0.5,0.2);

centerx = centerx+Dx;
centery = centery+Dy;

if(centerx+radius > 1.0) Dx = - Dx;
if(centerx-radius < -1.0) Dx = - Dx;
if(centery+radius > 1.0) Dy = - Dy;
if(centery-radius <-1.0) Dy = - Dy;

glBegin(GL_TRIANGLE_FAN);
  glVertex2f(centerx, centery);
  for (int i=0; i <= N; i++)
  {
  float angle = i*Dtheta;
  glVertex2f(centerx+cos(angle)*radius,
  centery+sin(angle)*radius);
  }
glEnd();
}

//--------- quit

void quit(unsigned char key, int x, int y)
{
if(key == 'q')
  {
  cout << "Closing window " << endl;
  glutDestroyWindow(win);
  exit(0);
  }
}
```

A snapshot of the animation is shown in Figure 8.2.1(b).

Rescaling

If we resize the graphics window, the displayed image will be distorted: a circle will become an ellipse and a person will instantaneously lose or gain weight. To prevent this, we run the glutRshapeFunc callback in the double buffer mode.

The following code contained in the file *pac_man.cc* draws the image of a Pac-Man whose shape remains unaltered when the window is resized:

```
#include <iostream>
#include <cmath>
#include <freeglut.h>

using namespace std;

void pac_man(void);
void resize(int, int);
void quit(unsigned char, int, int);
int win;
const float pi = 3.14159265358;
int N=64; // for Pac-Man
float Dtheta = 1.5*pi/N; // for Pac-Man

/*---------- main--------------------*/

int main(int argc, char **argv)
{
glutInit(&argc, argv);

glutInitDisplayMode(GLUT_DEPTH | GLUT_DOUBLE | GLUT_RGBA);
glutInitWindowPosition(100,100);
glutInitWindowSize(320,320);
win=glutCreateWindow("GLUT shapes");
glOrtho(-1.2, 1.2, -1.2, 1.2, -1.2, 1.2);
glutDisplayFunc(pac_man);
glutIdleFunc(pac_man);
glutReshapeFunc(resize);
glutKeyboardFunc(quit);
glutMainLoop();
return 0;
}

/*---------- Pac-Man --------------------*/

void pac_man()
{
glClear(GL_COLOR_BUFFER_BIT);
glBegin(GL_TRIANGLE_FAN);
glColor3f(0.1,0.9,0.0);
glVertex2f(0,0);
for (int i=0; i <= N; i++)
  {
  float angle = i*Dtheta+0.5*pi;
  glVertex2f(cos(angle),sin(angle));
  }
glEnd();
glutSwapBuffers();
}
```

```
/*---------- resize ---------------------*/

void resize(int w, int h)
{

//--- Prevent dividing by zero:

if(h==0) h=1;

float ratio = 1.0* w / h;

//--- Reset the coordinate system before modifying

glMatrixMode(GL_PROJECTION);
glLoadIdentity();

//--- Viewport is the entire window:

glViewport(0, 0, w, h);

//--- Set the correct perspective.

gluPerspective(45,ratio,1,1000);
glMatrixMode(GL_MODELVIEW);
glLoadIdentity();
gluLookAt(0.0,0.0,5.0,0.0,0.0,-1.0,0.0,1.0,0.0);

}

/*---------- quit ---------------------*/

void quit(unsigned char key, int x, int y)
{
cout << "Pressed key:" << key << endl;
cout << "Cursor position:" << x << " " << y << endl;
if(key == 'q')
  {
  cout << "Closing window " << endl;
  glutDestroyWindow(win);
  exit(0);
  }
}
```

Figure 8.2.2. shows the images of a Pac-Man in two windows. The first image is drawn in the primary window generated by the code, while the second image is drawn after the window has been resized using the window handles. The resize function involves a sequence of carefully designed OpenGL calls.

(a)   (b)

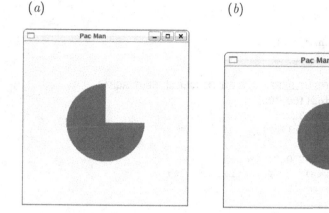

Figure 8.2.2 The same Pac-Man in the original and resized window.

Problems

8.2.1. Write a GLUT program to animate (a) a spinning, and (b) a rolling disk.

8.2.2. Write a GLUT program to animate the snowman with his head periodically turning left and right.

8.3 Drop-down menus

Programming drop-down menus can be a lot of fun. The sequence of callbacks must be designed carefully according to the OpenGL protocol.

The following code implemented in the file *mcnu.cc* generates a graphics window and produces a drop-down menu with a sub-menu that offers options for clearing the screen, drawing a teapot or a triangle, and quitting the application:

```
#include <freeglut.h>
using namespace std;

void showme(void);
void showmenu(void);
void menu(int);

int win;
int menuid;
int submenuid;
int draw_flag=2;
```

```
//--- main:

int main(int argc, char **argv)
{
glutInit(&argc, argv);
glutInitDisplayMode(GLUT_DEPTH | GLUT_SINGLE | GLUT_RGBA);
glutInitWindowPosition(100,100);
glutInitWindowSize(320,320);
win=glutCreateWindow("Goulis");

glClearColor(0.2,0.5,0.2,0.2);
glutDisplayFunc(showme);    // initial display
showmenu();
glutDisplayFunc(showme);
glutMainLoop();

return 0;
}

//--- showme:

void showme(void)
{
glClear(GL_COLOR_BUFFER_BIT);

if(draw_flag==1){
     glutPostRedisplay();}
else if(draw_flag==2){
     glutWireTeapot(0.5);}
else if(draw_flag==3){
     glBegin(GL_TRIANGLES);
     glVertex3f(-0.9,-0.5,0.0);
     glVertex3f( 0.3,-1.0,0.0);
     glVertex3f( 0.0, 1.0,0.0);
     glEnd();}
glFlush();
}

//--- showmenu:

void showmenu(void)
{
submenuid=glutCreateMenu(menu); // Create a sub-menu
glutAddMenuEntry("teapot", 2); // Add sub menu entries
glutAddMenuEntry("triangle", 3); // Create an entry

menuid=glutCreateMenu(menu); // Create the menu
glutAddMenuEntry("Clear", 1); // Create an entry
glutAddSubMenu("Draw", submenuid); // Create an entry
```

```
glutAddMenuEntry("Quit", 0); // Create an entry

glutAttachMenu(GLUT_LEFT_BUTTON);// respond to the left mouse button
glutAttachMenu(GLUT_RIGHT_BUTTON);// respond to the right mouse button
}

//--- menu:

void menu(int value)
{
glClear(GL_COLOR_BUFFER_BIT);
if(value == 0)
  {
  glutDestroyWindow(win);
  exit(0);
  }
else
  {
  draw_flag=value;
  }
}
```

Figure 8.3.1 shows the produced graphics window, including a drop-down menu generated by the user-defined function showmenu, which calls in turn the user-defined function menu. Each of these functions makes OpenGL and GLUT calls. The glutCreateMenu(menu) call returns to the menu function an integer mapping the menu items determined by the glutAddMenuEntry calls.

Problems

8.3.1. Modify the glut_menu.cc code to show the triangle at the initial display.

8.3.2. Modify the glut_menu.cc code to include the drawing of a rectangle as a third option.

8.3.3. Modify the glut_menu.cc code to incorporate a second sub-menu orig- inating from the triangle that offers the option for a red or yellow color.

8.4   GUI programming with GLUI

We have learned how to program graphics based on the GLUT library using OpenGL functions. To build a professional application incorporating a graph- ical user interface (GUI), we need further toolboxes offering *widgets*. The dic- tionary defines a widget as a contraption, a contrivance, a gadget, or a gizmo. In software engineering, widgets are programmed as objects of a drawing class.

Figure 8.3.1 A drop-down menu generated by GLUT. Clicking on an option changes the display.

GLUI is a GLUT-based user interface library providing buttons, check-boxes, radio buttons, spinners, and other controls to OpenGL applications (see: http://glui.sourceforge.net). The calls are window-system independent, relying on GLUT to handle all system-dependent processes such as window and mouse management. The GLUI distribution includes an informative user manual accompanied by a tutorial.

The library can be compiled readily using the makefile provided in the distribution to produce the library archive *lubglui.a*. We will assume that this file has been copied into the subdirectory *lib* of the working directory, while the header file *glui.h* has been copied into the subdirectory *include* of the working directory. More generally, the library and its header files can be put in appropriate system directories for use by others.

To compile a C++ program named *goulis.cc* and link it with GLUT, we use the Unix makefile:

```
LIB = -I/usr/include/GL -I/usr/include/GL/freeglut -I./include \
  -lX11 -lglut lib/libglui.a
goulis:  goulis.cc
    c++ -o goulis goulis.cc $(LIB)
```

where the backslash is a line continuation mark. Note that three libraries must be linked with the C++ code.

A simple GLUI code contained in the file *prime.cc* is listed below:

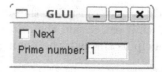

Figure 8.4.1 A GUI produced by GLUI. Data can be entered in the checkbox.

```
#include "glui.h"

using namespace std;
int prime;

int main(int argc, char* argv[])
{
glutInit(&argc, argv);
glutInitDisplayMode(GLUT_RGB | GLUT_DOUBLE | GLUT_DEPTH);
glutInitWindowPosition(50,50);
glutInitWindowSize(300,300);
GLUI *glui = GLUI_Master.create_glui( "GLUI");
new GLUI_Checkbox(glui,"Next",&prime);
(new GLUI_Spinner(glui,"Prime number:",&prime))
                      ->set_int_limits(10, 60);
glutMainLoop();
return 0;
}
```

Three GLUI functions are called by this program. Running the code produces the graphics display shown in Figure 8.4.1.

GLUI programming requires familiarization with the library nomenclature and protocols, which are explained in detail in the GLUI manual.

Problem

8.4.1. Adapt to C++ and run a GLUI code of your choice from the GLUI distribution.

8.5   GUI programming with GTK+

A powerful widget library is implemented in the GTK+ toolkit included in several Linux distributions (see http://www.gtk.org). GTK+ was originally developed for the gnu image manipulation program GIMP; accordingly, it is known as "the GIMP toolkit."

To develop an application, we must link the source code with the GTK+ header and object files, which is easier said than done. Fortunately, a fabulous application is available to help us through the linking process.

pkg-config is a public domain multi-platform application useful for compiling comprehensive codes that require a multitude of system libraries (see http://pkgconfig.freedesktop.org/wiki). The application inserts appropriate compiler options in the compilation line, thereby saving us from the painstaking task of manually citing all necessary header files and associated libraries.

For example, to compile the program horses.cc, we issue *in a single line* the command:

```
c++ -o horses horses.cc 'pkg-config --cflags gtk+-2.0' \
    'pkg-config --libs gtk+-2.0'
```

where the backslash in the first line is a line-continuation mark.

- The first directive 'pkg-config –cflags gtk+-2.0' runs pkg-config to list the header files of the gtk+-2.0 library.

- The second directive 'pkg-config –libs gtk+-2.0' runs pkg-config to list the implementations of the gtk+-2.0 library.

- The executable pkg-config itself is located in a system directory.

To install pkg-config on a Linux system, we download it from the Internet site http://pkgconfig.freedesktop.org/wiki, and follow the instructions, which prescribe issuing the command ./configure, followed by the command make install. The latter executes the *install* protocol described in the *makefile*. A great deal of gratitude is due to the authors of this truly useful application. configure is a *shell script*, that is, a program written in one of the Unix interpreted languages associated with a Unix shell, as discussed in Appendix A.

The following C++ code contained in the file *horses.cc* generates a window, displays a button, and prints the names of two horses on the button. When the button is clicked, the window disappears.

```
#include <gtk/gtk.h>
using namespace std;

int main( int argc, char *argv[] )
{
GtkWidget *window;
GtkWidget *button;
```

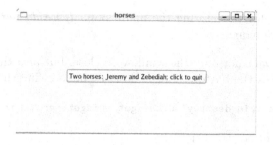

Figure 8.5.1 A window produced by the graphics toolkit GTK+. When the button
is clicked, the window disappears.

```
gtk_init (&argc, &argv);
window = gtk_window_new (GTK_WINDOW_TOPLEVEL);
gtk_container_set_border_width (GTK_CONTAINER (window), 100);
button = gtk_button_new_with_label ("Two horses:  Jeremy and Zebediah");
gtk_container_add (GTK_CONTAINER (window), button);

g_signal_connect_swapped (G_OBJECT (button), "clicked",
                          G_CALLBACK (gtk_widget_destroy),
                          G_OBJECT (window));
gtk_widget_show (button);
gtk_widget_show (window);
gtk_main ();

return 0;
}
```

GtkWidget in the fifth and sixth lines is the class type for the GTK+ widgets.
Running the code produces the window shown in Figure 8.5.1.

Note the similarities with the GLUT drawing code. Most of the GTK+
commands are self-explanatory. The first and last commands call the functions:

gtk_init(&argc, &argv)

This function parses the window-specific parameters transmitted to the
foundation graphics library or server.

gtk_main()

This function launches the graphics display in an infinite loop that can
be interrupted only by certain events.

In GTK+ programming, we first register the callbacks (widgets) and then start the graphics display by entering the main loop. *If we do not enter the main loop, nothing will happen.*

Now, we want not only the window to close, but also the application to quit when we click the button. This is done by introducing the function:

```
static void destroy( GtkWidget *widget, gpointer data)
{
  gtk_main_quit ();
}
```

and adding the callback:

```
g_signal_connect (G_OBJECT (window), "destroy",
                  G_CALLBACK (destroy), NULL);
```

immediately before the `g_signal_connect_swapped` callback. In this way, we associate the "destroy" with a signal handler event that occurs when the command `gtk_widget_destroy()` is executed.

Programming in GTK+ requires familiarization with the application protocols. Once the widgets have been mastered, the development of GUIs is tedious yet straightforward. A user interface designer with an integrated development environment (IDE) is available for rapid application development (RAD) (see `http://glade.gnome.org`).

Problems

8.5.1. Modify the `horses.cc` code so that the window closes and the application quits when the "q" button is pressed.

8.5.2. Adapt to C++ and run a GTK+ code of your choice from the GTK+ distribution.

Using Matlab

9

MATLAB is a software product for interactive numerics and graphics applications produced by *The Mathworks* corporation. MATLAB was initially developed as a virtual laboratory for matrix calculus and linear algebra. Today, MATLAB can be described both as a *programming language* and as a *computing environment*.

As a programming language, MATLAB is roughly equivalent, in some ways superior and in some ways inferior to traditional upper-level languages such as FORTRAN 77, C, or C++.

As a computing environment, MATLAB is able to run indefinitely in its own workspace. Thus, a session defined by the values of all initialized variables and graphical objects can be saved and reinstated at a later time. In this sense, MATLAB is an operating system running inside the operating system empowering the computer. Symbolic algebraic manipulation is available through an add-on library (toolbox) that uses a kernel borrowed from the all-purpose mathematical softoware product *Maple*.

An attractive feature of MATLAB is the availability of a broad range of utility commands, intrinsic functions, and computational toolboxes, especially graphics. A simplifying feature of MATLAB is that the dimensions of vectors and matrices used in the calculations are automatically assigned and can be changed in the course of a session, thereby circumventing the need for variable declaration and memory allocation.

Appendix F explains the basic syntax and grammar of the language and outlines the use of MATLAB functions. Documentation is available at: http://www.mathworks.com/access/helpdesk/help/techdoc/. Tutorials on general and special topics can be found on the Internet, and links are provided at this book's Internet site.

MATLAB must be purchased and installed with a proper license. Inexpensive licenses are available for students and educators through educational editions. On Linux, the educational version of MATLAB is installed as a standalone application. On Windows, the installation CD-ROM must be present in the drive at all times.

In this chapter, we explain how MATLAB can be called from C++ code for the purpose of using the MATLAB mathematical functions and generating graphics. The converse, calling C++ functions from a MATLAB code, is also possible, though of limited interest to the C++ programmer.

9.1   Invoking Matlab

To invoke MATLAB in Windows, we double-click on the MATLAB icon. This runs a starter program, currently a disk operating system (DOS) batch script, that launches the main MATLAB executable. Alternatively, we can start MATLAB from a DOS command line by a procedure similar to that discussed next for Unix.

To invoke MATLAB in Unix, we run the Unix script `matlab` by issuing the command:

```
matlab
```

Assuming that the script is in the execution path, this will launch MATLAB executable in some graphical used interface (GUI) or command line mode. To suppress the memory consuming GUI, we issue either the command:

```
matlab -nodesktop
```

or the command:

```
matlab -nojvm
```

where `jvm` is an acronym for java virtual machine. Starting MATLAB by issuing the command:

```
matlab -nodesktop -nosplash
```

suppresses both the GUI and the splash screen during start-up.

In Unix, MATLAB can be launched with a number of options. To obtain a list accompanied by explanations, we request help by issuing the command:

```
matlab -help
```

MATLAB uses a number of shared libraries, parameters, and environmental variables. To obtain a list, we issue the command:

```
matlab -n
```

9.2   The Matlab engine library

The MATLAB *engine* library contains a collection of functions in the form of an application program interface (API). For an official description, visit: `http://www.mathworks.com/access/helpdesk/help/techdoc/matlab_external`.

The engine interface allows us to start MATLAB from a C++ program, establish a MATLAB workspace, transfer data to the workspace, carry out calculations in the workspace, and transfer the results back to the C++ domain. Technically, the engine functions communicate with the C++ functions by a separate process using pipes in Unix, and through a component object model (COM) interface in Windows.

Dependencies and linking

To use MATLAB, the C++ code must be compiled and linked with a number of libraries, header files, and data files implementing the *engine* interface to produce a stand-alone binary executable. The MATLAB libraries

`libeng.xx`   `libmx.xx`   `libut.xx`

are required, where the suffix xx is `so` (shared object) in Unix, `dll` (dynamic link library) in Windows, and `dylib` (dynamic library) on Apple computers.

The `libeng` library requires (depends on) additional third-party libraries that support Unicode character encoding and data compression. While the ASCII code covers the letters of only the English alphabet, the Unicode includes text and symbols of writing systems from all over the world. The associated library files must reside in the directory hosting `libmx` and `libut`.

To ensure proper linking in Windows, we download the *Dependency Walker* utility from: `http://www.dependencywalker.com`, and then drag and drop the file *matlabroot/bin/win32/libeng.dll* into the *Depends* window. On newer systems, we drop the file *matlabroot/bin/win64/libeng.dll*.

Assume that MATLAB has been installed in the `/usr/local/matlab` Unix directory. To obtain a list of the required libraries, we navigate to the directory */usr/local/matlab/bin/glnx86* and issue the command:

`ldd -d libeng.so`

The option -d requests a list of dependencies.

Compilation makefile

A Linux makefile that compiles the C++ file *sapouni.cc* and produces the executable *sapouni* reads:

```
LIB1 = -leng -lmx -lut -licuuc -licuio
LIB2 = -lmat -licudata -licui18n -lMTwister
LIB3 = -I/usr/local/matlab/extern/include
LIB4 = -L/usr/local/matlab/bin/glnx86
mexec:  mexec.cc
     c++ -o sapouni sapouni.cc $(LIB1) $(LIB2) $(LIB3) $(LIB4)
```

The first four lines define libraries and header files participating in the executable. We see that nine libraries must be linked with the C++ object of our code, accompanied by corresponding header files. To produce the executable, we issue the command

```
make mexec
```

Library path

A system environmental variable permeates all processes to define the values of important system parameters. Examples are the executable search path, the choice of a display device, and a printer's name or address. The environmental variable LD_LIBRARY_PATH tells the linker where to find libraries not found in standard system directories.

For the compiled program *sapouni* to run, the environmental variable LD_LIBRARY_PATH must be set properly. Assume that MATLAB has been installed in the directory /usr/local/matlab. In the Unix tcsh shell, we issue the command:

```
setenv LD_LIBRARY_PATH '/usr/local/matlab/bin/glnx86'
```

In the Unix bash shell, we issue the command:

```
export LD_LIBRARY_PATH='/usr/local/matlab/bin/glnx86'
```

In other systems, this variable can be set through a graphical user interface.

9.3   The Matlab engine functions

C++ communicates with MATLAB through a small number of *engine* functions. A MATLAB session invoked from C++ is identified by a pointer declared as

```
Engine * ep;
```

where **ep** is a chosen pointer name. This declaration illustrates that **Engine** is a defined class.

Starting a MATLAB session

To start a MATLAB session identified by the pointer **ep**, we state:

```
ep = engOpen("matlab");
```

The launching command **matlab** can be replaced by any other string that invokes MATLAB with options. For example, to suppress the graphical user interface, we use:

```
ep = engOpen("matlab -nodesktop");
```

Equivalently, we can state:

```
char mstart[] = "matlab";
ep = engOpen(mstart);
```

In a third method, we explicitly use a pointer:

```
string invoke[] = "matlab";
char * pnt = invoke;
ep = engOpen(pnt);
```

Terminating a MATLAB session

To terminate the MATLAB session, we issue the statement:

```
engClose(ep);
```

The function **engClose** returns an integer.

Establishing a buffer

C++ has access to a character buffer that records the standard output of MATLAB, that is, it records output that ordinarily appears on the screen.

To establish this buffer, we select its size, declare a dedicated character string, and attach the character string to the MATLAB session by issuing the commands:

```
const int Bufsize = 256;
char Bufname[];
```

```
engOutputBuffer (ep, Bufname, Bufsize);
```

where `Bufsize` and `Bugname` are given names. The function `engOutputBuffer` returns an integer.

Executing a MATLAB command

We can execute (evaluate) a MATLAB command directly by invoking the function:

```
engEvalString (ep, "matlab command");
```

or indirectly by issuing the commands:

```
char mcom[] = "matlab command";
engEvalString (ep, mcom);
```

The function `engEvalString` returns an integer.

Putting variables into the MATLAB workspace

We can transfer a variable from the C++ domain to the engine workspace by invoking the function:

```
engPutVariable (Engine *ep, const char *string, const mxArray * string);
```

as discussed in Section 9.4. The function `engPutVariable` returns an integer.

Retrieving variables from the MATLAB workspace

We can transfer a variable from the MATLAB workspace to the C++ domain by invoking the function:

```
mxArray * engGetVariable (Engine *ep, const char *string);
```

as discussed in Section 9.5.

Running a MATLAB session

In the simplest application, we start MATLAB from a C++ program and carry out various computations in the MATLAB workspace. The commands are transferred from the C++ domain to the MATLAB workspace, and the MATLAB response becomes available through a buffer in the form of a long character string. Thus, direct data exchange does not take place.

The following C++ code contained in the file *mexec.cc* asks for MAT-
LAB commands, which are then processed by MATLAB. The result is put in a
memory buffer and displayed on the screen, and the session terminates when a
zero (0) is entered instead of a command:

```cpp
#include <iostream>
#include "engine.h"
using namespace std;

int main()
{
//--- Start a matlab engine session:

Engine * skilaki;
skilaki = engOpen("matlab -nodesktop -nosplash");

//--- Define a character buffer:

const int BUFSIZE=256;
char buffer[BUFSIZE];
engOutputBuffer(skilaki, buffer, BUFSIZE);

/*--- Define a character array to host a matlab command:
      Initialize the first character to 1 */

char matcom[50];
matcom[0]=1;
cout << "Please enter matlab commands:  0 to quit:"<< endl;

//--- Keep asking for commands until 0 is entered:

while(matcom[0] != '0')
{
  cin >> matcom;

  //--- Transfer the command to the matlab workspace:
  engEvalString(skilaki, matcom);

  //--- Display the matlab response:
  cout << buffer;
}

//--- End the session:

engClose(skilaki);

return 0;
}
```

Note that we have included the **engine.h** header file. A typical session is listed below:

```
a=4
>>
a =
        4
b=9
>>
b =
        9
c=a+b
>>
c =
       13
0
>>
ans =
        0
```

where >> is the MATLAB line prompt.

In retrospect, this code accomplishes little. This session could have been established by calling MATLAB directly rather than through the C++ code.

Problems

9.3.1. Use the code **mexec.cc** to compute and print (*a*) the square root of a number, and (*b*) the product of two matrices defined in MATLAB.

9.3.2. Investigate the significance of the buffer size.

9.4   Transferring data to the Matlab domain

In practice, we want to generate data in the C++ domain and ask MATLAB to lend us computational and graphics services.

Consider the array x[M][N] consisting of floating point numbers registered in double precision. To transfer this array into MATLAB, we work in three stages:

- First, we introduce an *mxArray*, with M rows and N columns, where the prefix *mx* stands for MATLAB executable. This is done using the command:

```
mxArray * arrayname = mxCreateDoubleMatrix (M, N, mxTYPE);
```

where the literal `mxTYPE` can be `mxREAL` for an array with real elements
or `mxCOMPLEX` for an array with complex elements consisting of a real and
an imaginary part.

- Second, we evaluate the *mxArray* using the command:

```
memcpy(mxGetPr(arrayname), xp, sizeof(x));
```

where `xp` is a pointer to the C++ array `x`.

- Third, we transfer the *mxArray* into the MATLAB-workspace using an
engine function:

```
engPutVariable(ep, "name", arrayname);
```

where `ep` is the declared engine session pointer name, and `name` is the
name of the array in the MATLAB domain.

The following code contained in the file *mtrans.cc* defines a numerical
variable, introduces its pointer, transfers the variable in the MATLAB domain,
and prints the variable:

```
#include <iostream>
#include "engine.h"
using namespace std;

int main()
{
double a = 5.0;
double * ap = &a;

//--- Start a session:

Engine * lva = engOpen("matlab12 -nojvm -nosplash");

//--- Define a character buffer:

const int BUFSIZE=256;
char buffer[BUFSIZE];
engOutputBuffer(lva, buffer, BUFSIZE);

/*--- Reserve the array ''mxa''
      Copy into memory
      Transfer the data */

mxArray * mxa = mxCreateDoubleMatrix(1, 1, mxREAL);
memcpy(mxGetPr(mxa), ap, sizeof(a));
engPutVariable(lva, "b", mxa);
```

```
//--- Matlab session:

engEvalString(lva, "b");

cout << buffer; // transfer back the matlab response

//--- End the session:

engClose(lva);

return 0;
}
```

The output of the code is:

```
>>
b =
    5
```

Two-dimensional graph

The following code contained in the file *mplot2d.cc* generates data and prepares a two-dimensional plot using MATLAB graphics functions:

```
#include <iostream>
#include "engine.h"
using namespace std;

int main()
{

//--- Define data:

const short sdata = 5;
double x[sdata] = {0.0, 0.1, 0.5, 0.8, 0.9};
double y[sdata] = {0.0, 0.2, 0.3, 0.4, 0.42};

//--- Start a Matlab session:

Engine * iams = engOpen("matlab -nojvm");

/*--- Reserve the array ''hronos''
      Copy into memory
      Transfer the data */

mxArray * hronos = mxCreateDoubleMatrix(1, sdata, mxREAL);
memcpy((void *)mxGetPr(hronos), (void *)x, sizeof(x));
```

```
engPutVariable(iams, "hrn", hronos);

/*--- Reserve the array ''position''
      Copy into memory
      Transfer the data */

mxArray * position = mxCreateDoubleMatrix(1, sdata, mxREAL);
memcpy((void *)mxGetPr(position), (void *)y, sizeof(y));
engPutVariable(iams, "pos", position);

/*--- Reserve the array ''distance''
      Evaluate in the Matlab domain */

mxArray * distance = mxCreateDoubleMatrix(1, sdata, mxREAL);
engEvalString(iams, "distance = 0.5*hrn.^2;");

/*--- Run a Matlab session:

engEvalString(iams, "plot(hrn,pos,'o-');");
engEvalString(iams, "hold on;");
engEvalString(iams, "plot(hrn,distance,'rs:');");
engEvalString(iams, "ylabel('metrisis','fontsize',15)");
engEvalString(iams, "xlabel('hronos','fontsize',15)");
engEvalString(iams, "set(gca,'fontsize',15)");

/*--- End the session:

cout << "Hit return to finish" << endl;
fgetc(stdin);

return 0;
}
```

Figure 9.4.1 shows the generated graphics display. The graph can be saved in a graphics file under various formats using menu options given in the graphics window.

Three-dimensional graph

The following code contained in the file *mplot3d.cc* produces a vector containing nodes along the x axis, and a second vector containing nodes along the y axis. The code then defines a two-dimensional Cartesian grid based on the x and y nodes, evaluates a function at the nodes, and finally prepares a three-dimensional plot:

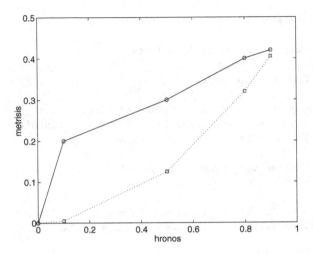

Figure 9.4.1 A two-dimensional plot generated by MATLAB through C++ code.

```cpp
#include <iostream>
#include <cmath>
#include "engine.h"
using namespace std;

int main()
{

//--- Define the nodes:

const short Nx = 33; // size of the data vector
const short Ny = 17; // size of the data vector
double x[Nx+1], y[Ny+1];
double z[Nx+1][Ny+1];

//--- x grid lines:

for (int i=0; i<=Nx; i++)
{
x[i]= (i-1.0+1.0)/Nx;
}

//--- y grid lines:

for (int j=0; j<=Ny; j++)
{
y[j]= (j-1.0+1.0)/Ny;
}
```

```
//--- z data:

for (int i=0; i<=Nx; i++)
{
  for (int j=0; j<=Ny; j++)
  {
  z[i][j]=cos(2*3.14159*(x[i]+y[j]))*exp(-3.0*x[i]);
  }
}

//--- Start a Matlab session:

Engine * gataki = engOpen("matlab12 -nodesktop");
engOutputBuffer(gataki, buffer, BUFSIZE);

/*--- Reserve the vector ''xx''
      Copy into memory
      Transfer the data */

mxArray * xx = mxCreateDoubleMatrix(1, Nx+1, mxREAL);
memcpy((void *)mxGetPr(xx), (void *)x, sizeof(x));
engPutVariable(gataki, "xplot", xx);

/*--- Reserve the vector ''yy''
      Copy into memory
      Transfer the data */

mxArray * yy = mxCreateDoubleMatrix(1, Ny+1, mxREAL);
memcpy((void *)mxGetPr(yy), (void *)y, sizeof(y));
engPutVariable(gataki, "yplot", yy);

/*--- Reserve the matrix ''zz''
      Copy into memory
      Transfer the data */

mxArray * zz = mxCreateDoubleMatrix(Ny+1, Nx+1, mxREAL);
memcpy((void *)mxGetPr(zz), (void *)z, sizeof(z));
engPutVariable(gataki, "zplot", zz);

//--- Matlab session:

engEvalString(gataki, "mesh(xplot,yplot,zplot);");
engEvalString(gataki, "hold on;");
engEvalString(gataki, "xlabel('x','fontsize',15)");
engEvalString(gataki, "ylabel('y','fontsize',15)");
engEvalString(gataki, "zlabel('z','fontsize',15)");
engEvalString(gataki, "set(gca,'fontsize',15)");
```

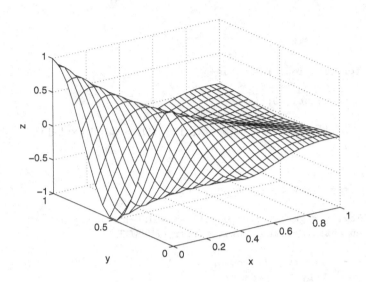

Figure 9.4.2 A three-dimensional plot generated by MATLAB through C++ code.

```
//--- End the session:

cout << "Hit return to continue\n";
fgetc(stdin);

return 0;
}
```

Figure 9.4.2. shows the generated graphics display.

It is important to note that the C++ data matrix z[Nx+1][Ny+1] is passed to MATLAB as an $(N_y + 1) \times (N_x + 1)$ matrix using the statement:

```
mxArray * zz = mxCreateDoubleMatrix(Ny+1, Nx+1, mxREAL);
```

This is because MATLAB stores the elements of a matrix by columns, whereas C++ stores the elements of a matrix in rows.

Drawing a sphere

As a further application, we now discuss a code contained in the file *msphere.cc* that generates a sphere by plotting surface patches defined by azimuthal and meridional divisions:

```cpp
#include <iostream>
#include <cmath>
#include "engine.h"
using namespace std;

//======================================

int main()
{

//--- Data:

double pi=3.14159265358;

const short Nt=16; // azimuthal divisions
const short Np=32; // meridional divisions

double x[Nt+1][Np+1], y[Nt+1][Np+1], z[Nt+1][Np+1];

double theta,ct,st,phi,cp,sp;

//--- Nodes:

double Dt = pi/Nt;
double Dp = 2*pi/Np;

for (int i=0; i<=Nt; i++)
{
theta = Dt*i;
ct = cos(theta);
st = sin(theta);
for (int j=0; j<=Np; j++)
  {
  phi = Dp*j;
  cp = cos(phi);
  sp = sin(phi);
  x[i][j]= ct;
  y[i][j]= st*cp;
  z[i][j]= st*sp;
  }
}

//--- Matlab:  gataki is the matlab session name

Engine * gataki = engOpen("matlab14 -nosplash -nodesktop");

//--- Establish a buffer:

const int BUFSIZE=256;
```

```
char buffer[BUFSIZE];
engOutputBuffer(gataki, buffer, BUFSIZE);

/* Matlab commands:  reserve the vector ''xx''
copy into memory
import the data */

mxArray * xx = mxCreateDoubleMatrix(Np+1, Nt+1, mxREAL);
memcpy((void *)mxGetPr(xx), (void *)x, sizeof(x));
engPutVariable(gataki, "xplot", xx);

/* Matlab commands:  reserve the vector ''yy''
copy into memory
import the data */

mxArray * yy = mxCreateDoubleMatrix(Np+1, Nt+1, mxREAL);


memcpy((void *)mxGetPr(yy), (void *)y, sizeof(y));
engPutVariable(gataki, "yplot", yy);

/* Matlab commands:  reserve the matrix''zz''
copy into memory
import the data */

mxArray * zz = mxCreateDoubleMatrix(Np+1, Nt+1, mxREAL);

memcpy((void *)mxGetPr(zz), (void *)z, sizeof(z));
engPutVariable(gataki, "zplot", zz);

//--- Matlab session:

engEvalString(gataki, "Nt=16;");
engEvalString(gataki, "Np=32;");
engEvalString(gataki, "xplot=xplot';yplot=yplot';zplot=zplot';");
engEvalString(gataki, "hold on");
engEvalString(gataki, "for i=1:Nt; for j=1:Np;
xp(1)=xplot(i,j);yp(1)=yplot(i,j);zp(1)=zplot(i,j);
xp(2)=xplot(i+1,j);yp(2)=yplot(i+1,j);zp(2)=zplot(i+1,j);
xp(3)=xplot(i+1,j+1);yp(3)=yplot(i+1,j+1);zp(3)=zplot(i+1,j+1);
xp(4)=xplot(i,j+1);yp(4)=yplot(i,j+1); zp(4)=zplot(i,j+1);
xp(5)=xplot(i,j); yp(5)=yplot(i,j); zp(5)=zplot(i,j);
patch(xp,yp,zp,zp); end; end");
engEvalString(gataki, "axis equal;");
engEvalString(gataki, "xlabel('x','fontsize',15)");
engEvalString(gataki, "ylabel('y','fontsize',15)");
engEvalString(gataki, "zlabel('z','fontsize',15)");
engEvalString(gataki, "set(gca,'fontsize',15)");
```

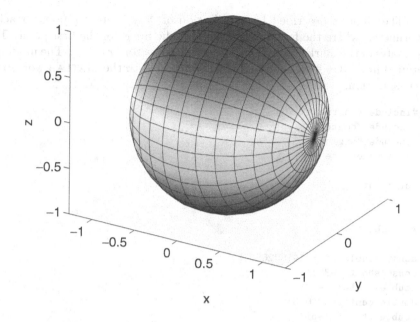

Figure 9.4.3 Drawing of a sphere generated by MATLAB through C++ code.

```
//--- Finish the session:

cout << "Hit return to continue\n";

fgetc(stdin);

return 0;
}
```

Figure 9.4.3 shows the generated graphics display.

Note that the C++ data matrix z[Nt+1][Np+1] is passed to MATLAB as an $(N_p + 1) \times (N_t + 1)$ matrix using the statement:

```
mxArray * zz = mxCreateDoubleMatrix(Np+1, Nt+1, mxREAL);
```

Animation of a bouncing circle

The following code contained in the file *animation.cc* animates the motion of a bouncing circle inside a square box. When the center of the circle hits one of the boundaries, the motion is reflected by switching the sign of the horizontal or vertical velocity.

The circle is described by a collection of $N + 1$ marker points tracing its perimeter, where the last point is the periodic image of the first point. The coordinates of the marker points are stored in the vectors x and y. The motion is computed in the C++ domain and then transferred to the MATLAB workspace for visualization:

```cpp
#include <iostream>
#include <cmath>
#include "engine.h"
using namespace std;

int main()
{

//--- Data:

const double pi=3.14159265358;
const short N=32;
double centerx = 0.0;
double centery = 0.0;
double step = 2*pi/N;
double x[N+1], y[N+1];

for (int i=0; i<=N; i++)
{
double arg = i*step;
x[i]= cos(arg)+centerx;
y[i]= sin(arg)+centery;
}

//--- Start a matlab session:

Engine * cokar = engOpen("matlab -nodesktop -nosplash");

/*--- Reserve the vector ``xx''
      copy into memory
      import the data */

mxArray * xx = mxCreateDoubleMatrix(1, N+1, mxREAL);
memcpy((void *)mxGetPr(xx), (void *)x, sizeof(x));
engPutVariable(cokar, "xx", xx);

/*--- Reserve the vector ``yy''
      copy into memory
      import the data */

mxArray * yy = mxCreateDoubleMatrix(1, N+1, mxREAL);
memcpy((void *)mxGetPr(yy), (void *)y, sizeof(y));
engPutVariable(cokar, "yy", yy);
```

```
//--- Matlab session:

engEvalString(cokar, "Handle1 = plot(xx,yy,'-','linewidth',2);");
engEvalString(cokar, "hold on");

engEvalString(cokar, "axis square");
engEvalString(cokar, "axis([-5 5 -5 5])");
engEvalString(cokar, "set(Handle1,'EraseMode','xor');");
engEvalString(cokar, "xlabel('x','fontsize',15)");
engEvalString(cokar, "ylabel('y','fontsize',15)");
engEvalString(cokar, "set(gca,'fontsize',15)");

//--- Animation:

float velx=1.0;
float vely=0.5;
float Dt = 0.1; // time step

//--- Loop over time:

for (int istep=0; istep<=10000; istep++)
{
      centerx = centerx+velx*Dt;
      centery = centery+vely*Dt;

      for (int i=0; i<=N; i++)
      {
      x[i]=x[i]+velx*Dt;
      y[i]=y[i]+vely*Dt;
      }

      memcpy((void *)mxGetPr(xx), (void *)x, sizeof(x));
      engPutVariable(cokar, "xx", xx);

      memcpy((void *)mxGetPr(yy), (void *)y, sizeof(y));
      engPutVariable(cokar, "yy", yy);

      engEvalString(cokar, "set(Handle1,'XData',xx,'YData',yy);");
      engEvalString(cokar, "drawnow;");

      if(centerx > 5.0) velx=-velx; //--- reflect if necessary
      if(centerx <-5.0) velx=-velx;
      if(centery > 5.0) vely=-vely;
      if(centery <-5.0) vely=-vely;
}

//--- End the session:
```

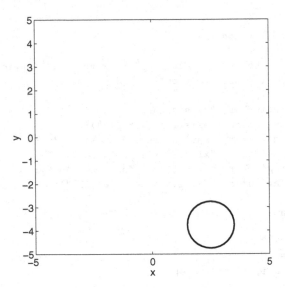

Figure 9.4.4 Animation of a bouncing circle inside a box generated by MAT-LAB through C++ code.

```
cout << "Hit return to finish\n";
fgetc(stdin);

return 0;
}
```

The graphics display is shown in Figure 9.4.4.

Problems

9.4.1. Write a code that defines data in the C++ domain and then calls MATLAB to display a cube.

9.4.2. Write a code that animates the rotation of a square. The data should be produced in the C++ domain and transferred to MATLAB for visualization.

9.5   Transferring data from Matlab to the C++ domain

Data generated in the MATLAB workspace can be retrieved and stored in appropriate variables in the C++ domain.

Matrix determinant and square

The following code contained in the file *muse1.cc* defines a matrix in the C++ domain, calls MATLAB to compute the determinant and the matrix square, and transfers the results back to the C++ domain:

```
#include <iostream>
#include "engine.h"
using namespace std;

int main()
{
const int BSZ=256;
char BuFFer[BSZ];

//--- Define a matrix in C++:

const short N = 2;
double x[N][N] = {{1.0, 2.0},
                  {4.0, 3.0}};

//--- Start an engine session:

Engine * oliver = engOpen("matlab12 -nojvm -nosplash");
engOutputBuffer(oliver, BuFFer, BSZ);

//--- Define a character buffer:

const int BufSIZE=256;
char buFFer[BufSIZE];
engOutputBuffer(oliver, buFFer, BufSIZE);

//--- Transfer the matrix x to matlab as xm:

mxArray * xm = mxCreateDoubleMatrix(N, N, mxREAL);
memcpy((void *)mxGetPr(xm), (void *)x, sizeof(x));
engPutVariable(oliver, "xm", xm);

//--- Evaluate and print the determinant:

engEvalString(oliver, "determinant = det(mat)");
cout << BuFFer;

//--- Retrieve the determinant:

mxArray * det = engGetVariable(oliver, "determinant");
double * orizousa = mxGetPr(det);
cout << *orizousa << endl;
```

```
//--- Evaluate the square:

engEvalString(oliver, "mat2 = mat^2");
cout << BuFFer;

//--- Retrieve the square:

mxArray * x2 = engGetVariable(oliver, "mat2");
double * square = mxGetPr(x2);
cout << "C++ domain:" << endl;
cout << square[0] << " " << square[2] << endl;
cout << square[1] << " " << square[3] << endl;

//--- End the session:

engClose(oliver);

return 0;
}
```

The session produces the following output on the screen:

```
>>
determinant =
      -5
>>
mat2 =
     9 16
     8 17
C++ domain:
9 16
8 17
```

The indented output originates from the MATLAB domain, and the non-indented output originates from the C++ domain. It is important to observe that the MATLAB matrix x2 is retrieved as the C++ vector square in a *column-wise* fashion.

Eigenvalues and eigenvectors

A complex number is composed of a real and an imaginary part. The real and imaginary parts of a scalar, vector, or matrix produced by MATLAB are placed in consecutive memory blocks.

The following code contained in the file muse2.cc defines a matrix in the C++ domain, calls MATLAB to compute the eigenvalues and eigenvectors, and transfers the results back to the C++ domain:

```
/* --------
Use matlab to compute the eigenvalues
and eigenvectors of a matrix
-----------*/

#include <iostream>
#include <iomanip>
#include "engine.h"

using namespace std;

int main()
{

//--- Define a matrix in C++:

const short N = 4; // size of the data matrix

double x[N][N] = {{ 1.0, 2.0, 3.0, 4.0},
                  {-4.0,-3.0, 5.0, 6.0},
                  { 8.0,-5.0, 5.0,-6.0},
                  {-0.8,-3.0,-5.0, 6.0},
                  };

//--- Start an engine session:

Engine * bouboulina = engOpen("matlab -nojvm -nosplash");

//--- Establish a buffer:

const int BSZ=1024;
char BuFFer[BSZ];
engOutputBuffer(bouboulina, BuFFer, BSZ);

//--- Transfer x to matlab as xm:

mxArray * xmat = mxCreateDoubleMatrix(N, N, mxREAL);
memcpy(mxGetPr(xmat), x, sizeof(x));
engPutVariable(bouboulina, "matrix", xmat);

//--- Compute the eigenvalues:

engEvalString(bouboulina, "[V,D]=eig(matrix)");

//--- Display the eigenvalues:

cout << BuFFer;

//--- Retrieve the eigenvector matrix:
```

```
mxArray * Eigv = engGetVariable(bouboulina, "V");
double * V = mxGetPr(Eigv);

//--- Define the real (EVR) and imaginary (EVI) parts
//--- of the eigenvalue matrix:

double EVR[N][N];
double EVI[N][N];
int Ic=-1, Jc;

for (int j=0; j<=N-1; j++)
{
  for (int i=0; i<=N-1; i++)
  {
  Ic=Ic+1;
  EVR[i][j]=V[Ic];
  Jc = Ic+N*N;
  EVI[i][j]=V[Jc];
  }
}

//--- Print the real part of the eigenvector matrix:

cout << setiosflags(ios::fixed | ios::showpoint);

cout << endl;
cout << "C++ domain:" << endl << endl;

for (int i=0; i<=N-1; i++)
{
  for (int j=0; j<=N-1; j++)
  {
  cout << setprecision(5) << setw(10) << EVR[i][j] << " ";
  }
cout << endl;
}

//--- Print the imaginary part of the eigenvector matrix:

cout << endl;

for (int i=0; i<=N-1; i++)
{
  for (int j=0; j<=N-1; j++)
  {
  cout << setprecision(5) << setw(10) << EVI[i][j] << " ";
  }
cout << endl;
```

```
}

//--- Retrieve the eigenvalue matrix:

mxArray * Eig = engGetVariable(bouboulina, "D");
double * D = mxGetPr(Eig);

//--- real (ER) and imaginary (EI) parts of the eigenvalue matrix

double ER[N][N];
double EI[N][N];
Ic=-1;

for (int j=0; j<=N-1; j++)
{
  for (int i=0; i<=N-1; i++)
  {
  Ic=Ic+1;
  ER[i][j]=D[Ic];
  Jc = Ic+N*N;
  EI[i][j]=D[Jc];
  }
}

//--- Print the real part of the eigenvalue matrix:

cout << endl;

for (int i=0; i<=N-1; i++)
{
  for (int j=0; j<=N-1; j++)
  {
  cout << setprecision(5) << setw(10) << ER[i][j] << " ";
  }
cout << endl;
}

//--- Print the imaginary part of the eigenvalue matrix:

cout << endl;

for (int i=0; i<=N-1; i++)
{
  for (int j=0; j<=N-1; j++)
  {
  cout << setprecision(5) << setw(10) << EI[i][j] << " ";
  }
cout << endl;
}
```

```
//--- end the session

engClose(bouboulina);

return 0;
}
```

The session produces the following output on the screen:

```
>>
V =
   0.1395 - 0.4469i    0.1395 + 0.4469i    0.8390   -0.6200
  -0.6325             -0.6325             -0.1584    0.0613
  -0.0107 + 0.4167i   -0.0107 - 0.4167i    0.4250   -0.6626
   0.0052 + 0.4550i    0.0052 - 0.4550i    0.3008    0.4157


D =
  -3.5013 + 6.8653i           0                      0    0
          0           -3.5013 - 6.8653i              0    0
          0                    0              5.5207      0
          0                    0                   0    10.4819


C++ domain:

    0.13951     0.13951     0.83896    -0.61997
   -0.63248    -0.63248    -0.15835     0.06126
   -0.01070    -0.01070     0.42498    -0.66261
    0.00515     0.00515     0.30077     0.41574

   -0.44691     0.44691     0.00000     0.00000
    0.00000    -0.00000     0.00000     0.00000
    0.41667    -0.41667     0.00000     0.00000
    0.45500    -0.45500     0.00000     0.00000

   -3.50127     0.00000     0.00000     0.00000
    0.00000    -3.50127     0.00000     0.00000
    0.00000     0.00000     5.52066     0.00000
    0.00000     0.00000     0.00000    10.48188

    6.86532     0.00000     0.00000     0.00000
    0.00000    -6.86532     0.00000     0.00000
    0.00000     0.00000     0.00000     0.00000
    0.00000     0.00000     0.00000     0.00000
```

We have computed and retrieved the real and imaginary parts of the eigenvalues and eigenvectors and stored them in individual matrices.

Problems

9.5.1. Write a code that defines a 3×3 matrix in the C++ domain, calls MATLAB to compute its inverse, and finally transfers the inverse back to the C++ domain into a 3×3 matrix.

9.5.2. Write a code that defines two 3×3 matrices in the C++ domain, calls MATLAB to compute their product, and finally transfers the product back to the C++ domain into a new 3×3 matrix.

Unix Primer

A

By any measure and all accounts, Unix is the most efficient and dependable operating system.

Like C++, Unix is case sensitive. The command or name `aginara` is not the same as `Aginara`.

To use a Unix computer, we need an account. Once this is established, we log in by typing the username and password in response to a prompt. To log out, we type:

`logout`

To change the password, we type:

`passwd`

A Unix file system can be regarded as a file cabinet accessible at a *mount point*. A file system can be mounted or unmounted manually or automatically when a recordable medium, such as a hard drive or a CD-ROM, is attached. File systems have different types such as `ext3`, or `ntfs`.

Each folder (directory) of a file system contains subfolders (subdirectories) and documents (files). Ancillary files whose names begin with a dot, such as *.simos*, are hidden from plain view. The directories are thus arranged in a pyramidal, tree-like structure. The top directory at the apex, denoted by a slash (/), is called the root. A typical directory structure is shown below:

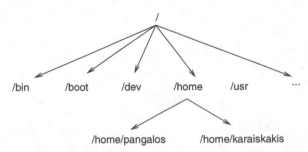

mkdir koulis	Generate a directory named koulis
rmdir kekos	Remove the directory named kekos
	(a directory can be removed only if empty)
rmdir -R kekos	Remove directory kekos and its contents
	(the argument -R stands for "recursive")
mv kekos koulis	Rename directory kekos to koulis
cp -R kekos koulis	Copy directory kekos to koulis
ls kekos	List files and folders in directory kekos
ls -a kekos	Include hidden files beginning with a dot
ls -l kekos	Long list of directory contents
pwd	Print the name of the working directory
cd koulis	Go to directory named koulis
	(koulis can be the absolute or relative name)
cd /	Go to the root directory
cd	Go to the home directory
cd ..	Go up one directory from working directory
cd ../..	Go up two directories from working directory
~	Home directory
~username	A user's home directory
.	Working (current) directory
..	Parent of working directory
../..	Grandparent of working directory
../../..	Ancestor of working directory

Table A.1 Unix commands for manipulating directories. The "working directory" is an abbreviation of the "current working directory."

The *absolute name* of the file or directory named "karaiskakis" in this tree is: /home/karaiskakis. If we are situated in directory /home, the *relative name* of this file or directory is: karaiskakis.

Assume that the absolute name of a directory is: /usr/local/lib/vogle. If we are situated in directory /usr/local, the relative name of this directory is: lib/vogle.

Every user has a home (login) directory accessed at log in, denoted with a tilde: ~ .

Unix commands are interpreted by a program called the Unix *shell*. Examples are the *csh*, the *tcsh*, the *bourne*, and the *bash* (bourne again) shell. While the basic commands are the same, each shell has its own dialect. We can change the current shell by typing the name of a new shell. To exit the shell, we type: exit .

The tables in the rest of this appendix illustrate basic Unix commands.

vi simos	Create or edit file simos using the vi editor
view simos	Read-only version of vi
cat > simos	Type text in a file named simos; end the session with Ctrl-D
mv simos siomadis	Rename file simos to siomadis
mv simos kekos	Move file simos into directory kekos
mv -i simos kekos	Inquire before overwriting
cat simos	Display contents of file simos
more simos	Display contents of file simos one screen at a time
less simos	A new version of more
rm simos	Remove (delete) file
rm -i simos	Inquire before deleting
diff simos siomadis	Show the differences between files simos and siomadis
cmp simos siomadis	Byte-by-byte comparison
grep string file1 file2 ...	Show lines containing string in listed files
grep -v string file1 file2 ...	Show lines not containing string
grep -i string file1 file2 ...	Show lines containing string, ignore case

Table A.2 Manipulating files in Unix. A file is generated and modified using a text editor. Because *vi* runs in the non-graphics mode, it is the most important editor. Type man vi to obtain further information. Popular graphics editors are *gedit* and *emacs*.

chown user file1 directory1 ...	Change ownership
chgrp group file1 directory1 ...	Change group
chmod mode file1 directory1 ...	Change the permission mode
chmod -R mode directory1 directory2 ...	Change all files in listed directories; R stands for recursive

Mode:

u	g	o	user (owner)	group	other
+	-		add or remove permission		
r	q	x	read	write	execute

Table A.3 In Unix, directories and files have an owner and a designated group of users. Read, write, and execute permissions are set for the owner (user), the group, and others. For example, issuing the command "chmod go+rwx katsarola" grants read, write, and execute permissions to the group and others for the file or directory katsarola.

lpr file	Print file on default printer
lpr -Pseftalia file	Print file on printer named seftalia
lpr -cn file	Print n copies
lpr -d file	Interpret file as a device-independent (dvi) file
lpq	Show printing queue on default printer
lpq -Pseftalia	Show printing queue on printer named seftalia
lprm #	Remove print request # listed with lpq

Table A.4 Unix printing commands.

ps	List processes and identification numbers (pid)
jobs	Report current jobs and job id numbers
ctrl-c	Terminate an active job
ctrl-z	Suspend an active job
kill pid#	Terminate an active process
history	Show session history
!1958	Repeat command with history number 1958
!str	Repeat last command beginning with string str
!!	Repeat entire last command line
!$	Repeat last word of last command line
man command	Display manual for a command
man -k string	List one-line summaries of manual pages containing the string
alias ouzo command	Abbreviate command to: ouzo
?	Single-character wild card
*	Arbitrary number of characters wild card
command > file	Direct output of command to file instead of the standard output (screen), replacing content
command >> file	Output is appended to the current contents
command < file	Command receives input from file instead of the standard input (keyboard)
cmd1	cmd2	"Pipe" (send) output of cmd1 to input of cmd2
script file	Log everything displayed on the screen to a file; end with exit
date	Display date and time
hostname	Display the computer name
ping goulis	Probe computer goulis on the Internet
users	Show logged-in users
env	Display the environmental variables

Table A.5 Miscellaneous Unix commands.

Summary of VOGLE Functions

B

The VOGLE reference manual is available from the Internet site hosting this book: http://dehesa.freeshel.org/vogle. The manual pages explain the syntax and arguments of the VOGLE graphics functions in C or C++, FORTRAN 77, and PASCAL. A summary is given in this appendix.

Setting up windows

prefposition(x, y)	Specify preferred position of the next window
prefsize(width, height)	Specify preferred width and height of the next window

Device control

vinit(device)	Initialize the graphics device. For example, device can be "X11" or "postscript"
vexit()	Exit VOGLE (last routine called) and reset the window or terminal
voutput("filotimo")	Redirect output for *next* vinit to file named *filotimo*
vnewdev(device)	Reinitialize to use a new device
char * vgetdev(device)	Returns the name of the current device
int getdepth()	Returns the number of bit planes (color planes) The number of colors displayable by the device is $2^{(nplanes-1)}$.

Color

color(hroma)	Set the current color: hroma can be: BLACK, RED, GREEN, YELLOW BLUE, MAGENTA, CYAN, WHITE mapped as a structure to: 0, 1, ... 7
clear()	Clear screen to current color
mapcolor(indx, red, green, blue)	Set color map index

Axes and projections

The projection routines define a new transformation matrix and consequently new world units. Parallel projections are defined by the functions ortho and ortho2. Perspective projections are defined by the functions perspective and window.

ortho (left, right, bottom, top, near, far)	Define x, y, and z clipping planes
ortho2 (left, right, bottom, top)	Define x and y clipping planes
perspective (fov, aspect, near, far)	Specify perspective
	for field of view (fov), aspect
	ratio (aspect), and distance
	from the eye to the near and far
	clipping planes
window (left, right, bot, top, near, far)	Viewing pyramid
clipping (onoff)	Turn clipping on or off;
	set onoff to 0 to turn off

Text

font (fontname)	Set the current font
int numchars()	Return number of characters
	in the current SOFTWARE font
textsize (width, height)	Set maximum size of a character
	in the current SOFTWARE font
	Negative size gives backward characters
textang (ang)	Set the SOFTWARE text angle
fixedwidth (onoff)	Turn fixed-width mode on or off
	for a SOFTWARE font
centertext (onoff)	Turns center-text mode on or off
	for SOFTWARE a font
getcharsize (c, width, height)	Get the width and height of a character
getfontsize (width, height)	Get maximum width and height
	of a character
drawchar (c)	Draw the character c
	and update the current position
drawstr (str)	Draw the text in string
	at the current position
float strlength (str)	Return the length of the string *srt*
boxtext (x, y, l, h, str)	Draw the SOFTWARE string *str*
	so that it fits in the imaginary box
boxfit (l, h, nchars)	Set scale for text so that a string
	of the biggest characters in the
	SOFTWARE font will fit inside an $l \times h$ box,
	where l and h are real values

Keyboard and cursor

int getkey()	Get the ASCII ordinal of the next key typed
int checkkey()	Returns zero if no key is pressed
	or ASCII ordinal if a key is pressed
int locator (xaddr, yaddr)	Locate the cursor: addr and yaddr are set
	to the current location in world coordinates
	The function returns a bit pattern indicating
	which buttons are held down
	If mouse buttons 1 and 3 are pressed,
	the locator returns the binary 101
	(decimal 7). The function returns -1 if the
	device has no locator capability
int slocator (xaddr, yaddr)	Locate the cursor in screen coordinates.
	The return value of the function is set up
	in the same way as with the locator
int getstring (bcol, string	Read in a string, echoing it in the current font
	with the current color and transformation
	bcol is the background color used for erasing
	characters after a backspace or delete key
	is received. The Backspace key (ASCII 8)
	and the Del key (ASCII 127) are interpreted as
	erasing characters. An EOT (ASCII 4)
	or a Carriage return (ASCII 13) will terminate
	the input. *getstring* returns the number of
	characters read. *getstring* does not check
	for overflow in the input buffer string

Moving the pen

move (x, y, z)	Move current graphics position to (x, y, z)
rmove (deltax, deltay, deltaz)	Relative move
move2 (x, y)	Move graphics position to point (x, y)
rmove2 (deltax, deltay)	Relative move in world units
smove2 (x, y)	Move current graphics position
	in screen coordinates (-1.0 to 1.0)
rsmove2 (deltax, deltay)	Relative move in screen units (-1.0 to 1.0)

Points

point (x, y, z)	Draw a point at x, y, z
point2 (x, y)	Draw a point at x, y

Drawing

draw (x, y, z)	Draw from the current graphics position to the point (x, y, z)
rdraw (deltax, deltay, deltaz)	Relative draw
draw2 (x, y)	Draw from the current graphics position to the point (x, y)
rdraw2 (deltax,deltay)	Relative draw
sdraw2 (x, y)	Draw in screen coordinates, -1.0 to 1.0
rsdraw2 (deltax, deltay)	Relative draw in screen units, -1.0 to 1.0

Viewport

It is possible to subdivide the screen into rectangular partitions called viewports, and then navigate inside each partition using screen coordinates ranging from -1.0 to 1.0.

viewport (left, right, bottom, top)	Specifies a portion of the screen for drawing; the box limits: left, right, bottom, and top are real values in screen coordinates.
pushviewport ()	Save the current viewport
popviewport ()	Retrieve last viewport
getviewport (left, right, bottom, top)	Returns limits of current viewport in screen coordinates

Aspect details

float getaspec t()	Returns the height-over-width ratio of the display device
getfactors (wfact, hfact)	Returns the width over the minimum of the width and height of the device, and the height over the minimum of the width and height of the device
getdisplaysize (w, h)	Returns width and height of device in pixels

Attribute stack

pushattributes ()	Save the current attributes on the attribute stack
popattributes ()	Restore attributes to what they were at last pushattributes

Matrix stack

pushmatrix ()	Save the current transformation matrix on the matrix stack
popmatrix ()	Reinstate the last matrix pushed

Viewpoint

polarview (dist, azim, inc, twist)	Specify the viewer's position in polar coordinates
up (x, y, z)	Specify the world up
lookat (vx, vy, vz, px, py, pz, twist)	Specify the viewer's position

Arcs and circles

circleprecision (nsegs)	Set number of line segments around a circle; default is 32
arc (x, y, radius, startang, endang)	Draw an arc in world units
sector (x, y, radius, startang, endang)	Draw a sector interpreted as a polygon
circle (x, y, radius)	Draw a circle interpreted as a polygon.

Curves

curvebasis (basis)	Define a basis matrix for a curve
curveprecision (nsegs)	Define the number of line segments to draw a curve
rcurve (geom)	Draw a rational curve
curve (geom)	Draw a curve
curven (n, geom)	Draw n-3 overlapping curve segments; n must be at least 4

Transformations

translate (x, y, z)	Set up a translation
scale (x, y, z)	Set up scaling factors for x, y, and z axes
rotate (angle, axis)	Set up a rotation for axis, where axis is x, y, or z

Flushing

vsetflush (yesno)	Set global flushing status
vflush ()	Call device flush or synchronization routine

Rectangles and polygons

rect (x1, y1, x2, y2)	Draw a rectangle
polyfill (onoff)	Set the polygon fill flag
polyhatch (onoff)	Set the polygon hatch flag
hatchang (angle)	Set the angle of the hatch lines
hatchpitch (pitch)	Set the distance between hatch lines
poly2 (n, points)	Construct an (x, y) polygon from an array of point
poly (n, points)	Construct a polygon from an array of points
makepoly ()	Open a polygon constructed by a series of move-draws and closed by closepoly
closepoly ()	Terminate a polygon opened by makepoly
backface (onoff)	Turn on culling of backfacing polygons
backfacedir (clockwise)	Set backfacing direction to clockwise or anti-clockwise

Patches

patchbasis (tbasis, ubasis)	Define the t and u basis matrices of a patch
patchprecision (tseg, useg)	Set minimum number of line segments making up curves in a patch
patchcurves (nt, nu)	Set the number of curves making up a patch
rpatch (gx, gy, gz, gw)	Draw a rational patch in the current basis, according to the geometry matrices gx, gy, gz, and gw
patch (gx, gy, gz)	Draw a patch in the current basis according to the geometry matrices gx, gy, and gz

Objects

makeobj (n)	Commence the object number n
closeobj ()	Close the current object
int genobj ()	Get a unique object identifier
int getopenobj ()	Get the number of the current object
callobj (n)	Draw object number n
int isobj (n)	Return non-zero if an object numbered n has been defined
delobj (n)	Delete the object number n
loadobj (n, filename)	Load the object number n in the file filename
saveobj (n, filename)	Save the object number n into file filename; does *not* save objects called inside object n

Double buffering

backbuffer ( )	Make vogle draw in the backbuffer; returns -1 if the device is not up to it
frontbuffer ()	Make vogle draw in the front buffer; this will always work
swapbuffers ()	Swap the front and back buffers

Position

getgp (x, y, z)	Get the current graphics position in world coordinates
getgp2 (x, y)	Get the current graphics position in world coordinates
sgetgp2 (x, y)	Get the current screen graphics position in screen coordinates ranging from -1 to 1

C++/Matlab/Fortran 77 Dictionary

In this Appendix, we summarize the main syntactic differences between C++ (and C), MATLAB, and FORTRAN 77, and present translation tables.

- Like C++, MATLAB is case-sensitive. FORTRAN 77 is case-insensitive, although this can be changed by raising an appropriate compiler flag.

- A C++ statement may begin at any place in a line and continue in the next line. A MATLAB statement may continue in the next line provided that a continuation mark represented by three dots (...) is inserted at the end of the *current* line. A FORTRAN 77 statement must begin after the sixth column and continue in the next line only if a character is inserted at the sixth column of the *next* line, representing a continuation mark.

- In C++ and MATLAB, the end of a statement is indicated by a semicolon representing a statement delimiter. If we omit the semicolon in MATLAB, the values of variables evaluated by the statement will be printed on the screen, sometimes flooding the output. No end-of-statement mark is required in FORTRAN 77.

- In C++ and MATLAB, two or more statements may be placed in the same line provided they are separated with semicolons. Only one statement per line is allowed in FORTRAN 77.

- In C++, MATLAB, and FORTRAN 77, white space is ignored. In C++ and MATLAB, a number cannot be split into two pieces separated by space. Thus, we may not write "3.141572" as "3.141 572".

- In C++, in-line comments may be inserted following the double slash (//). In MATLAB, we use the percentage sign (%); in FORTRAN 77, we use the exclamation mark (!).

- In C++, all text enclosed between a slash-asterisk pair (/*) and the converse asterisk-slash pair (*/) is reckoned to be commentary and ignored by the compiler. In MATLAB, we use the percent sign at the beginning of each line. In FORTRAN 77, we use the exclamation mark anywhere, or the "c" character at the beginning of each line.

- In C++, all variables must be declared. Variable declaration is not necessary in MATLAB; some declarations are necessary in FORTRAN 77.

  In FORTRAN 77, all variables beginning with the letters I,J,K,L,M,N (or i,j,k,l,m,n) are integers, while all other variables are real, registered in single precision. These defaults can be changed with appropriate data type declarations.

  For example, the statement:

  ```
  Implicit Double Precision (a-h,o-z)
  ```

  declares that all variables whose names begin with a–h and o–z (or A–H and O–Z) are registered in double precision.

- In C++ and FORTRAN 77, variables are not necessarily initialized to zero. In MATLAB, all variables must be given initial values.

- In MATLAB, a variable can change from integer to real, and vice versa, in the course of a calculation. Not being bothered with variable types is an extremely appealing feature of MATLAB. The penalty possible confusion and a prolonged CPU time.

Arrays

In C++, array indices can be zero or positive. In MATLAB, array indices can only be positive. These extremely annoying restrictions can be bypassed by shifting the indices.

In FORTRAN 77, array indices can have any positive or negative value.

In C++, the lower limit of an array index is 0. Thus, a vector v with 20 slots begins at $v(0)$ and ends at $v(19)$. Similarly, the indices of the 10×5 matrix $A[10][5]$ begin at $i, j = 0$ and end at $i = 9, j = 4$.

In MATLAB, the lower limit of an array index is 1.

In FORTRAN 77, the default lower limit of an array index is 1. However, this can be reset by stating, for example,

```
double precision A(-30:200)
Dimension B(-4:14,-10:29)
```

The vector A begins at A(-30) and ends at A(200). The first index of the matrix B begins at -4 and ends at 14; the second index begins at -10 and ends at 29.

Functions and subroutines

The structure of functions in C++ was discussed in this book, and the structure of functions in MATLAB is discussed in Appendix F.

FORTRAN 77 uses functions and subroutines. The structure of a subroutine is:

```
subroutine poulaki (a, b,...,s)
...
return
end
```

The parentheses enclose input and output arguments listed in arbitrary order, and the three dots indicate additional lines of code. The statement calling the subroutine is:

```
call poulaki (peace, train, ..., cat)
```

All arguments in FORTRAN 77 are passed by reference. Thus, a FORTRAN 77 function or subroutine is able to change any input argument.

FORTRAN 77 subroutines are written either in the file hosting the main program or in other files contain one subroutine or multiple subroutines, listed in arbitrary order. The names of the files containing the subroutines are arbitrary and bear no relationship to the names of the subroutines. `include` files are not necessary in FORTRAN 77.

In contrast, MATLAB functions are placed in individual files, one function per file. Strangely, the name of the function is determined by the file name, with the function name stated in the function declaration inside the file being irrelevant. This explains why each file must contain only one function, possibly resulting in a huge collection. `include` files are not necessary in MATLAB.

Translation tables

Table C.1 displays the relational and logical operands in the three languages. The similarities between MATLAB and C++ are noteworthy.

A MATLAB or FORTRAN 77 code can be translated into C++ code using the language syntax explained in Tables C.2-4.

Examples

The following C++ code prints on the screen the greeting "Hello Themistocles" and moves the cursor to the next line:

MATLAB   FORTRAN 77   C and C++

MATLAB	FORTRAN 77	C and C++
==	=	==
<	.lt.	<
<=	.le.	<=
>	.gt.	>
>=	.ge.	>=
~=	.ne.	!=
&	.and.	&&
|	.or.	||

Table C.1 Relational and logical operands in MATLAB, FORTRAN 77, and C++.
The MATLAB and C++ columns are nearly identical.

```
#include <iostream>
using namespace std;

int main()
{
cout << "Hello Themistocles \n";
return 0;
}
```

The output of the code is:

```
Hello Themistocles
```

In MATLAB, the same code consists of one line alone:

```
disp "Hello Themistocles"
```

In FORTRAN 77, the same code consists of two lines:

```
write (6,*) "Hello Themistocles"
end
```

Note that six blank spaces must be inserted at the beginning of each line.

MATLAB	C++
%———	/* ———
% AUTHOR: J Doe	AUTHOR: J Doe
%———	——— */
	int main()
	{
No formal structure	...
	return 0;
	}
Variable declaration	float a[30], b[4];
is not required	double a[10];
	double b[6][68];
Non-positive indices	int argos[100];
are not permitted	const int WED= 0;
	const int dim = 40;
	double a[dim];
i=6; % integer	int i=6; // integer
a=10.0; % double	float a=10.0; // real
b=10.0D0; % double	double b=10.0; // double
C=[0.1 0.2. 0.7];	double C[3]={0.1, 0.2, 0.7};
A=[0.1 0.2; -1.0 -0.4];	double A[2][2]={ {0.1, 0.2}, {-1.0, -0.4} };
B=[0.9 0.4; ...	double B[2][2]={ {0.9, 0.4}
-3.0 -0.3];	,{-3.0, -0.3} };
A(1,1)=0.1;	A[0][0] = 0.1;
break	exit(1);

Table C.2 MATLAB/C++ equivalent structures and statements. Statements, but not variable names, are written in lower case in both languages.

FORTRAN 77	C++
c AUTHOR: J Doe	/* AUTHOR: J Doe */
program main	int main()
...	{
stop	...
end	return 0;
	}
Dimension a(0:29), b(0:3)	float a[30], b[4];
Double precision a(0:9)	double a[10];
Double precision b(0:5,0:67)	double b[6][68];
Integer argos(100)	int argos[100];
Dimension argos(-23:89)	
Integer WED	const int WED= 0;
Parameter(WED=134)	
Double precision a(0:39)	const int dim = 40;
	double a[dim];
i = 6 ! integer	int i = 6; // integer
a = 10.0 ! real	float a = 10.0; // real
b = 10.0D0 ! double	double b = 10.0; // double
Dimension b(0:1)	float b[2] = {0.1, 0.3};
b(0) = 0.1	
b(1) = 0.3	
Dimension A(0:1,0:1)	float A[2][2] ={ {0.1, 0.2}, {-1.0, -0.4} };
A(0,0) = 0.1	
A(0,1) = 0.2	
A(1,0) =-1.0	
A(1,1) = 0.4	
Stop	exit(1);
Go to 34	goto melitzana;
34 Continue	melitzana:

Table C.3 FORTRAN 77/C++ equivalent structures and statements.

MATLAB	FORTRAN 77	C++

for i=1:n
  a=a+3;
  b=b+4;
end
	Do i=1,n
	  a=a+3
	  b=b+4
	End Do
		for (i=1;i<=n;i++)
		{ a=a+3;
		  b=b+4;
		}

for i=1:n
  a=a+3
end
	Do i=1,n
	  a=a+3;
	End Do
		for (i=1;i<=n;i++)
		  a=a+3; // only one
		// statement is allowed

for i=j:s:n
...
end
	Do i=j,n,s
	...
	End Do
		for (i=j;i<= n;i=i+s)
		{ ...
		}

while (i~=0)
...
end
	Do while (i.ne.0)
	...
	End Do
		while (i!=0)
		{ ...
		}

if(i==1)
...
end
	If(i.eq.1) then
	...
	End If
		if(i==1)
		{ ...
		}

if(i==1)
  x=3.0;
elseif(i==2)
  x=4.0;
else
  x=5.0;
end
	If(i.eq.1) then
	  x=3.0
	Else If(i.eq.2) then
	  x=4.0
	Else
	  x = 5.0
	End If
		if(i==1)
		  x=3.0;
		else if(i==2)
		  x=4.0;
		else
		  x=5.0;

if(i==1 & j==2)
  k=3;
end
	If(i.eq.1.and.j.eq.2) k=3	if(i==1 && j==2) k=3;

if(i==1 | j==2)
  k=3;
end
	If(i.eq.1.or.j.eq.2) then
	  k = 3
	End If
		if(i==1 || j==2) k=3;

Table C.4 MATLAB/FORTRAN 77/C++ equivalent structures. Note that elseif is one word in MATLAB.

MATLAB	C++
	#include <iostream>
a=input(" ");	cin >> a;
b=input('Please enter b:')	cout << "Please enter b:\n"; cin >> b;
disp(a)	cout << a << endl;
fprintf('%10.5f\n',a)	#include <iomanip> cout << setprecision(5) << setw(10); cout << a << endl;
name = fopen('input.dat');	#include <iostream> ifstream name; name.open("input.dat");

name = fopen('input.dat','wt')
 	
 fprintf(name, '%f %f %f \n',a,b,c)
 	
 fprintf(name, '%f',a(i,j))
 fclose(name)
	#include <fstream>
	 ifstream name("input.dat");
	 name >> a >> b >> c
	 >> endl;
	 name >> a[i][j];
	 name.close();

name=fopen('output.dat','wt');	#include <fstream> ofstream name; name.open("output.dat");

name=fopen('output.dat','wt');
 fprintf(name,'%f',a)
 fclose(name)
	#include <fstream>
	 ofstream name("output.dat");
	 name << a;
	 name.close();

Table C.5 Equivalent MATLAB/C++ structures and calls regarding input and output (I/O). The #include statements are placed at the top of the file containing the C++ code. iostream contains the header files of the standard input/output (keyboard/monitor) stream. fstream contains the header files of the *file* stream.

FORTRAN 77	C++
	#include <iostream>
read (5,*) a	cin >> a;
read (5,*) a,b,c	cin >> a >> b >> c;
write (6,*) a,b,c	cout << a << b << c << endl;
write (6,*)	cout << "\n";
write (6,*) "Please enter a:"	cout << "Please enter a: \n";
write (6,*) "temp=", tmp	cout << "temp=" <<tmp<< "\n";
	#include <iostream>
write (6,100) a	#include <iomanip>
100 Format (f10.5)	cout << setprecision(5) << setw(10);
	cout << a;
	#include <fstream>
open (1, file="input.dat")	ifstream dev_name;
	dev_name.open("input.dat");
	#include <fstream>
open (1, file="input.dat")	ifstream dev_name("input.dat");
read (1,*) a,b,c	dev_name >> a >> b >> c;
read (1,*) a(i,j)	dev_name >> a[i][j];
close (1)	dev_name.close("input.dat");
	#include <fstream>
open (2, file="output.dat")	ofstream othername;
	othername.open("output.dat");
	#include <fstream>
open (2, file="output.dat")	ofstream othername("output.dat");
write (2,*) a,b,c	othername << a << b << c << endl;
write (2,*) a(i,j)	othername << a[i][j] << endl;
close (2)	othername.close("output.dat");

Table C.6 FORTRAN 77/C++ equivalent structures and calls regarding input and output (I/O). The *#include* statements are placed at the top of the file containing the C++ code. iostream contains the header files of the standard input/output (keyboard/monitor) stream. fstream contains the header files of the *file* stream.

The following C++ code computes the sum of the inverses of the squares of the first N integers,

```
double s=0;
int i;

for (i=1; i<=N; i+1)
   {
   s=s+1.0/(i*i);
   }
```

In MATLAB, the same code reads:

```
s=0;
for i=1:N
   s=s+1.0/i^2;
end
```

In FORTRAN 77, the same code reads:

```
s=0
Do i=1,N
   s=s+1.0/i**2
End
```

Note the obligatory six blank spaces at the beginning of each line.

In Chapter 3, we discussed the bubble-sort code for sorting an array of numbers or names. The Internet site:

http://www.codecodex.com/wiki/index.php?title=Bubble_sort

lists the bubble-sort code in some twenty languages, including C++ and Fortran. Some of these codes, including Fortran, almost read like English.

In Section 4.5, we discussed the code *bits.cc* that computes the maximum integer that can be described with an available number of bits. The equivalent FORTRAN 77 program contained in the file *bits.f* is:

```
Program bits

Implicit Double Precision (a-h,o-z)
Integer p,q

write (6,*) " Will compute the greatest integer "
write (6,*) " that can be described with n bits "

98    write (6,*) " Enter the number of bits"
      write (6,*) " (should be less than 32)"
```

```fortran
        write (6,*) " 0 to quit "
        write (6,*) " ------------------------------"
        read (5,*) n

        If (n.eq.0) Go to 99

        write (6,101)
c--
        q = 0.0D0
        Do i=0,n-1
          p = 2**i
          q = q+p
          write (6,100) i+1,p,q
        End Do

        Go to 98 !  return to repeat
c--
99      Continue !  done
100     Format (1x,i5,2(1x,i15))
101     Format (" bits",5x,"increment",5x,"largest integer")
        Stop
        End
```

At the beginning of Section 4.6, we discussed the code *prj.cc* that computes the inner product (projection) of two vectors. The equivalent FORTRAN 77 program contained in the file *prj.f* is:

```fortran
        Program prj

        Double precision a(2), b(2), prod

        a(1) = 0.1
        a(2) = 0.2
        b(1) = 2.1
        b(2) = 3.1

        call prj (a, b, n, prod)

        write (6,*) " inner product:   ", prod

        Stop
        End

c-------

        subroutine prj (a, b, n, prod)

        Double precision a(2), b(2), prj
```

```
prod = 0.0D0

Do i=1,n
  prod = prod + a(i)*b(i)
End Do

Return
End
```

Why C++?

Although MATLAB makes life easy, the substantial memory requirements and CPU cost are important considerations. FORTRAN 77 is free, efficient, and easy to learn. Why then consider C++? Knowledge of C++ endows us with a wide selection of important programming tools related to object-oriented programming.

Perhaps more important, methods and ideas of object-oriented programming can be translated into physical concepts in the various fields of physical sciences and engineering. This correspondence has not been yet explored to its full extent due to the extreme specialization of the scientific disciplines. Initiatives are under way to foster an interdisciplinary approach.

ASCII Code

The ASCII code maps characters to integers. Characters include letters of the English alphabet, numbers, control characters, and other special symbols.

- Control characters for printers and other devices are encoded by the first 32 integers, 0–31. Code 32 represents the space between words.

- Codes 22–126 represent printable characters.

- The capital or upper-case letters of the English alphabet, A–Z, are encoded by successive integers in the range 65–90.

- The lower-case letters of the English alphabet, a–z, are encoded by successive integers in the range 97–122.

- Code 127 is the Escape character.

Decimal	Octal	Hex	Character	
0	0	00	NUL	Null character
1	1	01	SOH	Start of header
2	2	02	STX	Start of text
3	3	03	ETX	End of text
4	4	04	EOT	End of transmission
5	5	05	ENQ	Enquiry
6	6	06	ACK	Acknowledgment
7	7	07	BEL	Bell
8	10	08	BS	Backspace
9	11	09	HT	Horizontal tab
10	12	0A	LF	Line feed
11	13	0B	VT	Vertical tab
12	14	0C	FF	Form feed
13	15	0D	CR	Carriage return
14	16	0E	SO	Shift out
15	17	0F	SI	Shift in
16	20	10	DLE	Data link escape
17	21	11	DC1	Device control 1 (usually XON)
18	22	12	DC2	Device control 2

19	23	13	DC3	Device control 3 (usually XOFF)
20	24	14	DC4	Device control 4
21	25	15	NAK	Negative acknowledgment
22	26	16	SYN	Synchronous idle
23	27	17	ETB	End of transmission block
24	30	18	CAN	Cancel
25	31	19	EM	End of medium
26	32	1A	SUB	Substitute
27	33	1B	ESC	Escape
28	34	1C	FS	File separator
29	35	1D	GS	Group separator
30	36	1E	RS	Record separator
31	37	1F	US	Unit separator
32	40	20	SPC	Space between words
33	41	21	!	
34	42	22	"	
35	43	23	#	
36	44	24	$	
37	45	25	%	
38	46	26	&	
39	47	27	'	
40	50	28	(	
41	51	29	)	
42	52	2A	*	
43	53	2B	+	
44	54	2C	,	
45	55	2D	-	
46	56	2E	.	
47	57	2F	/	
48	60	30	0	
49	61	31	1	
50	62	32	2	
51	63	33	3	
52	64	34	4	
53	65	35	5	
54	66	36	6	
55	67	37	7	
56	70	38	8	
57	71	39	9	
58	72	3A	:	
59	73	3B	;	
60	74	3C	<	
61	75	3D	=	
62	76	3E	>	
63	77	3F	?	

64	100	40	@
65	101	41	A
66	102	42	B
67	103	43	C
68	104	44	D
69	105	45	E
70	106	46	F
71	107	47	G
72	110	48	H
73	111	49	I
74	112	4A	J
75	113	4B	K
76	114	4C	L
77	115	4D	M
78	116	4E	N
79	117	4F	O
80	120	50	P
81	121	51	Q
82	122	52	R
83	123	53	S
84	124	54	T
85	125	55	U
86	126	56	V
87	127	57	W
88	130	58	X
89	131	59	Y
90	132	5A	Z
91	133	5B	[
92	134	5C	\
93	135	5D	]
94	136	5E	^
95	137	5F	_
96	140	60	'
97	141	61	a
98	142	62	b
99	143	63	c
100	144	64	d
101	145	65	e
102	146	66	f
103	147	67	g
104	150	68	h
105	151	69	i
106	152	6A	j
107	153	6B	k
108	154	6C	l

109	155	6D	m
110	156	6E	n
111	157	6F	o
112	160	70	p
113	161	71	q
114	162	72	r
115	163	73	s
116	164	74	t
117	165	75	u
118	166	76	v
119	167	77	w
120	170	78	x
121	171	79	y
122	172	7A	z
123	173	7B	{
124	174	7C	l
125	175	7D	}
126	176	7E	~
127	177	7F	DEL

C++ Keywords

E

The words listed in the following table are reserved for C++ declarations and operations and may not be employed as variable names in a program.

Keyword	Use
asm	Insert an assembly language instruction
auto	Declare a local variable
bool	Declare a Boolean variable
break	Break out of a loop
case	Introduce a block of code in a switch statement
catch	Handle exceptions from throw
char	Declare a character variable
class	Declare a class
const	Declare immutable data or functions that do not change data
const_cast	Cast from const variables
continue	Bypass iterations of a loop
default	Default handler in a case statement
delete	Delete an object to free memory
do	Looping construct
double	Declare a double precision floating-point variable
dynamic_cast	Perform runtime casts
else	Alternate case for an if statement
enum	Create enumeration types
explicit	Use constructors only when they exactly match
export	Allow template definition to be separated from declaration
extern	External variables are defined in another program or file and evaluated upon linking
false	Boolean value of false
float	Declare a floating-point variable
for	Looping construct
friend	Grant a non-member function access to private data
goto	Jump to a different part of the program

if	Execute code based on the result of a test
inline	Optimize calls to short functions
int	Declare a integer variable
long	Declare a long integer variable
mutable	Override a *const* variable
namespace	Partition the global namespace by defining a scope
new	Allocate dynamic memory for a new variable
operator	Create overloaded operator functions
private	Declare private members of a class
protected	Declare protected members of a class
public	Declare public members of a class
register	Request that a variable be optimized for speed by storing it in the CPU registers instead of the RAM
reinterpret_cast	Change the type of a variable
return	Return from a function
short	Declare a short integer variable
signed	Modify variable type declarations
sizeof	Return the size of a variable or type
static	Create permanent storage for a variable in a function so that the value is preserved when we exit the function
static_cast	Perform a non-polymorphic cast
struct	Define a new structure
switch	Select code based on different values for a variable
template	Create generic functions
this	Pointer to the current object
throw	Throw an exception
true	Boolean value of true
try	Execute code that can throw an exception
typedef	Create a new type name from an existing type
typeid	Describe an object
typename	Declare a class or undefined type
union	A structure that assigns multiple variables to the same memory location
unsigned	Declare an unsigned integer variable
using	Import complete or partial namespaces into the current scope
virtual	Create a function that can be overridden by a derived class
void	Declare functions or data with no associated data type
volatile	Warn the compiler about variables that can be modified unexpectedly
wchar_t	Declare a wide-character variable
while	Looping construct

Matlab Primer

F

Only elementary computer programming skills are necessary to read and write MATLAB code. The code is written in one file or a collection of files, called the *source* or *program* files, using a standard file editor, such as the *vi* editor. The source code includes the main program, also called a script, and the necessary user-defined functions. The names of these files must be suffixed with .m

Execution begins by typing the name of the file containing the main program in the MATLAB environment. Alternatively, the code can be typed one line at a time followed by the RETURN keystroke in the MATLAB environment.

MATLAB is an interpreted language, which means that the instructions are translated into machine language and executed in real time, one at a time. In contrast, a source code written in FORTRAN, C, or C++ must first be compiled to produce the object files, which are then linked together with the necessary system libraries to produce the executable binary file.

F.1 Grammar and syntax

Following is a list of general rules regarding the grammar and syntax of MATLAB. When confronted with an error after issuing a command or during execution, this list should serve as a first check point:

- MATLAB *variables are (lower and upper) case sensitive:*
  The variable **echidna** is different than the variable **echiDna**. Similarly, the MATLAB command **return** is not equivalent to the erroneous command **Return**; the latter will not be recognized by the interpreter.

- MATLAB *variables must start with a letter:*
  A variable name is described by a string of up to thirty-one characters including letters, digits, and the underscore; punctuation marks are not allowed.

- MATLAB *string variables are enclosed by a single quote:*
  For example, we may define the string variable:

  ```
  thinker_764 = 'Thucydides'
  ```

- *Beginning and end of a command line:*
  A MATLAB command can begin at any position in a line, and may continue practically indefinitely in the same line.

- *Line continuation:*
  To continue a command onto the next line, we put three dots at the end of the line.

- *Multiple commands in a line:*
  Two or more commands can be placed in the same line provided they are separated with a semicolon (;).

- *Display:*
  When a command is executed directly or by running a MATLAB code, MATLAB displays the numerical value assignment or the result of a calculation. To suppress the output, we put a semicolon (;) at the end of the command.

- *White space:*
  More than one empty space between words are ignored by the compiler. However, numbers cannot be split in sections separated by blank spaces.

- *Range of indices:*
  Vectors and arrays must have positive and non-zero indices; the vector entry v(-3) is unacceptable in MATLAB. This annoying restriction can be circumvented in clever ways by redefining the indices.

- *Comments:*
  A line beginning with the % character, or the tail-end of a line after the % character, is a comment, and is ignored by the MATLAB interpreter.

- *Mathematical symbols and special characters:*
  Table F.1.1 lists mathematical symbols and special characters used in MATLAB interactive dialog and programming.

- *Logical control flow commands:*
  Table F.1.2 lists the basic logical control flow commands.

- *Input/Output commands:*
  Tables F.1.3-5 list basic Input/Output (I/O) commands, functions, and formatting statements. Once the output format is set, it remains in effect until changed.

+	Plus
-	Minus
*	Matrix multiplication
.*	Array multiplication
^	Matrix power
.^	Array power
kron	Kronecker tensor product
\	Backslash or left division
/	Slash or right division
./	Array division
:	Colon
()	Parentheses
[]	Brackets
.	Decimal point
..	Parent directory
...	Line continuation
,	Comma
;	Semicolon, used to suppress the screen display
%	Indicates that the rest of the line is a comment
!	Exclamation point
'	Matrix transpose
"	Quote
.'	Non-conjugated transpose
=	Set equal to
==	Equal
~=1	Not equal
<	Less than
<=	Less than or equal to
>	Greater than
>=	Greater than or equal to
&	Logical *and*
|	Logical *or*
~	Logical *not*
xor	Logical *exclusive or*
i, j	Imaginary unit
pi	number $\pi = 3.14159265358\ldots$

Table F.1.1 MATLAB operators, symbols, special characters, and constants.

break	Terminate the execution
else	Use with the if statement
elseif	Use with the if statement
end	Terminate a for loop, a while loop, or an if block
error	Display a message and abort
for	Loop over commands a specific number of times
if	Conditionally execute commands
pause	Wait for user's response
return	Return to the MATLAB environment, invoking program or function
while	Repeat statements an indefinite number of times until a specified condition is met

Table F.1.2 MATLAB logical control flow commands and construct components.

disp	Display numerical values or text
	Use as: disp disp() disp('text')
fclose	Close a file
fopen	Open a file
fread	Read binary data from a file
fwrite	Write binary data to a file
fgetl	Read a line from a file, discard newline character
fgets	Read a line from a file, keep newline character
fprintf	Write formatted data to a file using C language conventions
fscanf	Read formatted data from a file
feof	Test for end-of-file (EOF)
ferror	Inquire the I/O error status of a file
frewind	Rewind a file
fseek	Set file position indicator
ftell	Get file position indicator
sprintf	Write formatted data to string
sscanf	Read formatted string from file
csvread	Read from a file values separated by commas
csvwrite	Write into file values separated by commas
uigetfile	Retrieve the name of a file to open through dialog box
uiputfile	Retrieve the name of a file to write through dialog box

Table F.1.3 MATLAB Input/Output (I/O) commands.

F.2 Precision

MATLAB stores all numbers in the long format of the floating-point representation. This means that real numbers have a finite precision of roughly sixteen

input	Prompt for user input
keyboard	Invoke keyboard as though it were a script file
menu	Generate menu of choices for user input

Table F.1.4 MATLAB interactive input commands.

format short	Fixed point with 4 decimal places (default)
format long	Fixed point with 14 decimal places
format short e	Scientific notation with 4 decimal places
format long e	Scientific notation with 15 decimal places
format hex	Hexadecimal format

Table F.1.5 MATLAB formatting commands.

significant digits, and a range of definition roughly varying between 10^{-308} and 10^{+308} in absolute value. Numbers smaller than 10^{-308} or larger than 10^{+308} in absolute value cannot be accommodated.

MATLAB performs all computations in double precision. However, this should not be confused with the ability to view and print numbers with a specified number of significant figures using the commands listed in Table F.1.5.

F.3 Matlab commands

Once invoked, MATLAB responds interactively to various commands, statements, and declarations issued by the user in the MATLAB window. These are implemented by typing the corresponding name, single- or multi-line syntax, and then pressing the ENTER key.

Table F.3.1 lists general utility and interactive-input MATLAB commands. Issuing the command *demos* initiates various demonstrations and illustrative examples of MATLAB code, well worth exploration.

To obtain a full explanation of a MATLAB command, statement, or function, we may use the MATLAB **help** facility, which is the counterpart of the UNIX **man** facility. For example, issuing the command **help break** in the MATLAB environment produces the description:

```
BREAK Terminate execution of WHILE or FOR loop.
   BREAK terminates the execution of FOR and WHILE loops.
   In nested loops, BREAK exits from the innermost loop only.
   If you use BREAK outside of a FOR or WHILE loop in a MATLAB
   script or function, it terminates the script or function at
   that point.  If BREAK is executed in an IF, SWITCH-CASE, or
   TRY-CATCH statement, it terminates the statement at that point.
```

clear	Clear variables and functions from memory
demo	Run demos
exit	Terminate a MATLAB session
help	On-line documentation
load	Retrieve variables from a specified directory
save	Save workspace variables to a specified directory
saveas	Save figure or model using a specified format
size	Reveal the size of matrix
who	List current variables
quit	Terminate a MATLAB session

Table F.3.1 General utility MATLAB commands.

The command `clear` is especially important, as it resets all variables to the "uninitialized" status, and thereby prevents the use of improper values defined or produced in a previous calculation. A detailed explanation of this command can be obtained by typing `help clear` .

F.4 Elementary examples

In the following examples, we demonstrate the interactive usage of MATLAB with simple sessions. A line beginning with two "greater than" signs (>>) denotes the MATLAB command line where we enter a definition or issue a statement. Unless stated otherwise, a line that does not begin with >> is MATLAB output. Recall that the command `clear` clears the memory from previous data to prevent misappropriation.

• Numerical value assignment and addition:

```
>> a = 1
a =
     1
>> b = 2
b =
     2
>> c = a + b
c =
     3
```

• Numerical value assignment and subtraction:

```
>> clear
>> a=1; b=-3; c=a-b
c =
       4
```

• Number multiplication:

```
>> clear
>> a = 2.0; b=-3.5; c=a*b;
>> c
c =
          -7
```

Typing the variable c displays its current value, in this case -7.

• Vector definition:

```
>> clear
>> v = [2 1]
v =
        2 1

>> v(1)
ans =
        2

>> v' % transpose
ans =
        2
        1
```

Typing v(1) produces the first component of the vector v as an answer. The comment "transpose" is ignored since it is preceded by the comment delimiter "%." The answer **ans** is, in fact, a variable evaluated by MATLAB.

• Vector addition:

```
>> v = [1 2]; u = [-1, -2]; u+v
ans =
      0 0
```

- Matrix definition, addition, and multiplication:

```
>> a = [1 2; 3 4]
a =
       1 2
       3 4

>> b = [ [1 2]' [2 4]' ]
b =
       1 2
       2 4

>> a+b
ans =
       2 4
       5 8

>> c = a*b
c =
       5 10
      11 22
```

- Multiply a complex matrix by a complex vector:

```
>> a = [1+2i 2+3i; -1-i 1+i]
a =
       1.0000 + 2.0000i 2.0000 + 3.0000i
      -1.0000 - 1.0000i 1.0000 + 1.0000i

>> v = [1+i 1-i]
v =
       1.0000 + 1.0000i 1.0000 - 1.0000i

>> c = a*v'
c =
       2.0000 + 6.0000i
      -2.0000 + 2.0000i
```

By taking its transpose indicated by a prime, the row vector, v, becomes a column vector that is conformable with the square matrix, a.

- Print π:

```
>> format long
>> pi
ans =
       3.14159265358979
```

- for loop:

```
>> for j=-1:1
   j
   end
j =
      -1
j =
      0
j =
      1
```

In this example, the first three lines are entered by the user.

- if statement:

```
>> j=0;
>> i=1;
>> if i==j+1, disp 'case 1', end
case 1
```

- for loop:

```
>> n=3;
>> for i=n:-1:2
disp 'i='; disp (i), end
i=
    3
i=
    2
```

The loop is executed backward, starting at n, with step of 1.

- if loop:

```
>> i=1; j=2;
>> if i==j+1; disp 'case 1'
   elseif i==j; disp 'case2'
   else; disp 'case3'
   end
case3
```

In this example, all but the last line are entered by the user.

- while loop:

```
>> i=0;
>> while i<2, i=i+1; disp(i), end
   1
   2
```

The four statements in the while loop could be typed in separate lines; that is, the commas can be replaced by the ENTER keystroke.

F.5 Matlab functions

MATLAB comes with an extensive library of internal functions for numerical computation and data visualization.

Table F.5.1 lists general and specialized mathematical functions. To obtain specific information on the proper usage of a function, use the MATLAB help facility. If you are unsure about the proper syntax or reliability of a function, it is best to write your own code from first principles. It is both rewarding and instructive to duplicate a MATLAB function and create a personal library of user-defined functions based on control-flow commands.

F.6 User-defined functions

In MATLAB, a user-defined function is written in a file whose name defines the calling name of the function. The file name must be suffixed with the MATLAB identifier: .m . Thus, a function named *pindos* must reside in a file named **pindos.m**, whose general structure is:

```
function [output1, output2, ...]  = pindos (input1, input2,...)
......
return
```

The three dots indicate additional input and output arguments separated by commas; the six dots indicate additional lines of code. The output string, `output1`, `output2`, ..., consists of numbers, vectors, matrices, and string variables evaluated by the function by performing operations involving the input string, `input`, `input2`, ... To execute this function in the MATLAB environment or invoke it from a program file, we issue the command:

```
[evaluate1, evaluate2, ...]  = pindos (parameter1, parameter2,...)
```

After the function has been successfully executed, `evaluate1` takes the value of `output1`, `evaluate2` takes the value of `output2`, and the rest of the output variables take corresponding values.

Function	Purpose
abs	Absolute value
acos	Inverse cosine
acosh	Inverse hyperbolic cosine
acot	Inverse cotangent
acoth	Inverse hyperbolic cotangent
acsc	Inverse cosecant
acsch	Inverse hyperbolic cosecant
angle	Phase angle
asec	Inverse secant
asech	Inverse hyperbolic secant
asin	Inverse sine
asinh	Inverse hyperbolic sine
atan	Inverse tangent
atan2	Four quadrant inverse tangent
atanh	Inverse hyperbolic tangent
ceil	Round toward plus infinity.
cart2pol	Cartesian-to-polar coordinate conversion
cart2sph	Cartesian-to-spherical coordinate conversion
conj	Complex conjugate
cos	Cosine
cosh	Hyperbolic cosine
cot	Cotangent
coth	Hyperbolic cotangent
csc	Cosecant
csch	Hyperbolic cosecant
exp	Exponential
expm	Matrix exponential
fix	Round toward zero
floor	Round toward minus infinity
gcd	Greatest common divisor
imag	Complex imaginary part
lcm	Least common multiple
log	Natural logarithm
log10	Common logarithm
pol2cart	Polar-to-Cartesian coordinate conversion
real	Real part
rem	Remainder after division
round	Round toward the nearest integer

Table F.5.1 Common and specialized MATLAB mathematical functions. Continued on next page.

Function	Purpose
sec	Secant
sech	Hyperbolic secant
sign	Signum function
sin	Sine
sinh	Hyperbolic sine
sph2cart	Polar-to-Cartesian coordinate conversion
sqrt	Square root
tan	Tangent
tanh	Hyperbolic tangent
bessel	Bessel functions
besseli	Modified Bessel functions of the first kind
besselj	Bessel functions of the first kind
besselk	Modified Bessel functions of the second kind
bessely	Bessel functions of the second kind
beta	Beta function
betainc	Incomplete beta function
betaln	Logarithm of the beta function
ellipj	Jacobi elliptic functions
ellipke	Complete elliptic integral
erf	Error function
erfc	Complementary error function
erfcx	Scaled complementary error function
erfinv	Inverse error function
expint	Exponential integral
gamma	Gamma function
gammainc	Incomplete gamma function
gammaln	Logarithm of gamma function
legendre	Associated Legendre functions
log2	Dissect floating point numbers
pow2	Scale floating point numbers
rat	Rational approximation
rats	Rational output
eye	Identity matrix
ones	Matrix of ones
rand	Uniformly distributed random numbers and arrays
randn	Normally distributed random numbers and arrays
zeros	Matrix of zeros

Table F.5.1 Common and specialized MATLAB mathematical functions.

If a function evaluates only one number, vector, matrix, character string, entity or object, then the function statement and corresponding function can be simplified to:

```
function evaluate = pindos (input1, input2,...)
...
return
```

An example of a simple function residing in the function file `bajanakis.m` is:

```
function bname = bajanakis(isel)

if(isel == 1)
   bname = 'sehoon';
elseif(isel == 2)
   bname = 'phaethon';
else
   bname = 'alkiviadis';
end

return
```

F.7 Numerical methods

MATLAB includes a general-purpose numerical methods library whose functions perform numerical linear algebra, solve algebraic equations, carry out function differentiation and integration, solve differential equations, and execute a variety of other tasks. Special-purpose libraries of interest to a particular discipline are accommodated in *toolboxes*.

Table F.7.1 shows selected MATLAB numerical methods functions. While these functions are generally robust and reliable, it is wise to always work under the premises of the Arabic proverb: "Trust in Allah but always tie your camel."

F.8 Matlab graphics

A powerful feature of MATLAB is the ability to produce professional graphics, including animation. Graphics are displayed in dedicated windows appearing in response to the graphics commands.

Graphics functions are listed in Tables F.8.1. in several categories. To obtain a detailed description of a graphics function, use the *help* facility. Some useful tips are:

Function	Purpose
cat	Concatenate arrays
cond	Condition number of a matrix
det	Matrix determinant
eig	Matrix eigenvalues and eigenvectors
inv	Matrix inverse
lu	LU-decomposition of a matrix
ode23	Solution of ordinary differential equations by the second/third-order Runge-Kutta method
ode45	Solution of ordinary differential equations by the fourth/fifth-order Runge-Kutta-Fehlberg method
qr	QR-decomposition of a matrix, where Q is an orthogonal matrix and R is an upper triangular (right) matrix
poly	Characteristic polynomial of a matrix
quad	Function integration by Simpson's rule
root	Polynomial root finder
svd	Singular-value decomposition
trapz	Function integration by the trapezoidal rule
x = A\b	Solves the linear system $\mathbf{A} \cdot \mathbf{x} = \mathbf{b}$, where $\mathbf{A}$ is an $N \times N$ matrix, and $\mathbf{b}, \mathbf{x}$ are N-dimensional column vectors
x = b/A	Solves the linear system $\mathbf{x} \cdot \mathbf{A} = \mathbf{b}$, where $\mathbf{A}$ is an $N \times N$ matrix, and $\mathbf{b}, \mathbf{x}$ are N-dimensional row vectors

Table F.7.1 A partial list of general-purpose numerical methods Matlab functions.

- To generate a new graphics window, use the command: `figure`
- To produce a graphics file, use the **export** or **save** option under the *file* pull-down menu in the figure window.
- To manipulate axis properties, use the command *axis* and its options.
- To superimpose graphs, use the command `hold`.
- To close a graphics window, use the command `close`.

In the remainder of this section, we present several graphics sessions followed by the graphics output.

Two-dimensional graphs

bar	Bar graph
comet	Animated comet plot
compass	Compass plot
errorbar	Error bar plot
feather	Feather plot
fplot	Plot a function
fill	Draw filled two-dimensional polygons
hist	Histogram plot
loglog	Log-log scale plot
plot	Linear plot
polar	Polar coordinate plot
rose	Angle histogram plot
semilogx	Semi-log scale plot, x-axis logarithmic
semilogy	Semi-log scale plot, y-axis logarithmic
stairs	Stair-step plot
stem	Stem plot for discrete sequence data

Graph annotation and operations

grid	Grid lines
gtext	Mouse placement of text
legend	Add legend to plot
text	Text annotation
title	Graph title
xlabel	x-axis label
ylabel	y-axis label
zoom	Zoom in and out of a two-dimensional plot

Line and fill commands

fill3	Draw filled three-dimensional polygons
plot3	Plot lines and points

Two-dimensional graphs of three-dimensional data

clabel	Contour plot elevation labels
comet3	Animated comet plot
contour	Contour plot
contour3	Three-dimensional contour plot

Table F.8.1 Elementary and specialized MATLAB graphics functions and procedures. Continued on next page.

contourc	Contour plot computation (used by contour)
image	Display image
imagesc	Scale data and display as image
pcolor	Pseudocolor (checkerboard) plot
quiver	Quiver plot
slice	Volumetric slice plot

Surface and mesh plots

mesh	Three-dimensional mesh surface
meshc	Combination mesh/contour plot
meshgrid	Generate x and y arrays
meshz	Three-dimensional mesh with zero plane
slice	Volumetric visualization plot
surf	Three-dimensional shaded surface
surfc	Combined surf/contour plot
surfl	Shaded surface with lighting
trimesh	Triangular mess plot
trisurf	Triangular surface plot
waterfall	Waterfall plot

Three-dimensional objects

cylinder	Generate a cylinder
sphere	Generate a sphere

Graph appearance

axis	Axis scaling and appearance
caxis	Pseudocolor axis scaling
colormap	Color lookup table
hidden	Mesh hidden line removal
shading	Color shading
view	Graph viewpoint specification
viewmtx	View transformation matrices

Graph annotation

grid	Grid lines
legend	Add legend to plot

Table F.8.1 Elementary and specialized MATLAB graphics functions and procedures. Continued on next page.

text	Text annotation
title	Graph title
xlabel	x-axis label
ylabel	y-axis label
zlabel	z-axis label for three-dimensional plots

Graphics control

capture	Screen capture of current figure in UNIX
clf	Clear current figure
close	Abandon figure
figure	Create a figure in a new graph window
gcf	Get handle to current figure
graymon	Set default figure properties for gray-scale monitors
newplot	Determine correct axes and figure for new graph
refresh	Redraw current figure window
whitebg	Toggle figure background color

Axis control

axes	Create axes at arbitrary position
axis	Control axis scaling and appearance
caxis	Control pseudo-color axis scaling
cla	Clear current axes
gca	Get handle to current axes
hold	Hold current graph
ishold	True if hold is on
subplot	Create axes in tiled positions

Graphics objects

figure	Create a figure window
image	Create an image
line	Generate a line
patch	Generate a surface patch
surface	Generate a surface
text	Create text
uicontrol	Create user interface control
uimenu	Create user interface menu

Table F.8.1 Elementary and specialized MATLAB graphics functions and procedures. Continued on next page.

Graphics operations

delete	Delete object
drawnow	Flush pending graphics events
findobj	Find object with specified properties
gco	Get handle of current object
get	Get object properties
reset	Reset object properties
rotate	Rotate an object
set	Set object properties

Hard copy and storage

orient	Set paper orientation
print	Print graph or save graph to file
printopt	Configure local printer defaults

Movies and animation

getframe	Get movie frame
movie	Play recorded movie frames
moviein	Initialize movie frame memory

Miscellaneous

ginput	Graphical input from mouse
ishold	Return hold state
rbbox	Rubber-band box for region selection
waitforbuttonpress	Wait for key/button press over figure

Color controls

caxis	Pseudocolor axis scaling
colormap	Color lookup table
shading	Color shading mode

Table F.8.1 Elementary and specialized MATLAB graphics functions and procedures. Continued on next page.

Color maps

bone	Gray-scale with a tinge of blue color map
contrast	Contrast-enhancing gray-scale color map
cool	Shades of cyan and magenta color map
copper	Linear copper-tone color map
flag	Alternating RGB and black color map
gray	Linear gray-scale color map
hsv	Hue-saturation-value color map
hot	Black-red-yellow-white color map
jet	Variation of HSV color map (no wrap)
pink	Pastel shades of pink color map
prism	Prism-color color map
white	All white monochrome color map

Color map functions

brighten	Brighten or darken color map
colorbar	Display color map as color scale
hsv2rgb	Hue-saturation-value to RGB equivalent
rgb2hsv	RGB to hue-saturation-value conversion
rgbplot	Plot color map
spinmap	Spin color map

Lighting models

diffuse	Diffuse reflectance
specular	Specular reflectance
surfl	Three-dimensional shaded surface with lighting
surfnorm	Surface normals

Table F.8.1 Elementary and specialized MATLAB graphics functions and procedures.

- Graph of the function: $f(x) = sin^3(\pi x)$

```
>> x=-1.0:0.01:1.0; % define an array of abscissae
>> y = sin(pi*x).^3; % note the .^ operator (Table F.1.1)
>> plot(x,y)
>> set(gca,'fontsize',15)
>> xlabel('x','fontsize',15)
>> ylabel('y','fontsize',15)
```

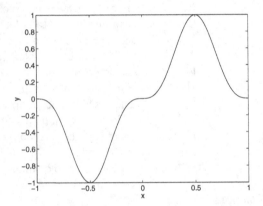

- Graph of the Gaussian function: $f(x) = e^{-x^2}$

```
>> fplot('exp(-x^2)',[-5, 5])
>> set(gca,'fontsize',15)
>> xlabel('x','fontsize',15)
>> ylabel('y','fontsize',15)
```

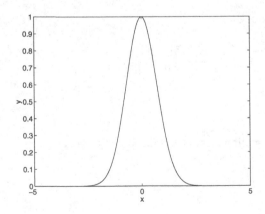

- Paint a polygon in black:

```
>> x =[0.0 1.0 1.0]; y=[0.0 0.0 1.0]; c='k';
>> fill (x,y,c)
>> set(gca,'fontsize',15)
```

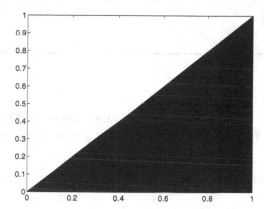

- mesh plot:

```
>> [x, y] = meshgrid(-1.0:0.10:1.0, -2.0:0.10:2.0);
>> z = sin(pi*x+pi*y);
>> mesh(z)
>> set(gca,'fontsize',15)
```

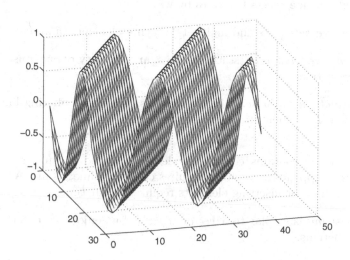

The Standard Template Library

C++ is endowed with the standard template library (STL), which offers a variety of utility functions and data structures generalized as templates and coined containers.

A comprehensive reference manual of the STL can be found at the Internet sites:

```
http://cppreference.com
http://www.josuttis.com/libbook/idx.html
```

The contents of STL can be broadly classified into the following categories:

- *Algorithms* containing various subroutines and utility functions

- *Sequence containers* (vectors, lists) holding sequences of data elements

- *Associative containers* (maps and multimaps) containing key/value pairs that provide access to values by way of keys

- *Ordered sets* (sets and multisets) storing elements in an orderly fashion

- *Container adapters* (stacks, queues, and priority queues) used to enforce access rules

- *Specialized containers* (bitsets, strings, valarrays) offering limited yet efficient implementations for specific data types

A *vector* contains contiguous elements stored in an array. Accessing members or appending elements requires constant time, as in RAM; locating a specific element or inserting elements requires linear time.

A *string* is similar to a *vector<char>*, but enjoys an extended menu of utility functions.

A *double-ended queue* offers fast insertion and deletion at the beginning and end of a vector.

A *list* is a sequence of elements stored in a linked list. Compared to vectors, the list offers fast insertion and deletion but slower random access.

A *queue* is a container adapter offering a FIFO (first-in, first-out) data structure.

A *priority queue* is a *queue*, but the elements inside the data structure are ordered by some predicate.

A *deque* provides a dynamic array structure with random access, and offers fast insertion and deletion of elements at the front and back of the array.

A *stack* is a container adapter offering the functionality of a stack – specifically, a FILO (first-in, last-out) data structure.

A *set* is an associative container encapsulating a sorted set of unique objects.

A *multiset* is an associative container allowing for duplicate objects.

A *map* is a sorted *associative container* containing unique key/value pairs. For example, a map can be defined to associate a string with an integer, and then used to associate the number of days in each month with the name of each month.

A *multimap* differs from a *map* in that it permits duplicate keys; that is, it allows a key to map more than one element.

A *bitset* allows a set of bits to be used as a data structure. Bitsets can be manipulated by various binary operators such as logical AND and OR.

An *iterator* is used to access members of the container classes in lieu of a pointer. For example, an iterator can be used to step through the elements of a vector.

A *valarray* offers efficient implementations for arrays, but lacks certain standard container functions.

Index